Build It Yourself VISUALLY™

The Ultimate Media Center PC for Under $999

by Kate J. Chase

Wiley Publishing, Inc.

Build It Yourself Visually™: The Ultimate Media Center PC for Under $999

Published by
Wiley Publishing, Inc.
111 River Street
Hoboken, NJ 07030-5774

Published simultaneously in Canada

Copyright © 2006 by Wiley Publishing, Inc., Indianapolis, Indiana

No part of this publication may be reproduced, stored in a retrieval system or transmitted in any form or by any means, electronic, mechanical, photocopying, recording, scanning or otherwise, except as permitted under Sections 107 or 108 of the 1976 United States Copyright Act, without either the prior written permission of the Publisher, or authorization through payment of the appropriate per-copy fee to the Copyright Clearance Center, 222 Rosewood Drive, Danvers, MA 01923, (978)750-8400, fax: (978)646-8600. Requests to the Publisher for permission should be addressed to the Legal Department, Wiley Publishing, Inc., 10475 Crosspoint Blvd., Indianapolis, IN 46256, (317)572-3447, fax: (317) 572-4355, online: www.wiley.com/go/permisssions.

Library of Congress Control Number: 2005931279

ISBN-13: 978-0-7645-9984-2

ISBN-10: 0-7645-9984-4

Manufactured in the United States of America

10 9 8 7 6 5 4 3 2 1

Trademark Acknowledgments

Wiley, the Wiley Publishing logo, Visual, the Visual logo, Simplified, Master VISUALLY, Teach Yourself VISUALLY, Visual Blueprint, Read Less - Learn More and related trade dress are trademarks or registered trademarks of John Wiley & Sons, Inc. and/or its affiliates. All other trademarks are the property of their respective owners. Wiley Publishing, Inc. is not associated with any product or vendor mentioned in this book.

LIMIT OF LIABILITY/DISCLAIMER OF WARRANTY: THE PUBLISHER AND THE AUTHOR MAKE NO REPRESENTATIONS OR WARRANTIES WITH RESPECT TO THE ACCURACY OR COMPLETENESS OF THE CONTENTS OF THIS WORK AND SPECIFICALLY DISCLAIM ALL WARRANTIES, INCLUDING WITHOUT LIMITATION WARRANTIES OF FITNESS FOR A PARTICULAR PURPOSE. NO WARRANTY MAY BE CREATED OR EXTENDED BY SALES OR PROMOTIONAL MATERIALS. THE ADVICE AND STRATEGIES CONTAINED HEREIN MAY NOT BE SUITABLE FOR EVERY SITUATION. THIS WORK IS SOLD WITH THE UNDERSTANDING THAT THE PUBLISHER IS NOT ENGAGED IN RENDERING LEGAL, ACCOUNTING, OR OTHER PROFESSIONAL SERVICES. IF PROFESSIONAL ASSISTANCE IS REQUIRED, THE SERVICES OF A COMPETENT PROFESSIONAL PERSON SHOULD BE SOUGHT. NEITHER THE PUBLISHER NOR THE AUTHOR SHALL BE LIABLE FOR DAMAGES ARISING HEREFROM. THE FACT THAT AN ORGANIZATION OR WEBSITE IS REFERRED TO IN THIS WORK AS A CITATION AND/OR A POTENTIAL SOURCE OF FURTHER INFORMATION DOES NOT MEAN THAT THE AUTHOR OR THE PUBLISHER ENDORSES THE INFORMATION THE ORGANIZATION OR WEBSITE MAY PROVIDE OR RECOMMENDATIONS IT MAY MAKE. FURTHER, READERS SHOULD BE AWARE THAT INTERNET WEBSITES LISTED IN THIS WORK MAY HAVE CHANGED OR DISAPPEARED BETWEEN WHEN THIS WORK WAS WRITTEN AND WHEN IT IS READ.

FOR PURPOSES OF ILLUSTRATING THE CONCEPTS AND TECHNIQUES DESCRIBED IN THIS BOOK, THE AUTHOR HAS CREATED VARIOUS NAMES, COMPANY NAMES, MAILING, E-MAIL AND INTERNET ADDRESSES, PHONE AND FAX NUMBERS AND SIMILAR INFORMATION, ALL OF WHICH ARE FICTITIOUS. ANY RESEMBLANCE OF THESE FICTITIOUS NAMES, ADDRESSES, PHONE AND FAX NUMBERS AND SIMILAR INFORMATION TO ANY ACTUAL PERSON, COMPANY AND/OR ORGANIZATION IS UNINTENTIONAL AND PURELY COINCIDENTAL.

Contact Us

For general information on our other products and services, please contact our Customer Care Department within the U.S. at 800-762-2974, outside the U.S. at 317-572-3993 or fax 317-572-4002.

For technical support, please visit www.wiley.com/techsupport.

Permissions

CPU Solutions

Wiley Publishing, Inc.

Praise for Visual Books

"Like a lot of other people, I understand things best when I see them visually. Your books really make learning easy and life more fun."

                              John T. Frey (Cadillac, MI)

"I have quite a few of your Visual books and have been very pleased with all of them. I love the way the lessons are presented!"

                              Mary Jane Newman (Yorba Linda, CA)

"I just purchased my third Visual book (my first two are dog-eared now!), and, once again, your product has surpassed my expectations."

                              Tracey Moore (Memphis, TN)

"I am an avid fan of your Visual books. If I need to learn anything, I just buy one of your books and learn the topic in no time. Wonders! I have even trained my friends to give me Visual books as gifts."

                              Illona Bergstrom (Aventura, FL)

"Thank you for making it so clear. I appreciate it. I will buy many more Visual books."

                              J.P. Sangdong (North York, Ontario, Canada)

"I have several books from the Visual series and have always found them to be valuable resources."

                              Stephen P. Miller (Ballston Spa, NY)

"Thank you for the wonderful books you produce. It wasn't until I was an adult that I discovered how I learn – visually. Nothing compares to Visual books. I love the simple layout. I can just grab a book and use it at my computer, lesson by lesson. And I understand the material! You really know the way I think and learn. Thanks so much!"

                              Stacey Han (Avondale, AZ)

"I absolutely admire your company's work. Your books are terrific. The format is perfect, especially for visual learners like me. Keep them coming!"

                              Frederick A. Taylor, Jr. (New Port Richey, FL)

"I have several of your Visual books and they are the best I have ever used."

                              Stanley Clark (Crawfordville, FL)

"I bought my first Teach Yourself VISUALLY book last month. Wow. Now I want to learn everything in this easy format!"

                              Tom Vial (New York, NY)

"Thank you, thank you, thank you...for making it so easy for me to break into this high-tech world. I now own four of your books. I recommend them to anyone who is a beginner like myself."

                              Gay O'Donnell (Calgary, Alberta, Canada)

"I write to extend my thanks and appreciation for your books. They are clear, easy to follow, and straight to the point. Keep up the good work! I bought several of your books and they are just right! No regrets! I will always buy your books because they are the best."

                              Seward Kollie (Dakar, Senegal)

"Compliments to the chef!! Your books are extraordinary! Or, simply put, extra-ordinary, meaning way above the rest! THANK YOU THANK YOU THANK YOU! I buy them for friends, family, and colleagues."

                              Christine J. Manfrin (Castle Rock, CO)

"What fantastic teaching books you have produced! Congratulations to you and your staff. You deserve the Nobel Prize in Education in the Software category. Thanks for helping me understand computers."

                              Bruno Tonon (Melbourne, Australia)

Credits

Project Editor
Dana Rhodes Lesh

Acquisitions Editor
Tom Heine

Product Development Manager
Lindsay Sandman

Copy Editor
Dana Rhodes Lesh

Technical Editor
David R. Briel

Editorial Manager
Robyn Siesky

Permissions Editor
Laura Moss

Manufacturing
Allan Conley
Linda Cook
Paul Gilchrist
Jennifer Guynn

Book Design
Kathie Rickard

Production Coordinator
Maridee Ennis

Layout
Carrie A. Foster
Mary J. Gillot
Jennifer Heleine
Amanda Spagnuolo

Screen Artist
Jill A. Proll

Illustrator
Ronda David-Burroughs

Proofreader
Arielle Mennelle

Quality Control
Leeann Harney
Joe Niesen

Indexer
Lynnzee Elze

Special Help
CPU Solutions

Vice President and Executive Group Publisher
Richard Swadley

Vice President and Publisher
Barry Pruett

Composition Director
Debbie Stailey

About the Author

Kate J. Chase has been helping people plan, assemble, configure, tweak, and troubleshoot PCs for more than 15 years. She has served as author, coauthor, and editor for nearly 30 books about the Internet, PC hardware (including certification), applications, utilities, and operating systems. Besides her role as a Microsoft MVP (most valuable professional), Kate has built and managed thriving online technical communities for America Online, The Microsoft Network, and ZDnet, where she is a recognized expert in a number of different areas. Beyond technical and consumer writing, she is a journalist, blogger, and Web community and telecommuting consultant.

Author's Acknowledgments

Thanks to the editorial and production team at Wiley & Sons, including Acquisition Editor Tom Heine, Project Editor Dana Lesh, and Technical Editor David Briel. Kudos also go to the very helpful folks at CPU Solutions, including sales representative Bo Bracey, who helped coordinate this book, design the system built here, and answer questions quickly and wisely.

Table of Contents

Chapter 1: Special Considerations for Media Center PCs

The Difference between an Average PC and a Media Center PC 4
Specific Differences in Windows Media Center 6
What You May Want and Need 7
What You Can Realistically Get 8
Plan Your System 10

Chapter 2: Preparing Your Shopping List

Decide on Essentials 14
Know More about the Basics 16
Worthy Extras 26
Assess Your Special Needs 28

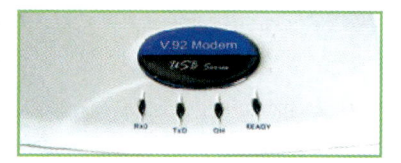

Chapter 3: Buying Your Components

Shop Smarter 30
Using CPU Solutions 32
What CPU Solutions Has Done for You 34
Compare Prices and Features 36
Customize Smarter 38
Order Windows 40
Double-Check Your Order 41
Place Your Order 42

chapter 4 — Preparing Your Tools and Workspace

Set Up Your Workspace 44
Pull Together Tools 48
Inspect and Inventory Your Parts 52
Store Until You Build 58
Avoid Problems 59

chapter 5 — Mapping Out the Case

My Choice for the Case 62
Alternative Case Choices 63
Open Up the Case 64
Determine What Is Inside 66
Remove Faceplates 72
Visualize Your Assembly 74

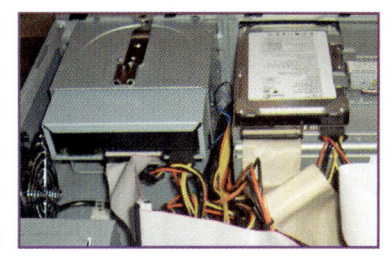

Table of Contents

chapter 6 — Installing the Power Supply

My Choice for the Power Supply 76
Alternative Power Supply Choices 77
Know Your Power Supply 78
Install the Power Supply 82
Check Your Power Cable 83
Think Beyond: Protect Power 84

chapter 7 — Installing the CPU

My Choice for the CPU 90
Alternative CPU Choices 91
Mount the CPU into the Motherboard 92
Connect the Heatsink and Fan to the CPU 94
Connect the Fan to the Motherboard 95
Check the Insertion 96

Chapter 8: Installing the Memory

My Choice for the Memory 98
Alternative Memory Choices 99
Check Your Memory 100
Know Your Memory Sockets 101
Install the Memory 102
Check the Seating 104
Add More Memory Later 105
Recognize Memory Problems 106
Find Memory Information 107

Chapter 9: Installing the Motherboard

My Choice for the Motherboard 108
Alternative Motherboard Choices 109
Check the Documentation 110
Orient and Prepare the Motherboard for the Case 112
Set the Jumpers 113
Mount the Motherboard 114
Connect the Power 118
Make Other Connections and Double-Check the Installation 120

Table of Contents

chapter 10 — Doing Your Drive Prep Work

Understanding the Physical Drive Setup 124
Determine Where Each Drive Goes 130
Prep Your IDE Drives for Use 132
Know the Difference between External and Internal Drives 136
Using Online Help Guides and Documents 138
Check Your Cables 142
Remove Screws and Retainers 143

chapter 11 — Installing Your Hard Drive

My Choice for the Hard Drive 144
Alternative Hard Drive Choices 145
Jumper and Prep the Drive 146
Install the Drive 148
Attach the Cable 150
Connect the Power Supply to the Hard Drive 152
Check the Drive Mounting 153

chapter 12 — Installing Your CD/DVD Drive

My Choice for the CD/DVD Drive 154
Alternative CD/DVD Drive Choices 155
Prepare the Drive 156
Install the Drive 157
Attach the Cable 158
Connect the Power 160
Verify Your Installation 161

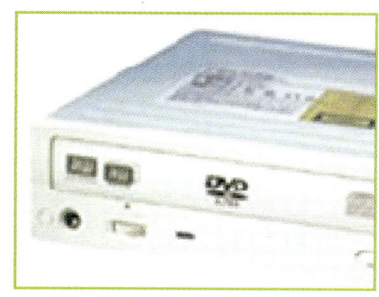

chapter 13 — Adding Additional Drives

My Choice for the Additional Drives 162
Alternative Additional Drive Choices 163
Add the Basics 164
Install the Drive 166
Affix the Cable 168
Connect the Power 169

Table of Contents

chapter 14 — Installing Your Graphics Card

My Choice for the Graphics Card	172
Alternative Graphics Card Choices	173
Understand Your Adapter Type	174
Install the Graphics Card	176
Check the Seating of the Graphics Card	178
Identify any Extra Cables	179

chapter 15 — Installing Your Sound Card

My Choice for the Sound Card	180
Alternative Sound Card Choices	181
Note the Connectors	182
Install Your Adapter	184
Connect the CD/DVD Drive to the Sound Card	186
Check the Installation	187

chapter 16 — Installing Your Modem

My Choice for the Modem 188
Alternative Modem Choices 189
Identify the Modem Type 190
Recognize the Connectors 191
Install Your Modem 192
Connect the Modem's Phone Line or Cable 193
Special Considerations 194

chapter 17 — Installing Your Network Interface Card

My Choice for the Network Interface Card 196
Alternative NIC Choices 197
The Wireless Network 198
Identify the Connections and Cable 200
Install the Adapter 202
Insert the Cable 203

Table of Contents

chapter 18 — Adding More Adapters

Know Your Options 204
Check Compatibility 208
Scope Out Space 209
Install the Additional Adapters 210

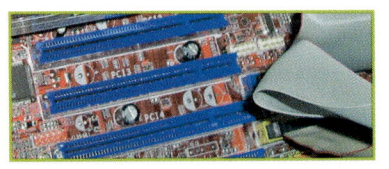

chapter 19 — Setting Up Your Monitor and Speakers

My Choice for the Monitor 214
Alternative Monitor Choices 215
My Choice for the Speakers 216
Alternative Speaker Choices 217
Considerations with Monitors 218
Review the Documentation 220
Check the Cables and Discs 221
Set Up the Monitor 222
Connect the Monitor 224
Install Your Speakers 225
Add Other Audio Devices 226

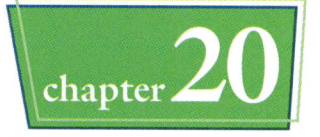

chapter 20 Installing Your Keyboard and Mouse

My Choice for the Keyboard and Mouse 228
Alternative Keyboard and Mouse Choices 229
Determine Your Connection Type 230
Install the Keyboard 232
Set Up Your Mouse 234
Install Other Input Devices 236

chapter 21 Installing Your Printer

My Choice for the Printer 238
Alternative Printer Choices 239
Determine Your Connection Type 240
Install the Printer 241

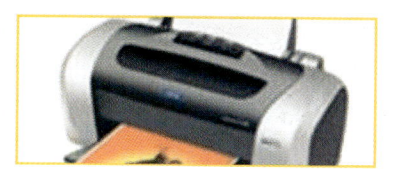

chapter 22 Installing USB/IEEE 1394 Devices

What to Know to Install USB/IEEE 1394 Devices 242
Connect the Devices 244

Table of Contents

chapter 23 Preparing to Boot

Check All Your Work .... .250
Install the Power Cord and Start the PC .... .252
Cover a Few Basics .... .253
Troubleshooting Boot Issues .... .254

chapter 24 Installing the Windows Media Center Operating System

Boot Your PC with the Windows Media Center CD .... .258
Set Up Your Operating System .... .260
Activate Windows .... .266

chapter 25 — Testing, Tweaking, and Tuning Your PC

About Testing Your Parts 268
Run Windows Update 270
Try Out Your Components 272
Open Device Manager 273
Consult and Use Device Manager 274
Update Drivers in Device Manager 282
Force Windows to Check for New Hardware 286
Fine-Tune Your PC 288

chapter 26 — Media Center PC Final Troubleshooting and Recovery

Final Troubleshooting 296
Getting Help 298
Before and After You Resolve Special Problems 302

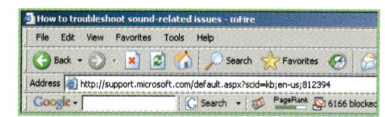

Glossary **308**

Part I

Planning Your PC

A Windows Media Center PC is anything but just a standard PC. Instead, this system needs more power, and its hardware must be able to process video graphics with both blazing speed and crisp accuracy so that you get the best results when you play movies and music and even watch and capture TV through your system.

Because of this, you need to be sure that you get all the components needed to assemble not only a fully functioning PC but also one that enables you to take full advantage of the media-creation and playing aspects of your customized system.

The chapters composing this first part of the book take you through everything you need to buy and help you determine what special extras you may want for the specific work and fun you want to enjoy through your new, personally designed system. Especially important, you will learn about the special Web store that our partner, CPU Solutions, has put together for you to make your shopping experience both easy and enjoyable. If you shop through CPU Solutions, you can take a substantial amount of the guesswork out of the PC part-buying process and then follow along with the step-by-step visual assistance offered throughout this book.

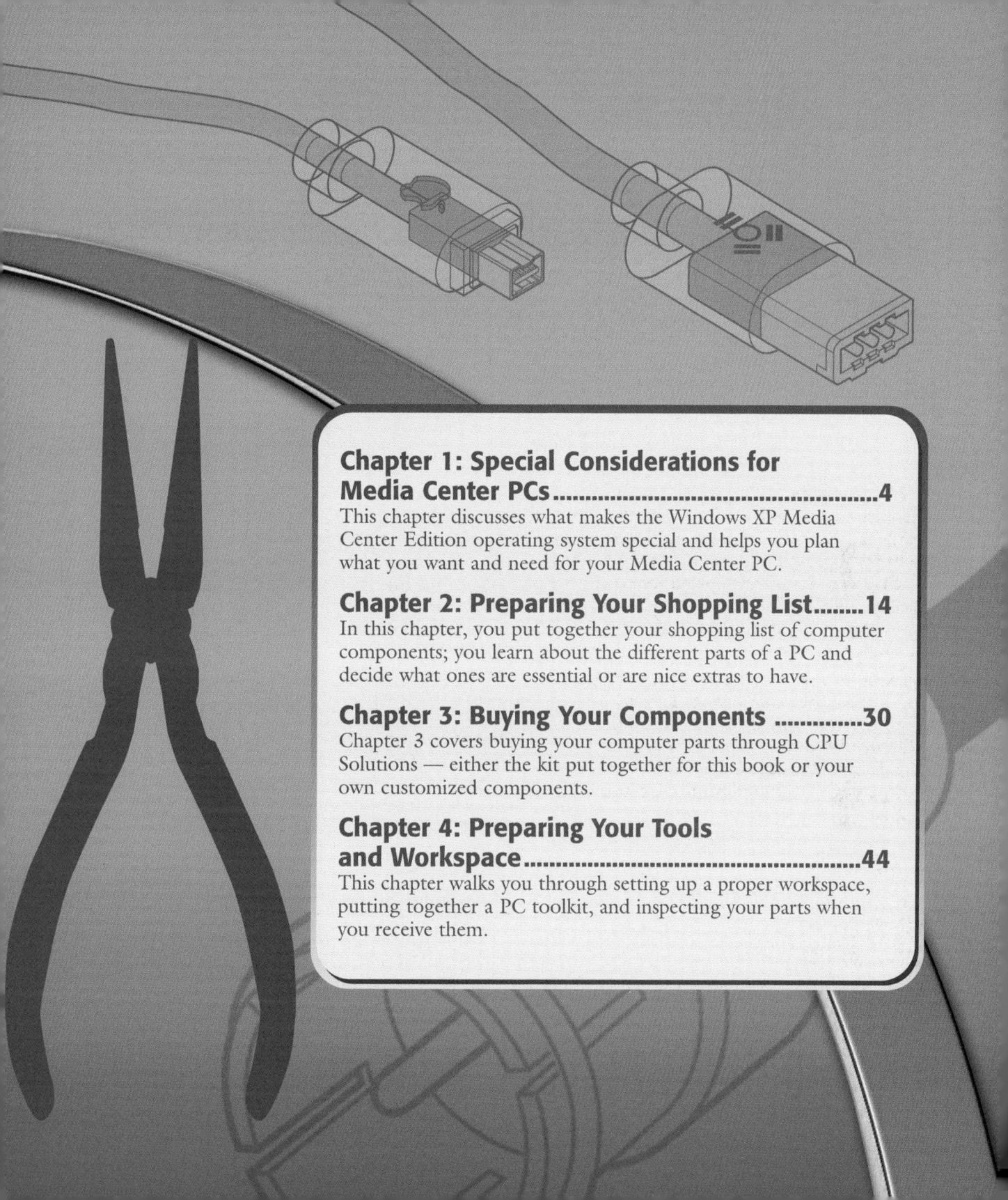

Chapter 1: Special Considerations for Media Center PCs 4

This chapter discusses what makes the Windows XP Media Center Edition operating system special and helps you plan what you want and need for your Media Center PC.

Chapter 2: Preparing Your Shopping List 14

In this chapter, you put together your shopping list of computer components; you learn about the different parts of a PC and decide what ones are essential or are nice extras to have.

Chapter 3: Buying Your Components 30

Chapter 3 covers buying your computer parts through CPU Solutions — either the kit put together for this book or your own customized components.

Chapter 4: Preparing Your Tools and Workspace 44

This chapter walks you through setting up a proper workspace, putting together a PC toolkit, and inspecting your parts when you receive them.

The Difference between an Average PC and a Media Center PC

Windows Media Center was engineered for consumer entertainment. A Windows Media Center PC needs hardware that can handle more video and audio demands than the average PC.

If the PC that you have currently is more than a few years old, it probably is not a good candidate for Microsoft Windows Media Center because it was designed for a much more general-purpose use.

A Standard PC

A standard PC from two to three years ago typically featured 128MB of memory, decent video including a 17" monitor, a nice but not particularly great sound system, and a 40GB hard drive. All of these components are fine if you are just playing some regular games, listening to sound files, browsing the Web, and running basic desktop applications.

A Media Center PC

A Windows Media Center PC needs hardware that can handle high video and audio demands, including a fast CPU (or a *processor*), a highly capable video adapter (or a *graphics card*), and an audio adapter (a *sound card*). A Media Center PC also needs a fair amount of hard drive space, memory, and extras such as strong speakers, a TV tuner/video capture card, and a monitor capable of drawing the graphics and handling video.

A New System

Because of the differences discussed here, you cannot turn just any PC into a Media Center system. Also, unlike other versions of Windows, you cannot just walk into a store and buy a copy to install on your existing system. Windows Media Center is only available either on a new PC manufactured to Windows Media Center standards or from a vendor of PC hardware who sells components to build such a system.

Windows Media Center Online

To learn more about Windows Media Center, go to www.microsoft.com/windowsxp/mediacenter/.

Specific Differences in Windows Media Center

Windows Media Center Edition is not quite the same as any other version of Windows. Windows Media Center is actually a special form of Windows XP that has been reengineered for the total entertainment experience.

Windows Media Center is optimized to take advantage of the special things that you do with it, including downloading movies and music, burning your own DVDs and CDs, and even watching cable or satellite TV directly from your desktop.

A Home Theater

Windows Media Center is designed to integrate with your home theater, so you can share a TV program or movie, listen to music, and even display photos. After you use this book to build a PC and equip it with Windows Media Center, you can decide whether you want to use the PC as a separate system or add it to the entertainment and information center that you have in your living room or den.

Enhancements and Features

Windows Media Player 10: The most recent version of the popular media player with many extras over previous incarnations.

Windows Movie Maker 2.1 with DVD burning: Creates movies and slideshows from still images that you add through your digital camera or grab from TV or videos using a TV tuner/video capture card.

Built-in DVD and CD burning: Windows Media Center makes it simple to burn your own DVDs, which can hold eight times the capacity of a CD, and your own CDs.

Enhanced digital photo tools: More special options for working with your digital photos are included within the Windows desktop system.

Digital media refinements: Here you get tools such as Audio Converter to save space either on your hard drive or on your handheld personal media player and Windows Party Mode to give you secure music playback so that you can be the deejay at get-togethers.

Better game playing: This version of Windows has been improved to give you a better gaming experience, complete with support for the newest games that require DirectX 9–capable hardware.

What You May Want and Need

Think about what you would like to have on your new PC. However, do not just think about what you want but also about what you need. Likely, your Windows Media Center PC will do double duty: both as entertainment and the standard jobs that you use a regular PC for.

The system built in this book can handle all its roles admirably while remaining within the budget of most people. Yet you should think ahead to the many ways you will use your customized system above and beyond the fun.

Suit Your PC to Your Needs

If you expect to do a great deal of video editing, you may want a graphics card with even more power than the one used for this customized Media Center PC. This is also true if you happen to do a fair amount of still photo editing.

Additional memory would be good, too; understand that memory is a relatively inexpensive way to give your system a big power boost. A much larger monitor may be wise, as well, because you need more screen space to manipulate many different editing windows simultaneously.

Ask Yourself Questions

As you consider what you want and need, ask yourself these questions:

- What are the kinds of work you expect to do with the system over the next year or two?
- Will you add the Media Center PC to your living room setup or put it to use in a different room as a media solution?
- Do you have existing PC hardware — such as a printer or a big screen monitor — that you can press into service so that you can free up money to spend on other equipment?
- If you choose a smaller new hard drive, what is the chance that you will run out of space in three to six months?
- Do you play a lot of graphics-intensive games? If so, you may need even better video.
- Who besides you will use the system and how?
- How much do you want to spend? Is it more or less than the target system in this book?
- Do you want to have a digital video camera for use with this PC? If so, you need a Firewire/IEEE 1394 port (also called *i.Link* for users of Sony video cameras) on the new PC.

If other questions crop up as you think, write them down or make a mental note so that you remember as you plan and shop.

What You Can Realistically Get

Another question to ask yourself is, "Why build rather than just buy a fully equipped Windows Media Center PC?" The answer to this is almost always just-for-your-specific-needs customization.

Unfortunately, money is always a factor, and you need to think about that as you plan. The system designed for this book was specifically put together to give you power where it is needed most, all the while staying under $1,000.

Bought Systems Offer Few Choices

Although many manufacturers, including big outfits such as Dell and Gateway, offer custom system configurations on their Web sites that enable you to pick and choose at least some of your components, you usually do not get that many different choices. For example, you may be able to select between two or three different hard disks, a small array of monitors, and a CD recording drive versus a DVD recording drive.

Cost Considerations

If you want Windows Media Center and a new PC but do not necessarily expect routinely to use this system to its fullest, you also may be able to cut some corners. Perhaps a CD burner that also plays DVDs would work rather than a DVD player/recording drive. Likewise, if you have some flexibility in your budget, you may be able to seriously jazz up the system that you build, fitting it with a high-powered audio and video system.

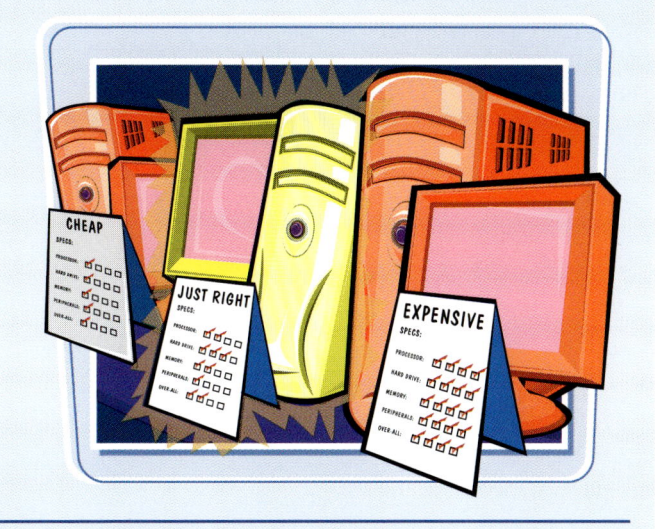

A Monitor for Your Budget

The monitor may be your biggest issue when it comes to your budget. The monitor used in the system built in this book is a very decent choice, but it is not a flat panel liquid crystal display (LCD) unit but a standard cathode ray tube (CRT) with a dense front-to-back profile. The thinner a monitor is and the greater its display area, the more you will spend.

For one of the better consumer-level very large monitors, you can easily spend $900 to $1500 just on this one piece of equipment. If you are passionate about media or do a certain amount of video editing as part of your regular work *and* you are not operating under a tight budget, you may be able to justify the expense. But if not, you may be able to go with a 17" LCD rather than CRT unit and add no more than $100 or so to the total cost of the PC.

Plan Your System

It is important to carefully plan your system before you buy your parts so that you get exactly the computer that you need. Stick to your plan; do not sabotage yourself and abandon all your planning by giving in to the temptation to buy the next computer that you see online or in a store.

Do not forget your objectives for the new PC as well as your wants and needs; these can be easily overlooked in impulse shopping.

Stick to Your Plan

There are smart reasons to go to the additional effort that you have in this chapter — and will continue in the next — before you start shopping. When you begin to actually look at the parts and prices, it may be too easy to get caught up in the moment or get impatient to start building. But although you want a new Windows Media Center PC, you want to avoid certain situations or behaviors in doing so.

Stick to Your Budget

Do not overspend your budget; this is something that is too easy to do. Although you can make exceptions based on particular wants or needs, you should decide on a set budget and try to choose smartly within that overall dollar range.

Watch for Hardware Compatibility

Be careful that you do not unwittingly choose incompatible hardware. Almost every PC hardware component is designed for use with specific operating systems. You need to check the product information to make sure that yours will work with Windows XP Media Center Edition.

Check for All Your Parts

Check and recheck your parts list, which is covered in Chapter 2, to be sure that you obtain absolutely everything that you need to assemble your PC. This includes everything from major components such as a monitor and motherboard to small details such as power cords, cables, and screws used to mount drives. Do not be afraid to ask questions of your sales representative about what is and is not included with a part.

Plan Your System (continued)

Understand one core truth: Salespeople exist to get you to buy something. Unfortunately, their need to sell is usually in direct opposition to your need to get the right parts to build the best system for you.

Do not get talked into either parts or a whole system that will not do what you want. Instead, use this book as your guide to shop and build intelligently with parts that will be compatible.

Avoid Sales Hype

Many sales representatives may not be all that knowledgeable about the equipment that they sell and how compatible something may be with what you want to achieve. Everyone has had the experience of walking into a store, asking smart questions, only to get answers — and a product — that ends up not being right. Unfortunately, you may end up spending more because many stores — online as well as brick-and-mortar — end up charging you a restocking fee when you take the product back; this fee may be as much as 10 to 15% of the total price.

Hidden Benefits

Want to know a secret about building your own PC that is too often overlooked? Building your system accomplishes more than allowing yourself to customize it just the way that you want it. You also learn an incredible lot about how a PC goes together, the hardware involved, and troubleshooting as part of the process. It is like instantly moving from PC novice to grizzled veteran status and is likely to give you a real sense of control.

Take Advantage of the Windows Media Center Design Studio

Are you completely mystified about what all these fancy terms can mean when it comes to tech and media? If so, you will be happy to know that you do not need to know, for example, the difference between the terms *hot plug* or *hot swap*. Microsoft provides a special feature online called Design Studio that helps you understand how you can integrate Windows Media Center into your total entertainment experience and bring rich media like sound and video into any room in your home.

Visit the Microsoft Windows Media Center support site at www.microsoft.com/windowsxp/mediacenter/ and choose Design Studio or, if that is not available, click Design Your Media Center PC Powered Home. There, you not only learn about the best new features of Media Center, but also how you can identify hardware that you may want to add to the system you build in this book as well as to your home theater setup. The guide lets you build a blueprint to revamp your existing equipment and get the best media experience. Tabs at the bottom of your browser window let you switch to different areas of focus in the Design Studio.

Decide on Essentials

You, as the builder rather than the buyer of a preassembled system, need to understand both the major components that you need as well as the smaller, yet still critical, items required, including cables to connect your various drives to the motherboard and to connect your CD or DVD player to the sound card.

You need to know the individual parts that are absolutely required, along with additional components that can empower a media-specific PC. Think of this as your basic shopping list.

Avoid Missing Parts

You do not have the luxury of assuming *anything*. One simple assumption can leave you missing an important component when you are right in the middle of assembling your system. This is not so bad if you live in an area where you can hop in the car and drive to a shopping mall that happens to sell small parts, but it is still inconvenient and can end up costing you extra money.

Start Your Shopping List

Every PC requires the following major components:

- A case
- A power supply
- A motherboard
- A CPU (central processing unit) and its fan and a heatsink
- Memory
- Required add-on adapters
- A hard drive
- A removable media drive such as CD or DVD drive
- A monitor
- A keyboard and mouse
- Speakers

Know More about the Basics

You now know the basic parts list for your PC build-it-yourself shopping. Remember, however, that this list is very basic. Here, you will learn about the important role each part plays in your system.

Later in this chapter, you will learn about other hardware that you may want to add based on what you plan to do with your system.

Know More about the Basics

THE CASE

The case and the power supply provide the structure and the electricity required for all the components in your PC.

The case serves as the housing for all the internal components and provides jacks or other connections for external ones such as speakers.

The case choice determines how many extras you can install. It also factors into how cool and well your system operates and how easy it will be to go inside and replace parts.

THE POWER SUPPLY

The power supply mounts inside the case and converts power from the household or office current. This unit also contains at least one fan for removing hot air from the case. You learn in Chapter 6 how the capacity of the power supply affects what can be added to the system and protections to prevent "dirty" power.

Note: Choose your CPU and motherboard first; then choose your case design and power supply. This works best.

THE MOTHERBOARD

The motherboard is the core printed circuit board to which almost everything else installs in a personal computer. It is also called a *mainboard* or a *system board*.

The motherboard mounts to the chassis inside the case. Certain other components such as the CPU and its fan, memory, and any adapters are installed directly on the motherboard, and almost everything else gets connected directly or indirectly to it.

- The CPU socket/slot: where your CPU gets mounted.
- Memory sockets: where your memory sticks are installed.
- Expansion board slots: where your adapters such as video and sound are installed.
- Onboard connectors: let you connect external and other internal devices such as drives.
- Integrated network adapter and sound adapter: this motherboard is already set up to connect this PC to a network and provide sound.

My preferred motherboard only works with AMD CPUs, yet my favored CPU is Intel. What can I do?

Check with CPU Solutions first. Usually, however, you need to couple an Intel CPU with an Intel-supported motherboard — and the same with AMD. Over the years, there have been just a very few dually compatible ones.

If I buy integrated components on my motherboard such as the graphics, sound, and network, will I regret it? I have heard they are not always very good.

You do not always sacrifice quality for integrated parts such as the functions that you mention. On bargain systems, this sacrifice happens a lot. But you are not putting together a super-cheap PC here, which helps. Also, you can replace most integrated components such as sound and networking with a separate adapter to take the place of those functions already on the motherboard.

continued

17

Know More about the Basics *(continued)*

The CPU, fan, and memory are often added to the motherboard before you actually mount the motherboard against the case chassis. The selection of these items must be done in concert with the type of case and motherboard you purchase, or you can run into serious problems.

The way you empower your PC with sound, video, and network capability is through the installation of adapters, also called *add-on* or *expansion boards* or *cards*.

Know More about the Basics *(continued)*

THE CPU AND ITS FAN

The CPU, or the "brain" of the PC, mounts into a CPU slot or socket on the motherboard and must be cooled usually by both a CPU fan and a *heatsink,* which is a piece of metal applied with a special compound to the CPU housing.

The motherboard and CPU have to match, meaning the motherboard has the right socket or slot to allow the CPU to be installed.

MEMORY

The memory is a "stick" or miniature printed circuit board in which special chips are mounted. Your memory type must be matched to the motherboard and CPU.

Understand that memory is what gives you the operating power to run applications on your desktop and to open and move between already open files. Too little memory cuts down on system performance.

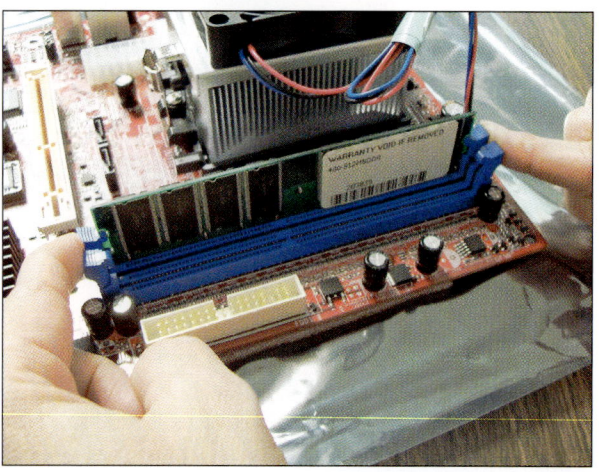

THE VIDEO ADAPTER

The video adapter, also called the *graphics card,* is a special circuit board designed to draw the images that you see on your monitor screen. A video card usually features a special CPU all its own called the *VPU* (video processing unit) to make the pictures draw much faster on your monitor without slowing down the main CPU.

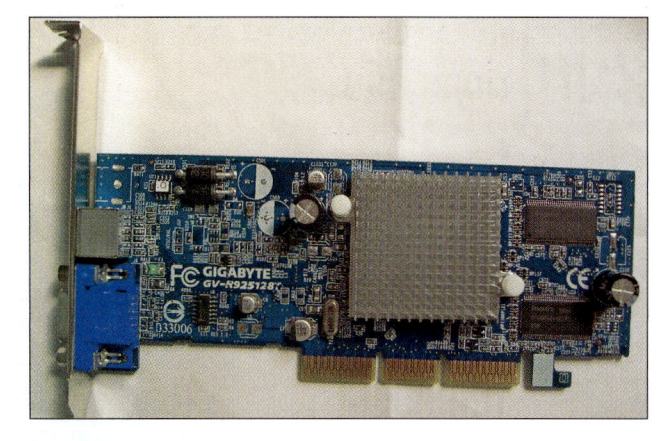

THE AUDIO ADAPTER

The audio adapter — also called the *sound card* — handles all the sounds that you hear through your PC speakers, which are connected to the audio adapter at the back of the PC.

The sound card is usually installed to one of the motherboard's PCI slots but may also be integrated directly into the motherboard. Other devices such as a microphone and headphones also plug in to jacks located on the sound card.

Where do adapters mount?

Adapters mount into expansion slots on the motherboard called AGP with video and PCI for video, sound, and network.

What does *integrated motherboard* mean? If I have one, do I need to add adapters?

Many motherboards are *integrated,* which means that they have video, sound, and/or networking built directly into them. But I suggest adding separate adapters, ones that boast more power and features than the integrated chips on the motherboard, because that will enable you to get better sound and video — more than the integrated motherboard allows.

Chapter 2: Preparing Your Shopping List

continued

19

Know More about the Basics *(continued)*

Other available adapter types include a network adapter, modem, and specialty boards that add features not already available on the motherboard.

The drives serve as your file storage area and are never built directly into the motherboard but attached to the motherboard using cables.

Know More about the Basics *(continued)*

THE MODEM

A modem, although not absolutely required, acts as a "translator" between your PC and either your phone line or your cable/DSL or satellite high-speed connection so that you can access the Internet. Many modems also enable you to send and receive faxes.

A modem may be integrated into the motherboard, installed as an adapter to a PCI slot on the motherboard, or available as an external unit that connects to the back of the PC.

THE NETWORK ADAPTER

The network adapter — also called the *network interface card* (NIC) — lets you connect different PCs together and share an Internet connection from one PC to others.

Like a modem, a network adapter may be integrated into the motherboard, installed into a motherboard slot, or external. A cable or wireless connection is required to connect multiple PCs together through a jack on the network adapter.

DRIVES

Every PC requires at least one hard drive that acts as the permanent file storage area where your operating system and applications are installed, but you may also have additional drives such as a second hard drive, a CD or DVD drive, and a floppy disk drive.

A floppy drive and main hard drive are almost always internal and are connected by a special ribbon cable to a connector on the motherboard. Other drives may be external and connect through a Universal Serial Bus (USB) or IEEE 1394 (Firewire) port on the motherboard.

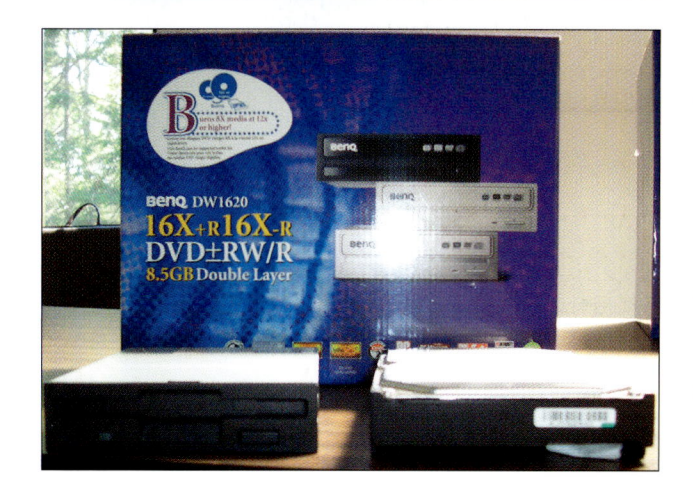

How many adapters can I install on my motherboard?

You are limited only by the number of expansion board slots available in your motherboard. Even after that, there are workarounds; for example, you can install an external modem or network card if your motherboard does not have a free expansion slot.

What can I use to back up my files?

You can use any of the different variety of drive types as backups, including hard disk, floppy, and CD or DVD drives. CD and DVD drives — whether only players, recordable, or rewriteable — and specialty drives are especially used for backups so that you can protect important files off the main hard disk.

continued

Know More about the Basics *(continued)*

Besides the internal key components that you need, there are also several basic ones that sit outside the case and attach via ports at the front or back of the PC. These include the monitor, keyboard, mouse or another pointing device such as a trackball, and speakers.

Know More about the Basics *(continued)*

THE MONITOR

The monitor is the TV-like device that draws the images rendered by the video adapter, or graphics card. The monitor connects to this card – or directly to the motherboard when video chips are integrated onto the motherboard – at the back of the PC.

KEYBOARD AND MOUSE

The keyboard and mouse are input devices through which you type and click. These devices are connected either to standard ports at the back of the PC or through a USB port that may be located either at the back or front of the PC.

SPEAKERS

Similar to the speakers on your home stereo, these connect to the audio adapter, or sound card, at the back of the PC or directly through jacks on the motherboard when sound is integrated into the motherboard.

Do I necessarily have to install a modem in my PC?

No. As a matter of fact, a modem is not included in the Media Center PC that I am showing you how to build in this book. The reason for this is that most people today use high-speed Internet connections that often require either just a special type of network adapter or a specific type of modem — something you probably already have as part of an existing PC or home network setup.

If I decide to go with one of the new, fancy, and big flat-screen monitors, will I experience problems using it with the video adapter?

As you learn later, most video adapters today either provide two ports — one of the standard monitor connections called the *video* or *VGA port,* and a second one for the DVI port used by the fancy flat screens. Where two ports are not present, you will usually find that the graphics card comes with an adapter to allow the newer monitors to plug in. But verify this with your choice of graphics card.

continued

Know More about the Basics *(continued)*

There are a number of smaller items you will also need to get to complete your assembly, including cables, cords, and specialty fans. Most of these should be included with the core components that you order, but you need to make sure that they are included when you place an order and that you receive them with your parts.

Although most of these may strike you as "pesky details," they are still quite essential, and you need to be sure that you have them before you actually build the system — or you will run into problems.

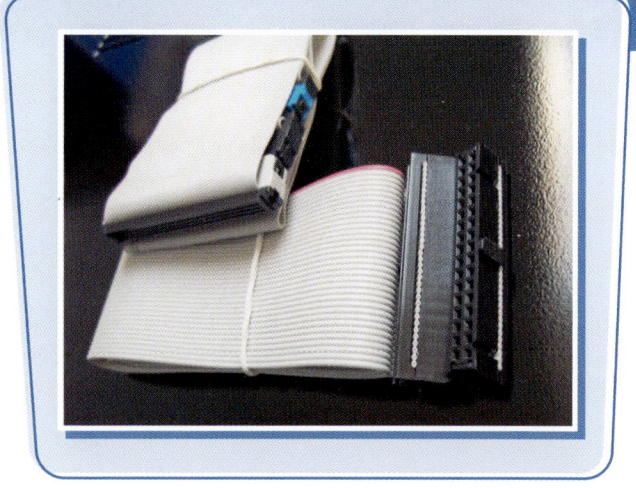

Know More about the Basics *(continued)*

THE MAIN POWER CORD

The main power cord connects the PC to electricity and usually is included with the case and/or power supply.

Power cords are available separately for between $4 and $10.

RIBBON CABLES

Ribbon cables are required for your all internal IDE/ATA drives. A standard PC motherboard features two IDE connectors where drives are connected by ribbon cables.

Two drives can be connected through a single ribbon cable if the cable has a slave connection in which the main cable is connected to the first drive and then a small extra loop of cable connects up the second drive.

THE MONITOR POWER CORD

The monitor power cord should ship with your monitor, sometimes attached permanently to the monitor and sometimes removable, which can be plugged into the back of the monitor and into the outlet.

THE VIDEO CABLE

The video cable should also ship with your monitor to connect the monitor to the back of the PC, usually directly to the video adapter (graphics card) or to a special connection on motherboards with integrated video.

THE CD/DVD-TO-SOUND CARD CABLE

There is a small cable that attaches the CD/DVD drive to the sound card for audio output; this usually is included with your CD or DVD drive and sometimes with a sound card.

SPECIALTY FANS

Specialty fans are used to improve airflow and reduce heat buildup within the case. These are available in all types, from special drive cooling fans that install to an available drive bay in the case to tiny fans that you can mount at strategic spots inside the case where special cooling is needed; the price ranges from a few dollars to $150 or more.

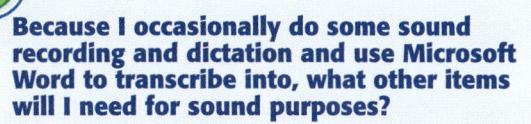

Q&A

Because I occasionally do some sound recording and dictation and use Microsoft Word to transcribe into, what other items will I need for sound purposes?

Other items that you may want to add include a microphone, which is needed for speech recognition software or when you want to create your own sound files, and a pair of headphones so that you can listen to your Media Center PC privately.

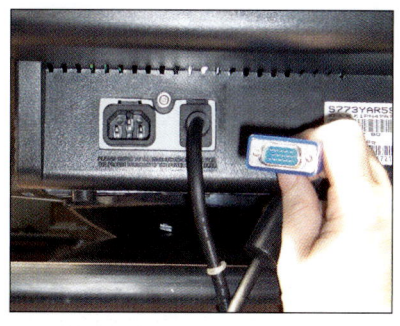

What if I cannot locate the cables or cords that are supposed to come with my hardware? Can I use just anything that fits?

Do not press "just anything" into service. Instead, contact your hardware vendor — such as CPU Solutions — to see if it can provide the exact cable or cord that you need. But also check again through the boxes your hardware was packed in. Cords and cables have a way of being missed when they are actually there.

Worthy Extras

Beyond the "must-have" components, there are a number of additional ones that you may either want or require, depending on the work you do and your considerations in Chapter 1. These can include one or more of the items listed here.

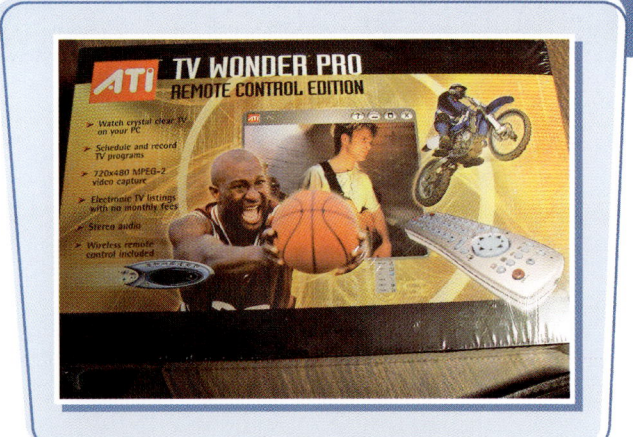

Worthy Extras

You may want additional adapters that perform special jobs such as the TV tuner/video capture board featured in the Media Center PC built for this book, a modem, or a network adapter.

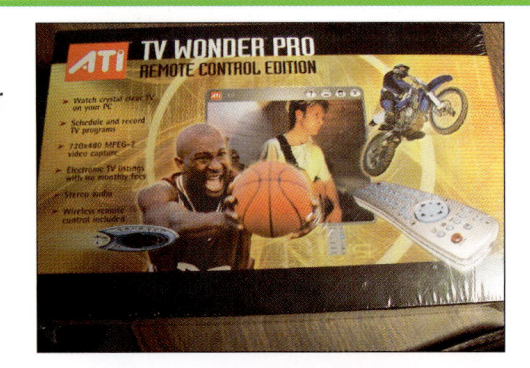

You may want extra drives — perhaps both a CD-RW drive for backups and a DVD-RW drive to play and record CDs. You also may want an additional hard drive.

You may want extra game devices, such as a joystick or a steering wheel, which often connect to the PC either through the sound card or through the USB ports.

You may want to add a printer if you do not already have one; if you do have a printer, you can share it on the network with your Media Center PC so that everyone can use a single printer. Likewise, a flatbed scanner is a great way to copy images and documents directly into your PC.

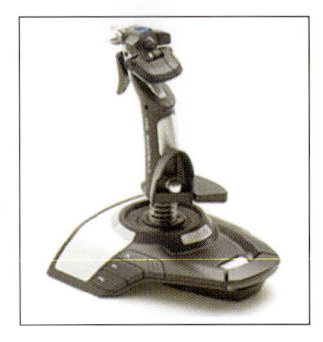

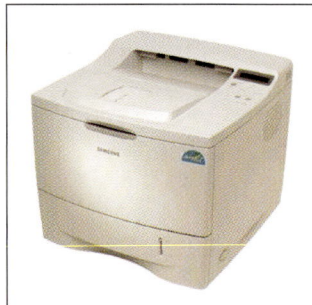

You may want a digital camera — either a still camera or Webcam or a digital video camera.

Personal media players, such as iPods and other handheld MP3 players, are a hot addition to any media desktop system. Some personal media players feature an extremely sensitive microphone and enough storage to record up to an hour of a conversation or music.

A graphics tablet enables you to draw images using a special stylus and electronic board and store the images directly on your PC.

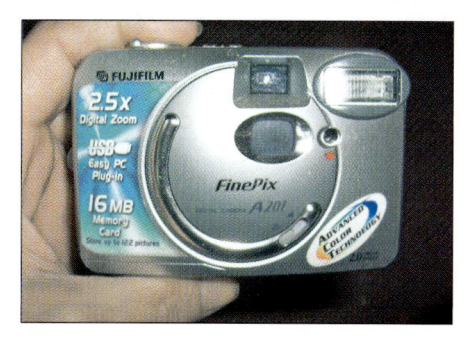

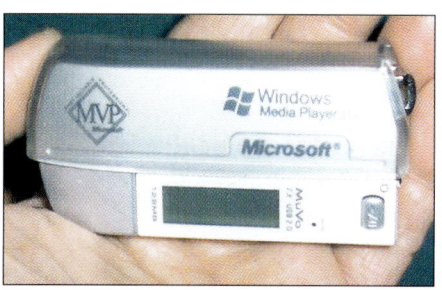

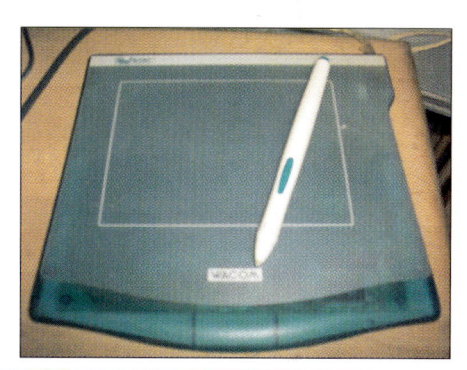

How do I connect my digital camera to my computer?

The target PC built in this book includes both USB ports where most still cameras connect as well as an IEEE 1394 (Firewire) port where you can connect digital movie cameras. You may be able to connect an older style camera through either your video adapter or the video capture board included with the Media Center PC.

I have a really old digital camera that connects through the COM ports. Do you think I can continue to use this one, or should I consider a new purchase?

You probably want a new camera for several reasons. Cameras that download through the COM port at the back of the PC are notoriously slow. More importantly, cameras have gotten so much better in the years since COM port cameras were around. Your old one will take much fuzzier pictures.

Chapter 2: Preparing Your Shopping List

27

Assess Your Special Needs

Can you think of anything else you may need beyond what you have already learned about? If not, what about other items you simply want? Although the list provided in this chapter is pretty comprehensive, you may want to look around — both on the CPU Solutions site you visit in Chapter 3 as well as in your local consumer electronics/computer shop — to see if you can find any other must-haves for special work or play that you may be involved in.

Assess Your Special Needs

The Roland sound mixing board shown here, which connects via a USB port, can turn your Media Center PC into a more sophisticated sound recording studio.

An uninterruptible power supply (UPS) can save your computer from taking a direct hit from a power surge, a lightning strike, or overloaded circuits that may otherwise fry your power supply and/or motherboard. A UPS plugs in between your wall outlet and the PC itself.

A UPS also packs a battery that gives you time, usually at least 5-15 minutes, for you to work beyond the point you lose power so that you can close your applications and shut down your PC normally.

Although not quite as powerful at saving your PC as a full UPS, a surge suppressor also acts to protect your PC from power problems. Often looking very much like a slightly large power strip (some power strips include surge suppressors, but not all), a surge protector takes a power surge or spike directly that would otherwise hurt your PC. The price range is between $6 and $80.

It is a good idea to have a modem and dial-up as a back-up Internet connection, for those times when your high-speed Internet connection is not available. A dial-up modem costs between $15 and $50.

Note: You can use one of the free Internet services if you do not want the cost of a back-up dial-up Internet account. Juno at www.juno.com and NetZero at www.netzero.net both offer free accounts that give you up to four hours a month to be online without a fee.

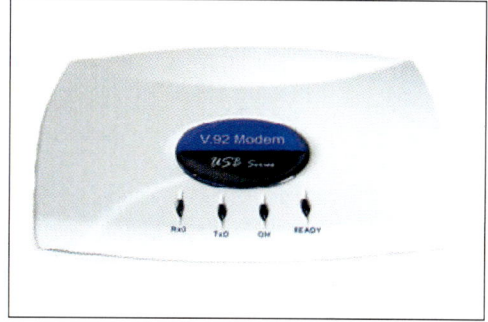

Q&A

I cannot spend the extra money on special items. Why should I take the time to assess any special needs?

Even if your budget does not allow any special additions right now, you may want to keep a wish list. Then later, as more money becomes available, you can add on more bells and whistles.

Why does the PC I will create with this book not include a modem?

The system that you build here does not include a modem because you may already have high-speed Internet access in your home and office and can share that connection with this new PC. One of the great benefits of Windows Media Center is that it makes it much easier for you to download not just sound files but entire movies, so to take full advantage of this, you will want high-speed Internet access.

Shop Smarter

Before you get to the actual shopping, you need to prepare. Take what you have already done in asking yourself questions about what you need and want, add to it the research you did through the Microsoft Windows Media Center Design Studio, and then review all your material.

First, review your notes, your wish list, and your needs before you do your shopping. This helps guarantee that you do not forget anything or short-change the system if you customize above and beyond the system designed for you in this book.

CPU Solutions

As you will learn here, CPU Solutions has partnered with Wiley, the publisher of this book, to make it a cinch for you to find what you need. CPU Solutions has even built a special area on its Web site devoted to you, the reader using this book, to build your own Windows Media Center PC. There is more about this later in the chapter.

Understand as you go that there is always the chance that you may want to explore other hardware not outlined for this project. For example, you may see a really great deal on another monitor that you may want to get to replace an older monitor on another PC you have.

Fit Your Needs

You are not limited in any way. CPU Solutions will be happy to work with you in choosing more than just what is covered in this book and the target system here. You also may need additional hardware to install a home network if you do not already have one. If you question whether you should buy now or later, appreciate that it may make more sense to take care of all your computer needs now in one shopping session.

CPU Solutions Coupons

At the back of this book, you will find coupons that can help you cut costs as you shop through CPU Solutions. Be sure to check these out before you go online to buy. Remember also that each parts chapter includes some alternative hardware selections, so you can customize your new PC beyond what is built in this target system.

Using CPU Solutions

Your very first step is to visit the CPU Solutions online store and begin to explore what it has available as well as its prices. You want to look around thoroughly before you buy. Also, do not be afraid to ask questions; contact information for customer service representatives is available online.

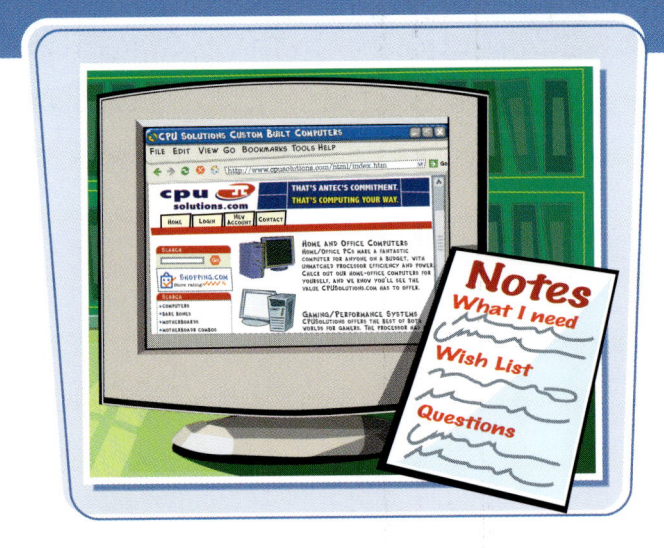

Using CPU Solutions

1. Connect to the Internet.
2. Open your Web browser.
3. Type in the address **http://www.cpusolutions.com**.
4. When the CPU Solutions site loads, begin your exploration.

5. Click the **Contact** tab to see how you can contact CPU Solutions and its helpful customer service representatives to ask questions that you may have or get custom configuration information.

Note: This contact information includes e-mail addresses.

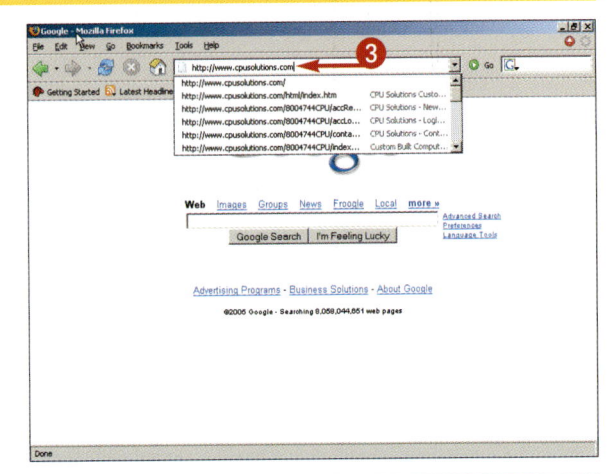

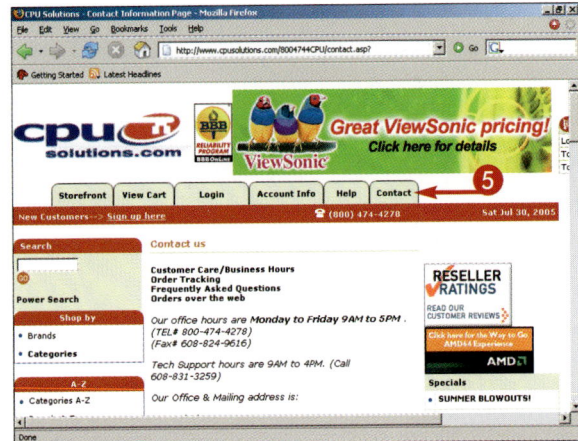

32

6 Click one of the **Specials** links to see what products may be offered under special discounting to enable you to augment your new system at a price savings.

7 Click **New Products** under Just Arrived to view hardware CPU Solutions has just acquired in its inventory that may not have been available at the time this book was written.

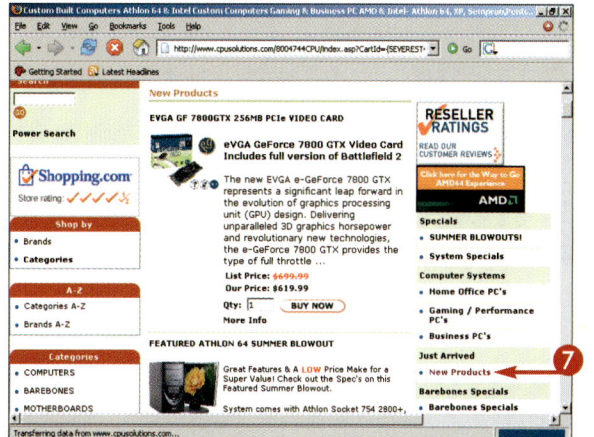

Can I start purchasing my products now?

No, please wait until you go through everything on the site and make all your choices before you actually begin to place your order. This will help you stay organized and focused.

Is there any problem if I decide to order extra parts or wholly different parts through CPU Solutions?

Absolutely none. This book — and the CPU Solutions online store — provides you with a guide for what you will need. But what you choose and order is strictly up to you and your specific needs and desires. For example, although this system was put together on a budget, you have the freedom to add lots of great extras on your own.

Chapter 3: Buying Your Components

33

What CPU Solutions Has Done for You

CPU Solutions has worked closely with the development of this book to select hardware that should work very well with the Windows Media Center PC operating system and give you a great experience for the special qualities of a media center system.

You can select the basic setup available to save you time in shopping for pieces individually, which means that you would be basically done until the order arrives and you can pick up your work in Chapter 4, or you can go through the site yourself and pick options using instructions that you will find in the remainder of this chapter.

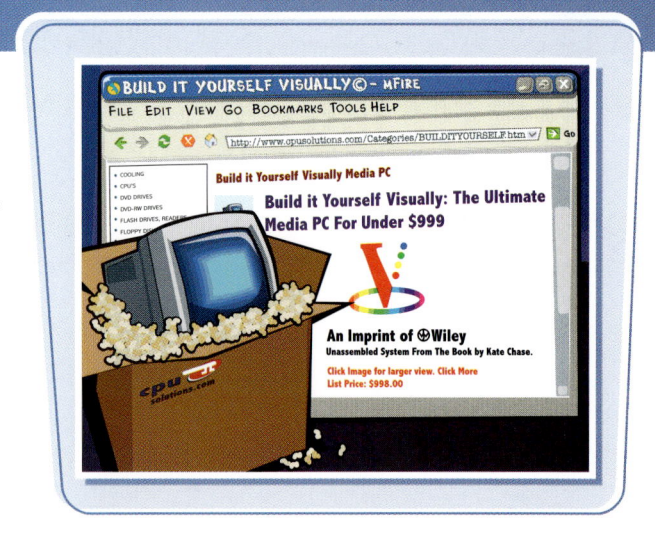

What CPU Solutions Has Done for You

1. At the CPU Solutions site, scroll down and click **BUILD IT YOURSELF VISUALLY**.

The *Build It Yourself Visually* page appears.

2. Scroll down and click **Build It Yourself Visually Media PC**.

- Alternatively, you can save time by simply clicking **Buy Now** to order the specific setup for the Windows Media Center PC, including all the parts that you need.

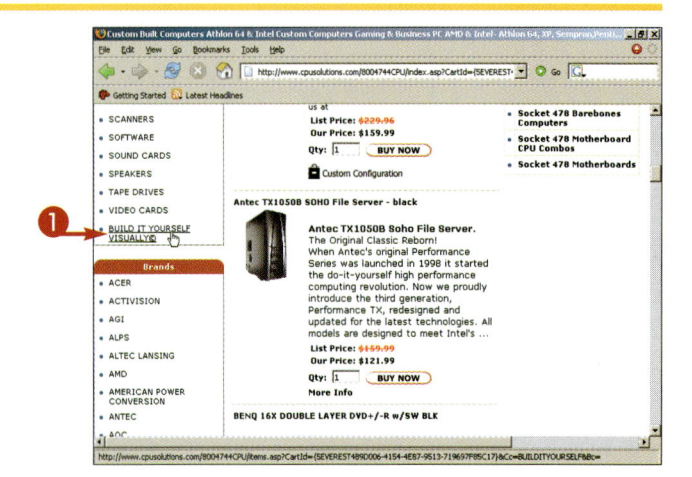

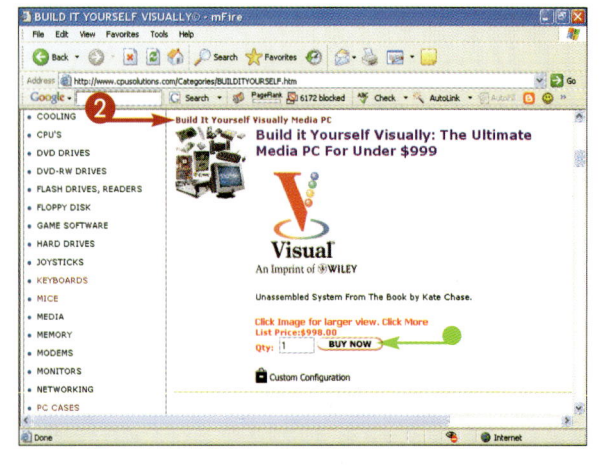

The *Build It Yourself Visually: The Ultimate Media Center PC for Under $999* page appears.

③ To see what is available for this build, scroll down and review the hardware components.

● You can create your own custom configuration by starting with the basic setup as your core order but then selecting varying hardware to fit your needs. Just click ⌄s and select different pieces of hardware.

Note: You can also click **Custom Configuration** *on the initial* Build It Yourself Visually *page to access this customization list.*

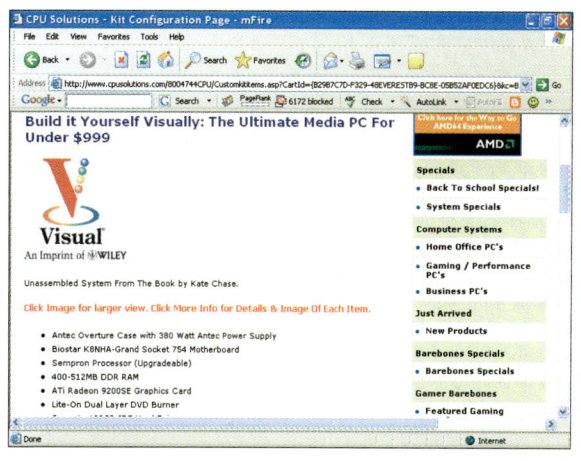

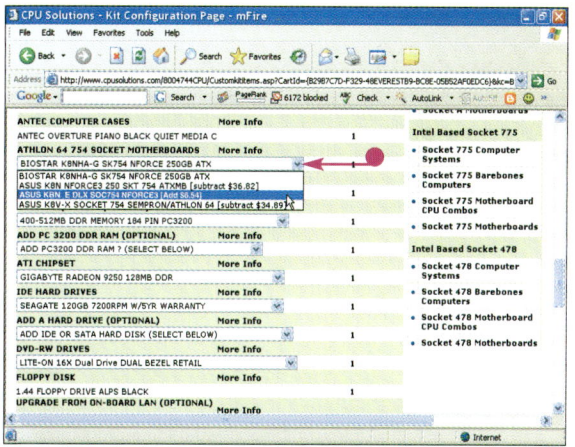

Q&A

What are the components that you chose for the target system?

Case: Antec Piano Console, $108.81 (with power supply)

CPU: Sempron 2600, $83.60

Memory: 400-512MB DDR, $62.99

Motherboard: Biostar K8NHA-G, $79.99

Hard drive: Seagate Barracuda, $80.61

CD/DVD drive: Benq DVD-R/RW, $61.99

Additional drive: Floppy disk, $10.99

Graphics card: Gigabyte Radeon 9250 125MB, $47.40

Additional adapter: TV Wonder Pro TV tuner/video capture card, $100.43

Monitor: AOC 17" CRT, $124.99

Speakers: Altec Lansing, $38.01

Keyboard and mouse: Logitech Internet Pro, $16.60

Operating system: Windows XP Media Center Edition, $138.42

Chapter 3: Buying Your Components

35

Compare Prices and Features

If you opt to shop for yourself rather than use the easy configuration center under the area named for this book, you can achieve great results by doing your homework. Consult this book as you go along because it tells you everything that you need to order along with recommended alternative hardware.

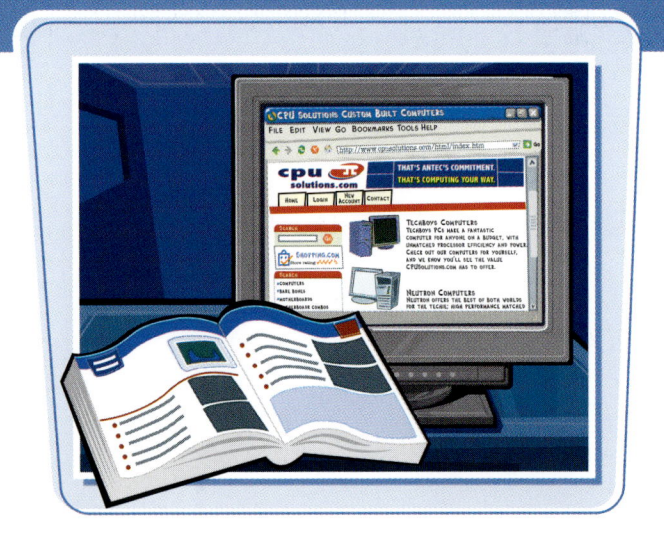

Compare Prices and Features

BROWSE BY CATEGORY

① Scroll down and look through the Categories section.

You can browse through individual components and bundle selections offered by the store.

BROWSE BY MANUFACTURER

① Scroll down below the Categories list to the Manufacturer section.

● If you know the name of the manufacturer of a specific product, such as Altec Lansing, Benq, and Seagate — and those listed in the chosen and recommended alternative pages at the beginning of each hardware component chapter — you can browse through the products available from that manufacturer.

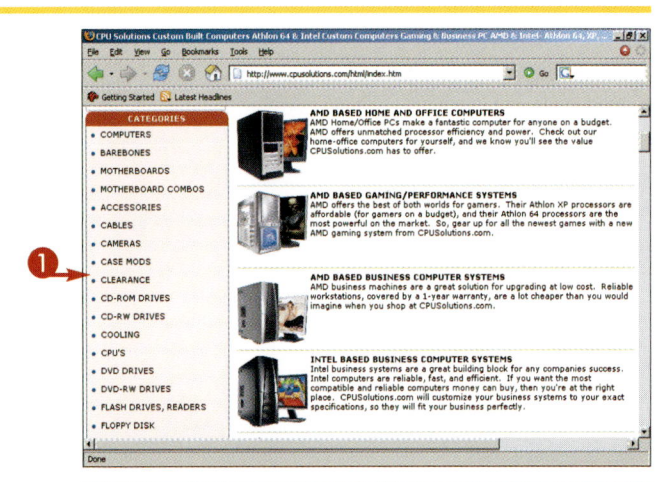

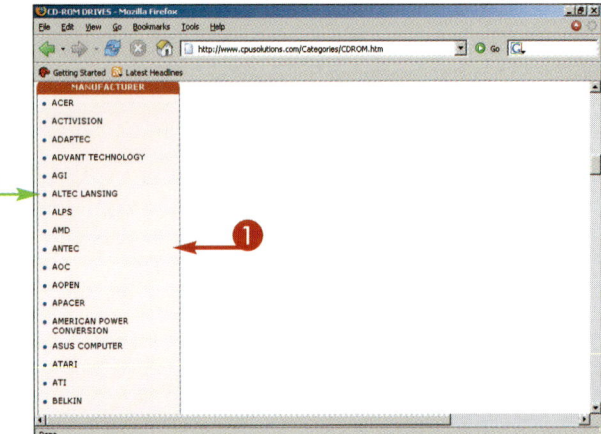

CHECK SPECIFIC PRODUCTS

① Go through the products one by one in the Categories and Manufacturer lists.

② Click the link for an individual product to reach its details.

③ Read through the specific information about each product, including the technical details and what is included with the product.

④ Compare the features and prices for each product.

⑤ When you make a final selection, write the product name down to help you identify exactly what you will order.

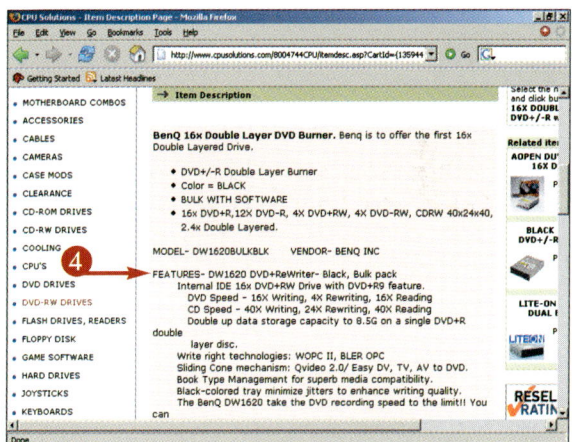

Q&A

How should I keep track of the different items through which I am browsing?

You may want to have a notepad or even a PC spreadsheet open to let you note specific features and prices to later help you compare and make a final choice.

Is there anything extra that I should look for?

Verify that any needed accessories such as cables and power cords are listed under the product information to ship with the device.

Chapter 3: Buying Your Components

Because it is very possible you will opt to make some custom changes to the target system as put together in this book, you want to follow recommendations on smart customization, so you are sure that everything you order will be compatible and exactly what you want and need.

Recommended Alternatives

Whenever possible, you want to make your custom choices from the list of recommended alternative products listed in each component chapter after the selected item. This recommended list takes into account the requirements of a Windows Media Center PC and what you are most likely going to need, while also considering budgetary concerns. So you will find products that are usually cheaper than the chosen one as well as those with special options that may cost quite a bit more.

Ask Questions

As you browse through CPU Solutions's site, take advantage of the knowledgeable staff who can aid you in making intelligent custom selections that meet not only the requirements of your Windows Media Center PC but also your unique needs for how you will put this system to use.

As I was putting together the best system that I could for under $1,000, I went shopping for the best possible package with as many extras as I could pack in there. But before I made my final selection, I consulted with Bo, one of CPU Solutions's highly capable sales reps, who suggested some alternatives that may work better and result in a much more powerful system while still coming in just a hair beneath my ideal price.

A List of Questions

What you may find most effective is to go through your various choices and then draft a list of questions you have related to all your choices. Then, when you contact CPU Solutions directly, such as by phone, you will know what to ask. Doing this also reduces the chance that you will need to make several repeat calls, just trying to cover all bases.

Windows Media Center and Windows XP

Remember, Windows Media Center is a form of Windows XP. Most products rated to work with Windows XP should work with this version of Windows. Still, it does not hurt to ask CPU Solutions if you have any doubts.

Read the Product Details

Take special care to read through the technical specifics for each product. This is where you may discover some of the questions you may want to ask of CPU Solutions, perhaps because the detail does not specify whether cables are included or does not indicate that it is compatible with Windows Media Center.

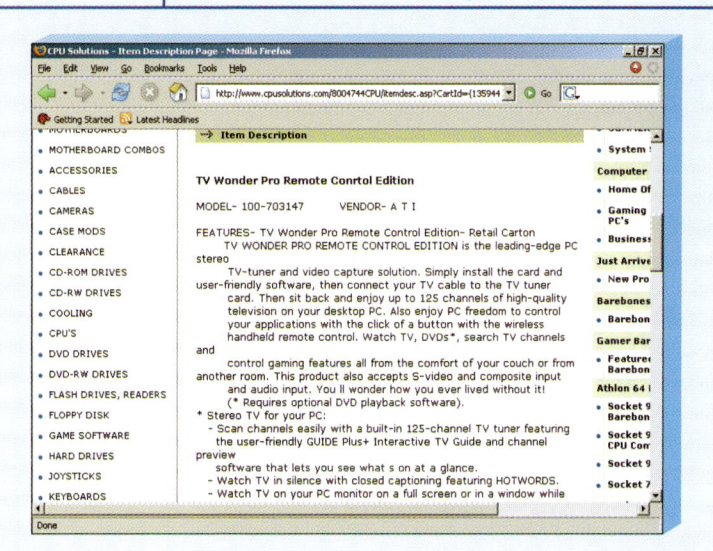

Order Windows

Do not forget to order a copy of Windows Media Center when you place your order for your hardware. Without this disc, you can only build the PC. You cannot go any farther than that. However, if you buy the Windows Media Center PC parts via the CPU Solutions *Build It Yourself Visually* kit, the operating system is included in the package and package price.

Order Windows Media Center Online

Although the Windows Media Center installation CD is not specifically mentioned in the various hardware components section, it is vital that you obtain this disc. Also, understand that you can only get a copy from a vendor of new PC hardware; you will not be able to order it from Microsoft or buy it off the shelf at your local PC store.

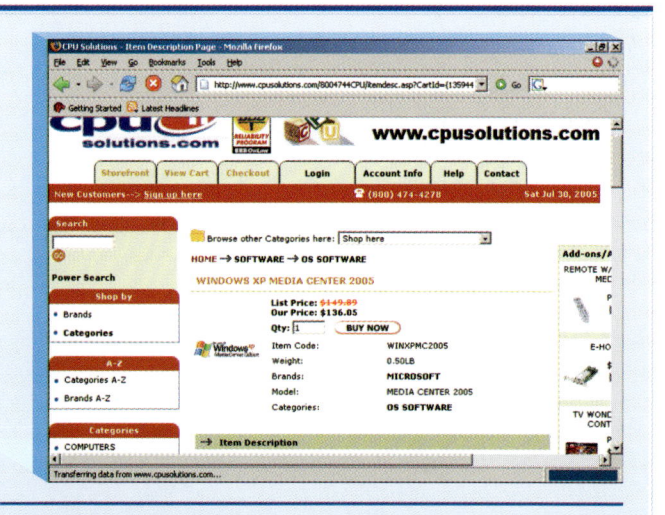

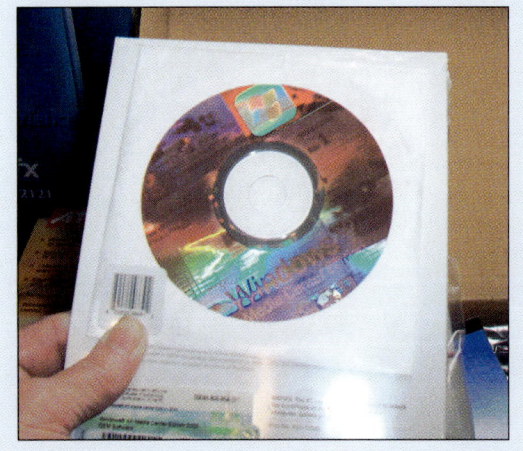

Do Not Take Shortcuts

Understand, too, that you do not want to try to take shortcuts here — specifically:

- Although you could order just Windows XP to install on your new PC, this will not have the media-rich features of Windows Media Center.

- Do not plan to borrow a copy of Media Center from someone else to install it. Not only is this illegal, but it usually also ends up being a nightmare because you will need the disc again at times later — such as when you change something about the PC — and you probably will not have your "borrowed" disc available to use.

- You may find that some online ads and spam you receive in your electronic mailbox promise you a copy of Windows Media Center for a cut-rate cost without having to buy new hardware as well. Likely, these copies are not legal, and you will not be able to activate and register them IF you are able to install from them in the first place — and you may not be able to do so.

Double-Check Your Order

After you have selected each component that you need, there is still one more thing you need to do before you actually place your order.

Make Sure That You Have Everything

Double-check your order to be certain that you have absolutely everything you need, such as the following:

- Your Windows Media Center installation disc.
- All your hardware components, including the case, the CPU and its fan, the motherboard, memory, the power supply, the hard drive, the CD/DVD drive, any additional drives, the graphics card, any additional adapters, the monitor, speakers, the keyboard, and the mouse.
- All the connecting hardware, such as power cords for the devices that require them, cables to install your drives, screws, and a grounding wrist strap. CPU Solutions does not offer a wrist strap for sale, but you can obtain one at your local electronics shop.

Place Your Order

Now that you have your list complete, your details covered, and everything double-checked, you are ready to go through the CPU Solutions site again to place your order. This final section walks you through the basic steps to place your order.

Place Your Order

1. Have your list handy along with your credit card or debit card.

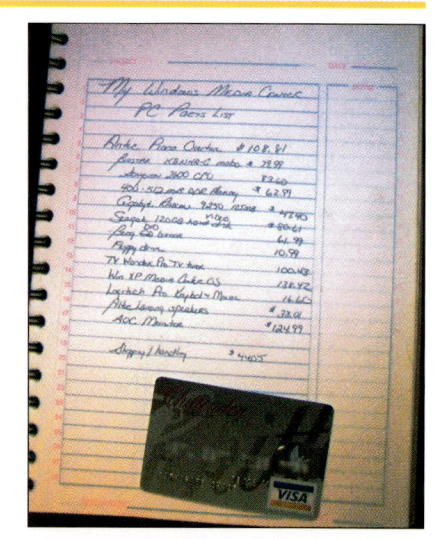

2. Go to www.cpusolutions.com.

3. Click the category for the first item on your list, such as **PC Cases** for the case.

4. Scan through the list of products until you locate the one that you want to order.

5. Click to open the product detail page for that product.

6. Click **Buy Now**.

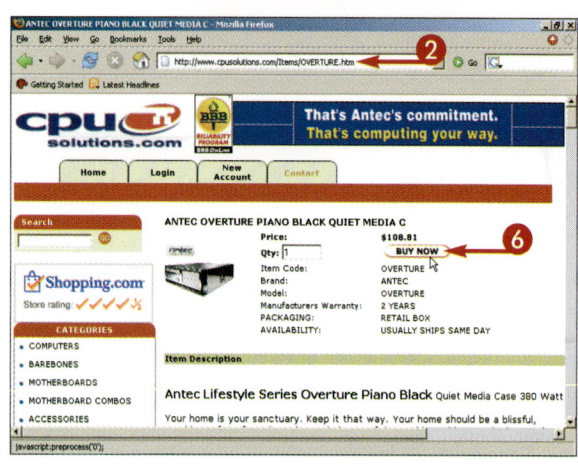

The View Cart page appears.

7 Review the item that you selected.

● A running total of your order appears here.

8 Click **Continue Shopping**.

9 Proceed to order all the other items on your list, including your Windows Media Center install disc.

10 After you have clicked **Buy Now** on the final item, compare the order form to your shopping list and make sure that everything you need is there.

11 Click **Checkout**.

The Account page appears.

12 Click **Sign Me Up Now**.

13 Fill out the basic information, such as your name, address, and other details.

14 When prompted, provide your shipping address details, along with your credit/debit card information.

15 After the order is processed, check your e-mail; a summary of your order details should arrive there momentarily.

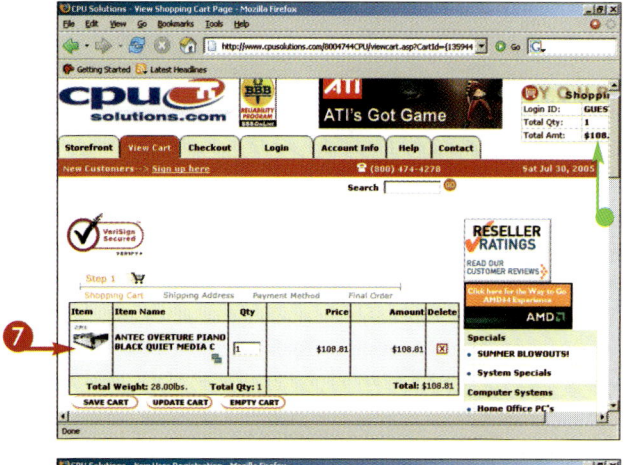

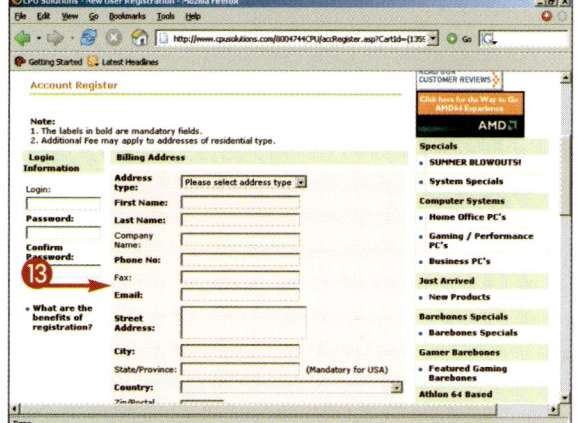

Chapter 3: Buying Your Components

What methods of payment does CPU Solutions accept?

To order online, you will need a credit card or debit card. Did you know that most debit cards can be used to shop online, just like credit cards? However, you may incur a small surcharge for the use of a debit card over a credit card. You can also arrange to send a check or money order to CPU Solutions.

Can I place my order late at night?

Yes, you can place an online order at any time. Try to pick a time when you will not be distracted by other phone calls, children, or other factors.

43

Set Up Your Workspace

Whatever you do, do not just assume that as the parts begin to come in, you can and should start ripping the items out of boxes and sticking them together. First, some of the parts can be fairly delicate, and you could damage them. Second, you have other tasks to perform.

Without taking some extra steps in the time before you assemble, you run a much greater risk of hitting an unforeseen problem that can result in issues that may be harder to solve than they would have been before the fact.

The Appropriate Workspace

The first thing that you need to do is find a space both to go through your system parts and ultimately to do the assembly. But it cannot be just any space. This workspace should fit some special requirements. Also, do yourself a big favor and begin to figure out your workspace either before or right after you place your order. After the boxes begin to arrive may be a little late and may lead to your "just making do."

What You Should Have in Your Workspace

Your workspace should have certain features that will work to your advantage in preparing for and then assembling your new system. Although some of these points may seem picky, you will discover that if you follow the plan, you will have fewer headaches and less frustration than if you ignore them.

Good Lighting
You need good lighting. Where possible, light should come not just from above but from the side, preferably the side where your open case will be angled.

Phone Access
You need access to a phone. After all, you may have to call for support, and you do not want to be in a wholly different room. If you have a cordless or cell phone, this is perfect because then you do not have to fight the cord.

Your Tools
Have your tools available. In the next section, "Pull Together Tools," you will learn about the tools that you should have for your assembly. Try to keep these in a designated place so that you can go back to them rather than lose them because you keep moving them. Also, consider this book part of your toolkit, so you want to have a place to keep the book and open it as you work.

No Distractions
You should avoid any distractions in the area. To assemble a PC properly can be a tough job, and it is only made more difficult if your attention is divided.

Nothing in Your Way
You need room to move about your workspace. Move any boxes, chairs, or anything else that may be in your way so that you can work unimpeded.

A First Aid Kit
Have a first aid kit available or at least some bandages and antiseptic. This is hardly a laughing matter; emergency rooms everywhere see people come in each day with serious lacerations, shocks, and even burns suffered from mistakes in working with PC hardware. Some cases and parts, for example, have jagged or razorsharp edges. Of course, you are going to learn the right way to do your work, so you will not suffer injury. Still, it is better to be safe just in case you do hurt yourself.

continued

Set Up Your Workspace *(continued)*

What to Avoid in Your Work Area

Now that you know exactly what you should have — or should make available — in your PC assembly work area, you also need to know certain elements that you must avoid in this space. If you decide on a particular area and find it violates one of these rules, you may want to reconsider and find a different space in which to work.

Few Visitors and No Clutter

Avoid clutter and lots of traffic. The more people go through your space, the more chance someone may poke around, accidentally knock something off your worktable, or decide to borrow a tool or part that you have set up. Likewise, you do not want lots of boxes, books, or other items limiting your area. You need room to move.

No Children and Pets

Keep the space clear of children and pets. It can be difficult enough for adults to handle some of these parts, but PC assembly is filled with horror stories of pets who got sick on a circuit board, toddlers who decided to chew on a toxic and sensitive part, and similar tales that create a real problem during assembly.

No Food or Drink

Avoid food or beverages. Even very neat people can suffer beverage spills or have a bag of chips wind up all over a table. Extend the same care to anything else that may be moist or sticky.

No Moisture, Dust, or Grease

Try to limit the amount of moisture, dust, and grease or greasy smoke that can get into your work area. If you consider setting up your workspace in a garage, basement, or even an attic, consider how clean and dry the area is.

No Open Windows or Fans

Avoid setting up a worktable near an open window, fan, or air conditioner. This is because you run the risk of sending dust, moisture, or even dirt right into your assembly area, which can cause problems and even damage your equipment.

No Magnets or Sharp Items

Do not have magnets or sharp items in the work area. Magnets are bad for magnetic media such as hard disk drives. Sharp items can nick or otherwise scratch or damage circuit boards and other parts.

Not Too Cold or Too Hot

Avoid extremes of temperature. Either too hot or too cold conditions can affect your delicate PC parts. For this reason, never store PC parts — or a finished PC — in an unheated garage or basement. Condensation can develop when parts inside a PC begin to heat up, which can fry your motherboard and other components. Also, it is best if you do not set up your workspace in front of a window where strong sunshine enters that can shine directly on your parts.

Nothing You Do Not Need

Finally, remove anything else from your workspace that absolutely does not have a role to play in your PC assembly.

Safety Concerns

Keep Parts Away from Children

Some PC parts may strike you as not particularly delicate or clean. In fact, in handling them, you may notice that your fingers become dirty or have a smell. Sure enough, these are not pieces that you want near mouths, especially the mouths of children or pets.

Clean-Room Issues

Understand that many PC components are manufactured in strictly controlled, clean-room conditions where people wear the same kind of gear that you may expect to find in a biohazard lab. One of the reasons for this is that some of the parts inside a hard disk, a CPU, or a circuit board are so tiny that you could easily lose individual pieces. But a bigger issue is that dust, the normal grease that comes from human skin, and the results of a simple sneeze can actually damage those parts.

Be Careful When Handling Parts

Beyond that, however, PC components contain a fair amount of toxic material. Think lead, mercury, and some really noxious compounds. There are also precious materials such as copper and gold that can be easily corroded. Other parts are extremely delicate and can break with little effort. Most parts will not tolerate any stress or flexing or pressure. The majority of them probably will not survive being handled roughly and certainly not being dropped either on a worktable or on the floor.

You do not have to wear a clean-room getup to review your parts and assemble your PC. But you should always start the process with very clean hands and then wash your hands thoroughly afterward. Everything you pull out to look over or work with must either be installed or put away in the same package that you got it. Do not leave parts out and unprotected and *never* put one piece on top of another in a stack.

Chapter 4: Preparing Your Tools and Workspace

47

Pull Together Tools

You need some basic tools and helpful items to assemble your PC. None of these are terribly exotic, and you may have some of these already available to you in one form or another.

Resist the urge to pull out the big household or garage toolchest. You do not need that many tools. You also do not want to use dirty or banged-up tools; your PC tools should be clean and in good condition. For example, a screwdriver should have a clean, smooth head free of gouge marks or crusted dirt.

A PC Toolkit

If you — or someone you know who may let you borrow one — happen to have a small PC toolkit, this may work for you in your assembly. If you do not have a PC toolkit, you can obtain or locate the needed tools fairly easily. Many stores even sell prepackaged kits with basic items for $15 or under.

Tools for Your Toolkit

I recommend that you include these tools in your toolkit.

Two Screwdrivers

You need two screwdrivers — one regular and one Phillips head — of a comfortable size for both your hands and the smaller size screws used for PC assembly.

A Mallet

You need a small mallet or something else that you can use to help push a part into place if you do not happen to have much hand strength. Although you normally will not have — and should avoid — situations in which you need to use a mallet, such a tool comes in handy when you need to seat something and apply some careful, delicate pressure. Remember, no pounding!

Containers

You need one or two small cups or containers, suitable for holding screws or other tiny parts.

continued

Pull Together Tools *(continued)*

I do not recommend wearing gloves to assemble your PC because they may reduce your overall dexterity. But keep your hands clean and dry.

Tools for Your Toolkit *(continued)*

Tweezers

You can use tweezers with protected or rubberized edges to help you install smaller connections or plugs if you cannot easily grip them with your fingertips.

Antistatic Wrist Strap

An antistatic wrist or grounding strap, which you can buy for a few dollars at most consumer electronics/computer stores, is used to reduce the chance that static electricity will be transferred inside the case as you work. Although you are assembling a PC from scratch here, before any power is applied to it, you will need the grounding strap whenever you have to go back inside the system later.

Other Smart Additions

Besides the tools already discussed, there are some very savvy additions you can make — without much expense or fuss — that can help you immensely.

- All the documentation and disks that come with your parts.
- An additional work light that you can easily move as needed to illuminate inside the case as you work. Some pros even get one of those headbands with a battery-operated light that shines light in whatever direction they need.
- Access to a working PC with an Internet connection. This can be invaluable when you need to stop and try to find the answer to a question.

Keep a PC Journal

You may want to start a PC journal as a sort of log about your new PC. This can be simply a small notebook with at least one protective pocket — preferably one that you can fold or snap closed.

Your PC Journal

Use your journal to do the following:

- Document what is included on your system, both in terms of hardware and the operating system.
- Note where you bought the PC or its various parts.
- Hold warranty information, any floppy disks or CDs that came with the system or parts, and any additional paperwork.
- Jot down problems, solutions, replacements, repairs, part names and numbers, and upgrades/updates along with tech support numbers, Web site addresses, and other details.
- Keep a recorded CD or DVD with your journal with a copy of a full system backup or disk image that you create right after you get the system up and running with the programs you plan to use on it. See Part VII, "Turning Your Components into the Ultimate Media Center PC," for more information about this.

Prepare to Work

If you expect to get right to work once you inspect and inventory your parts, there are a couple of additional steps you should take first. If instead, you expect to do the assembly at another time, consult this list again before you begin building.

Prepare Yourself

Before you begin your assembly, make sure that you do the following:

- Remove jewelry, including rings, bracelets, and even your watch. Jewelry and watches can catch on delicate parts and — in some cases — damage delicate components. They can also scratch printed circuit boards.
- Tie back long hair.
- Remove or secure a necktie or a necklace that could dangle down into the case.
- Bandage any open cuts or sores on your hand to prevent dust or dirt from getting inside the wound; make certain that the bandage is tight rather than loose so that it cannot catch on a protruding part or a sharp edge.

Inspect and Inventory Your Parts

Do not assume that you have received everything you ordered for your PC assembly. You may discover midway through your work that you cannot locate an item you need or that a part you got is either the wrong one or is defective or damaged.

If you order all your parts at the same time from CPU Solutions, it is likely that everything will arrive simultaneously — usually in one huge box with all the parts and a separate box that contains your monitor.

Inspect Your Order

As soon as possible after you receive your order, you need to inspect all the components, as well as check your original order against the packing list you will find in the main box and then against each individual item packed within. Preferably, this should be done within 24 hours of getting the shipment because it may be harder to make the case that a box or item was damaged in shipment or missing from your order if you wait several days.

A Place for Safe-Keeping

If you cannot perform these steps immediately, put the main boxes in your work area or in another safe location until you can open them up and check the order. It is perhaps smartest not even to open the main boxes until you can do the inventory and inspection. This is because there is enough detail work here to make the job tougher if you do it piece-meal.

Do It All at Once

There is another reason you should not do this work in stages. You increase the chance you will miss something that is there or assume that you have all the parts when you do not.

Warning!

Avoid stacking the boxes one atop another. The top one could fall or something in the bottom box could be damaged.

Before you touch the boxes, look them over. If you see a shipping box that is damaged, indicate this to your delivery person before you take the box. Ask the delivery person how to proceed if there is a problem with the items inside.

If the shipping boxes look fine, which they probably will, then you can unpack when you want. But exercise real caution when you do unpack the individual items in your order. Some of the components are packed very carefully and securely to prevent damage during shipment.

Take Care of Packing Material

Try not to bust styrofoam packing forms or tear bubble wrap or the special antistatic bags certain items are packaged in. After all, if there is a problem with your order, you may need to repackage the item again to send it back. Furthermore, you can hurt an item if you just yank it out.

Carefully Unpack Your Boxes

With a box such as this one containing PC hardware, open the lid and try to get a feel for how you can lift it out carefully. First, remove any small parts or paperwork that may be inside; then gently lift the item out of its box.

Perform Your Inventory

Inside one of your shipment boxes — likely the main box containing the majority of your parts — you should find a copy of your order along with the packing list. Pull this out and use it as a checklist; verify that you received each component and mark it on the list as you go.

Look Twice for Small Items

What if you cannot find an item? Look again. Some very small parts may be packaged into bigger boxes with other items. Memory and your Windows Media Center operating system install disc may be packed into your motherboard or another box.

Chapter 4: Preparing Your Tools and Workspace

continued

53

Inspect and Inventory Your Parts *(continued)*

If you have never worked with PC hardware before, you may wonder what exactly you should check. If you have never seen a hard disk, you may not know what it looks like. Specifically, look for a product or model number to check against your order/packing list to be sure that what you got is what you ordered.

Inspect the Parts

Look not only at the product box but also at any labels or numbers printed on the part itself. This helps you identify a situation in which you got the right box but the wrong component inside it, which does not happen often but always remains a possibility.

Check for Damage

As you check your parts, also look for problems such as damage or dents in the housing of your monitor, drives, or case; a cable that appears to have a crack or a tear; tiny parts lying behind in a box after you remove the component; and cracked or broken printed circuit boards.

Hard-to-See Problems

Certain types of damage or defects will be fairly obvious — for example, a dent in the metal casing around a drive or cracked plastic on the front of a drive case. Yet not every type of damage or defect will be easy to identify.

Hairline Fractures

Your motherboard and adapters are built onto printed circuit boards, which can develop tiny cracks or hairline fractures, for example. When you first get these parts, you should look them over carefully. Examine them again before or during the installation, too, if you happen to apply too much pressure in trying to mount them inside the case.

Use Backlighting

You may be able to spot defects or hairline cracks in a circuit board that you cannot see otherwise if you hold it up to a light. But some fractures may occur where it is hard to see, regardless. Only a professional — such as your parts vendor — can test the equipment for you.

Chapter 4: Preparing Your Tools and Workspace

continued

55

Inspect and Inventory Your Parts *(continued)*

What to Do If Something Appears Wrong

If you received a damaged shipping box and it appears the parts inside were hurt in the process, you should contact the shipper immediately to begin a claim. If you caught the problem before the delivery person left, you may receive a claim form then and there. If not, the shipper can send one or deliver one to you or point you to an online site where you can fill out a claim online or download and print a form to send to them.

If you notice a problem other than that from a damaged shipment — such as a wrong or missing one or a damaged part that does not appear to be shipping-related — contact CPU Solutions immediately.

RMA

To return the part for replacement, you usually need both the address where you need to send the damaged component along with a return authorization number, sometimes also called a Return Merchandise Authorization (RMA). This number is important because it confirms that the company acknowledges an issue and agrees to accept it back.

Carefully Repackage the Item

Repackage the item carefully, duplicating the way it was packaged originally. Also include any and all materials that came with the item, including a cord or cable, documentation, and disks. You may pay more if you do not include all the material when you send it back. (If the original shipping box is not available, place the product package in an appropriate sturdy box and send it back marked with the RMA.)

Can I Continue If There Is Damage?

What happens if the part breaks after you have it? Unfortunately, this falls within your responsibility. Neither the shipping company nor the online store that you purchased from can be held liable if you mishandle the equipment. This is one of the reasons deliberation and care are stressed here.

Regardless of how the damage is caused, you probably need to replace such a part before you can proceed. Even if a broken or fractured part appears to work if you decide to try it, the chances are high that the part will die or otherwise stop working fairly soon thereafter.

The problem is that even if you are able to get the PC working if you press the damaged part into service, there is a greater potential for a part "frying" or overheating as the system heats up after you turn on the finished PC. When the problem part is a central one such as a motherboard, the risk increases that the damaged component can actually damage other parts. For example, a damaged motherboard could short circuit in a way that damages some or all of the other parts installed to it, such as add-on adapters or memory. Likewise, damaged memory may take the motherboard with it when it dies.

So although you may be tempted to use a damaged part, understand that you are taking a much bigger risk in doing so. It is usually much smarter to replace the damaged component before you assemble the PC because, in all likelihood, you are going to end up replacing the part fairly soon anyway. If you use it regardless, you may have to replace more than one part.

Store Until You Build

Resist the urge to just leave all the parts lying around your work area or wherever else you chose to unpack the boxes and do your inspection and inventory. Parts will go missing, accumulate dust or moisture, get greasy fingerprints, outright break, or develop some defect. Instead, you want to return your parts to their packaging.

Store Until You Build

Anything that came in an antistatic bag such as your memory should be returned to its bag. Likewise, return parts that came in boxes to their boxes.

Either return all documentation and disks to their individual packages or keep them all together with your PC journal or in a file folder or large envelope.

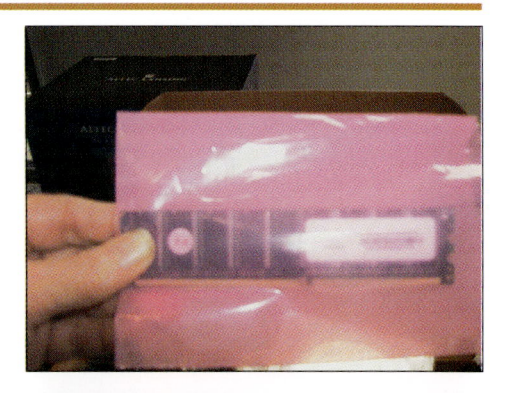

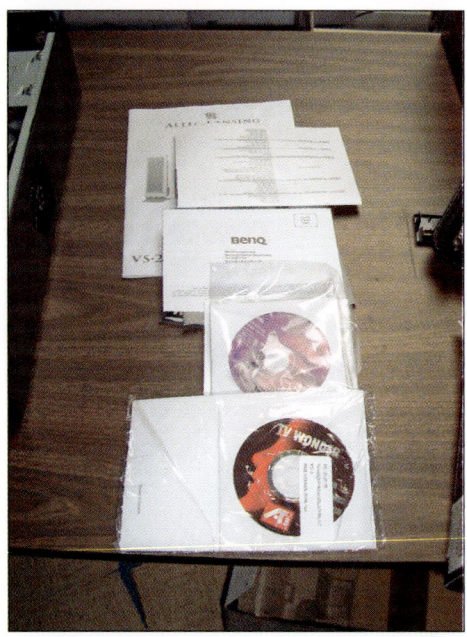

Avoid Problems

If you encountered any defects or damage or missing parts, make sure that you get these issues resolved and replacements parts in place before you go ahead. It is much harder to install some components after you have the rest of the PC together than it is to wait until you have everything you need.

If you follow all the tips and recommendations in this chapter, you should be ready to go.

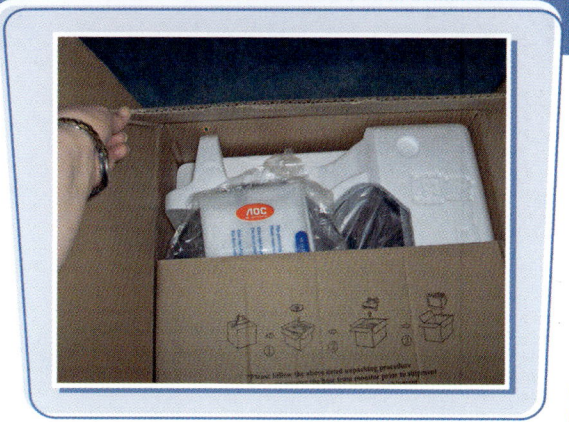

Avoid Problems

Should more than a few days intervene between the time you inspect your equipment and the time you assemble, it may not hurt to do another quick inventory and inspection after you remove the parts from their boxes, just before you begin to build.

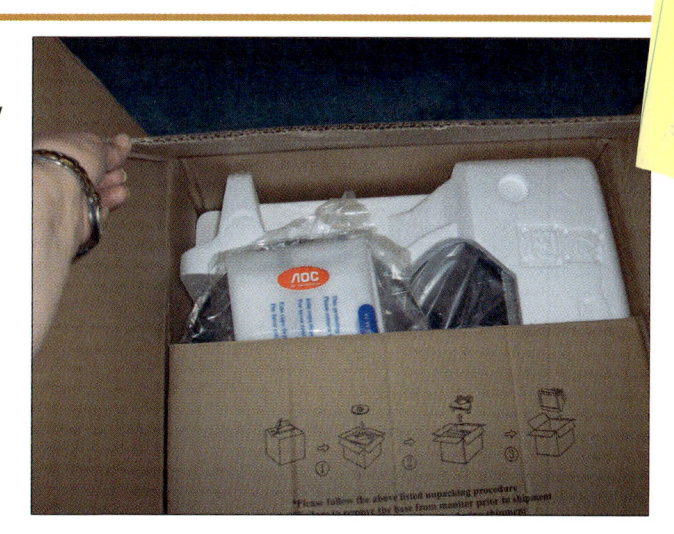

Q&A

I have done a lot of prep work. When will I start to build my Media Center PC?

You begin prepping the case and then performing some of the most basic — and critical — parts of your assembly in the next part of this book, Part II, "Beginning to Build." So be sure that your work area is ready, your tools and documentation — and the PC journal if you are keeping one — are in place, and you have done all the detail work outlined in this chapter.

Part II

Beginning to Build

Now that you have your various components and detail parts such as cables and power cords, along with your all-important copy of Microsoft Windows Media Center, you can begin the job of assembling your PC. If you find yourself amazed that all the components now sitting in your workspace will somehow fit in the rather compact case design, you are not alone. But they will, especially with careful attention to detail.

You start with the mostly empty PC case by preparing it to accept all the internal parts such as the motherboard. You start by mapping out where different components will go — a critical step before you actually get to work. You also prepare the case through the removal of faceplates that temporarily cover drive bays where your various drives will be installed as well as faceplates where add-on adapters will reside and connect to peripheral equipment at the rear of the PC.

Then you take the first major step in successful PC assembly as you install the power supply. Even if your case choice happens to come with the power supply already in place, you will want to review Chapter 6 because some time you may need to replace this unit during the lifespan of your PC. In this part, you also learn about critical equipment you can add to your system to help protect both the power supply and the PC itself from dangerous power fluctuations as well as sudden and severe power outages.

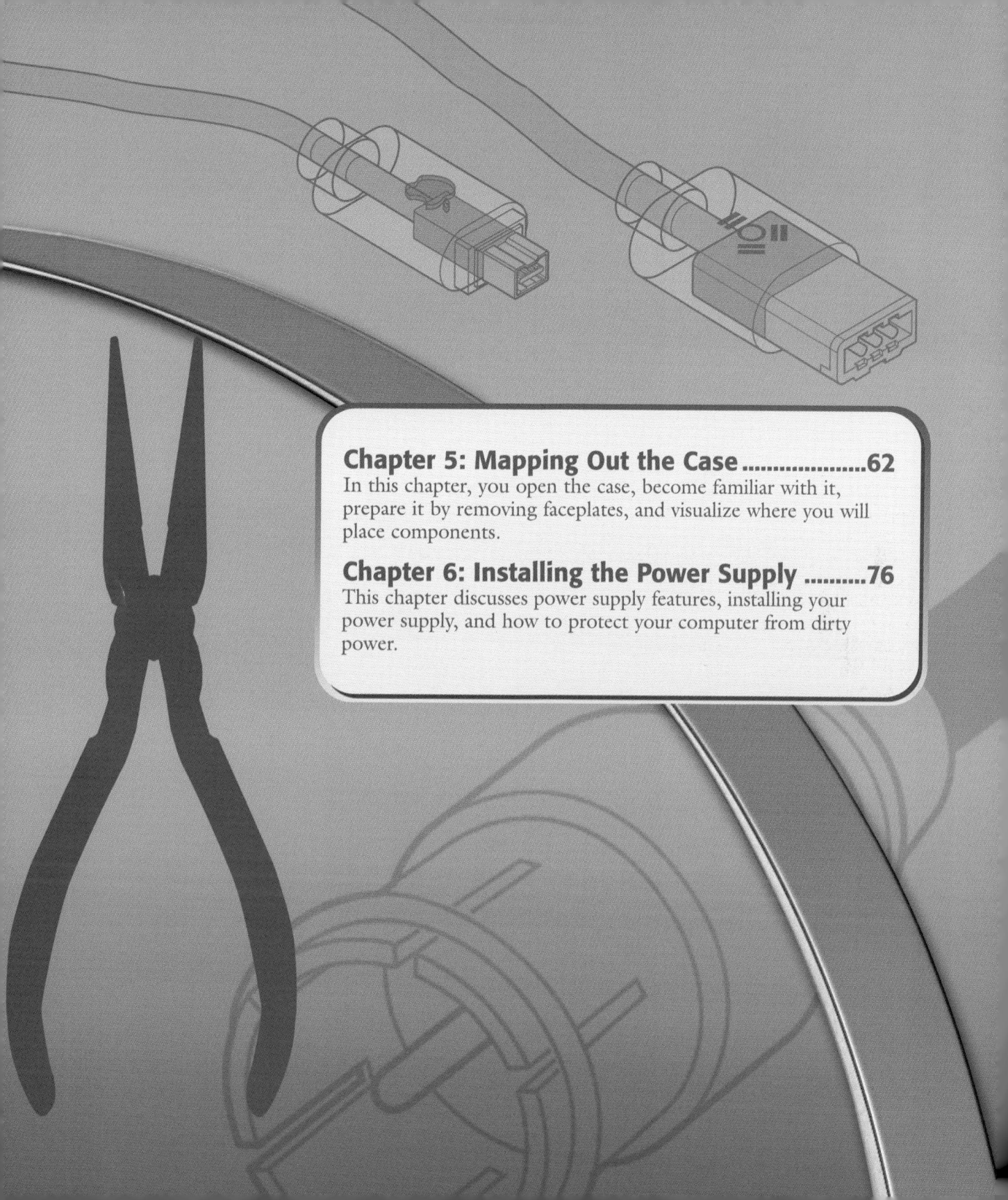

Chapter 5: Mapping Out the Case 62
In this chapter, you open the case, become familiar with it, prepare it by removing faceplates, and visualize where you will place components.

Chapter 6: Installing the Power Supply 76
This chapter discusses power supply features, installing your power supply, and how to protect your computer from dirty power.

My Choice for the Case

You may want to choose a case based on appearance, but there is more that matters. You want a strong and capable case.

Although the majority of PC shoppers and owners probably cannot tell you the color of their PC cases, others — eager to have an ultracool-looking system not colored the usual beige, gray, or black — will spend a decent amount of money to acquire something quite different than what anyone else has.

The Antec Case

The case shown here — the Antec Quiet Media Overture Piano ($108.71) — was chosen based on a few different factors. The manufacturer has a decent name and reputation. The case size is large enough to hold not just what will be added in this project but offers room to grow. Its design should result in adequate air circulation through the unit to keep internal components from overheating.

Inside the Case

Although the case, at its price, is not a bargain model, the price includes a 380-watt power supply also made by Antec. As you learn in Chapter 6, this unit has a fairly robust capacity for a PC and should work even if a few more components are added later.

Nice Appearance

The case's sleek appearance, in black, should work well in a high-visibility area such as a living room or den. The piano model, which is what you have with this horizontal case, is a departure from the standard tower or upright design.

Alternative Case Choices

Perhaps you want a different appearance or a less expensive model. For a case, you can go much cheaper — as well as much more expensive — than the Antec Quiet Media Overture case chosen for this build.

Factors to Consider

If you choose an alternative case, be sure of certain factors before you make your selection. The case must fit the style of motherboard — referred to as *form factor* — that you choose. CPU Solutions's online catalog descriptions specify this information to help you decide wisely. Also be sure that the case features a minimum of five drive bays to house the three drives you add to this system and others you may install later. Also, determine whether the price includes the power supply.

Different Cases

I recommend these cases as decent alternatives to the one that I have chosen for this book:

$

- CPU Solutions CPU Roadster with side window and 350W power supply ($38.12) (shown here)
- Irwin Beige Z720T MATX with 300W power supply and screwless design ($57.13)

$$$$

- Antec Aria MicroATX Cube with 300W power supply ($95.95)
- Thermaltake Tsunami Case with window and 11 drive bays, but no power supply ($126.13) (shown here)

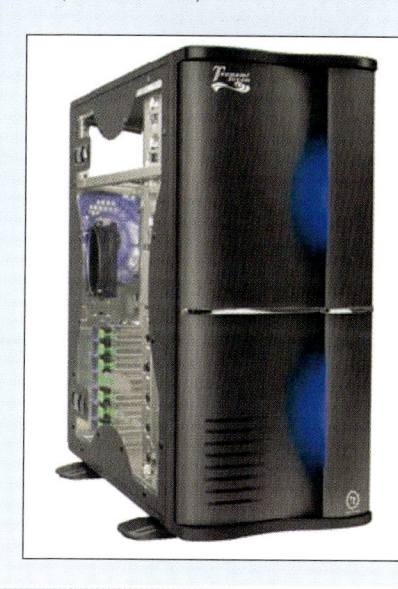

Open Up the Case

Exactly how you open your case to look inside depends on the case you chose and the features it offers. Access can range from extremely difficult to slide-out-a-drawer easy. There are usually just three basic ways to get inside.

Before you try to open your case, check the documentation and diagram that came with your case. This tells you how to open the case and what you need to do to set the case up.

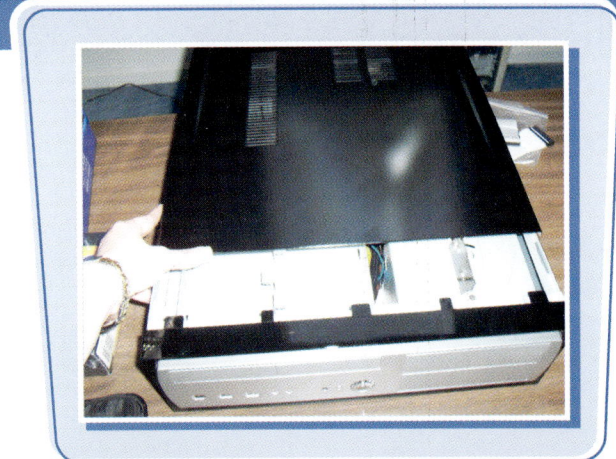

Open Up the Case

REMOVE SCREWS

1. Remove the screws located at the rear of the PC.
2. Pull or slide off one side of the cover.

USE A LEVER

1. Retract the lever.
2. Slide the chassis out — much like you pull out a drawer, although with more care.

OPEN A WINDOW

1. Open the window found on one side of the PC.
2. Reach inside.

CHECK THE DOCUMENTATION

1. Look for a diagram that points out the major features around and in the case.

   This will give you an idea about the special needs, if any, for your assembly and how you place components.

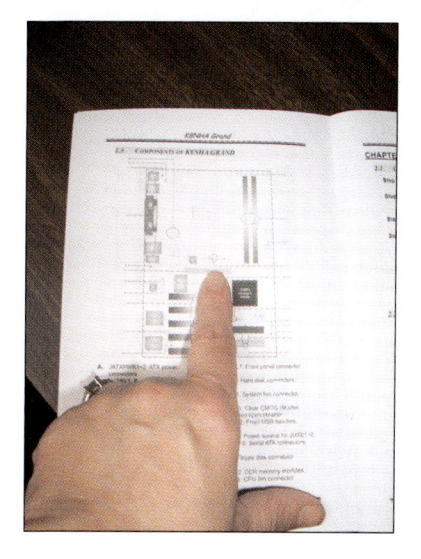

SLIDE-OUT DRIVE TRAY

1. As you check out the features, look at the drive bays.

   If it looks like you may have to work a bit harder to install and later access the drives, you can purchase and install slide-out drive trays to make your work easier.

Q&A

Can I just leave the cover off of my case?

No, PCs are not designed to be operated for extended periods of time with the cover off; you draw in dust and dirt, risk injury, and may actually defeat the cooling mechanisms. Normally, the case cover should always be in place when your PC is on.

What if where I want to place my PC does not have power plugs or is somewhat moist or high traffic? Is that really such a problem?

Yes, it could be. You do not want 20 feet of extension cord running from your PC and another room, so avoid a situation where there is no power outlet handy (although you may consider getting an electrician to install an extra one). High moisture and high traffic areas also present real problems, so do your best to minimize both to secure your system.

Chapter 5: Mapping Out the Case

65

Determine What Is Inside

In the Antec Overture model, you already know that there is a power supply preinstalled. But there happens to be more inside than just that unit. Notice, for example, that there are several different wires.

Determine What Is Inside

LABELS ON CONNECTORS

On this system, the wires' connectors are all labeled to tell you what they are, including USB (Universal Serial Bus), IEEE 1394/Firewire, and PWR for power. These you will connect once you install the motherboard and begin to connect the power supply to various other components.

TAKE CARE OF THE BAG OF HARDWARE

① Pull out the plastic bag containing hardware, but do not open it.

Inside you will see some of the little hardware parts that you will need for installing the motherboard, such as *standoffs,* screws for mounting add-on adapters and drives.

Note: You should also find a power cord, which connects into the big plug at the back of the PC and is then plugged into your power source. Do not plug the power cord in at this point.

66

② After you remove the bag of hardware, note its contents.

③ Set the bag aside in a good, safe location.

Note: If you cannot resist the urge to open the bag up, make certain that all the pieces get returned to the bag. You do not want to lose them.

INSIDE THE CASE

Take some time to familiarize yourself with the inside of the case — comparing it to the documentation. Begin to visualize how you will first orient and then install the motherboard, mount the drives, and so on.

Note: This step of familiarization is particularly important if you chose a different case design. A piano style case varies in layout from a tower design. So keep referring back to the documentation until you have a sense of the space.

I am having trouble distinguishing between the different wires and connectors. How can I tell which is which?

Your case manual or other documentation should help you identify what the various wires and connectors are there to do and how you will connect them.

Why should I not plug in the power cord now?

You should not connect the power cord to the PC and to an outlet yet. This will be done later, after the system is assembled. You have so much more work to be performed right now, work that is not safe — for either you or the hardware — to be done with the power connected.

continued

67

Determine What Is Inside (continued)

One of the very best ways to get some idea for what your finished system will look like — and to get an idea of the layout of a PC assembly — is to check a fully assembled PC that you may have somewhere else in your home or office.

Determine What Is Inside (continued)

CHECK THE INSIDE OF A COMPLETED PC

1. Shut down and turn off the PC.
2. Disconnect the power cord at the back of the PC.
3. Using the directions that came with it, put on your antistatic grounding strap. 
4. Remove the case cover.
5. Look inside, being careful not to touch anything.

Chapter 5: Mapping Out the Case

⑥ Take a digital photo of the working PC.

⑦ Replace the cover.

⑧ Turn on the PC.

⑨ Download the image into the PC.

⑩ Print out the image.

⑪ Diagram the print-out and use it as a reference tool for building your new PC.

Note: The following pages give you an idea of what you are looking at.

Rear of PC
CPU fan with CPU below it
Power supply connectors to motherboard
AGP video adapter
CD/DVD drive
Front of PC
Jumpers on IDE/ATA drives
Ribbon cables between drives and motherboard
PCI slot
Network adapter in PCI slot
Drive bays
Power supply

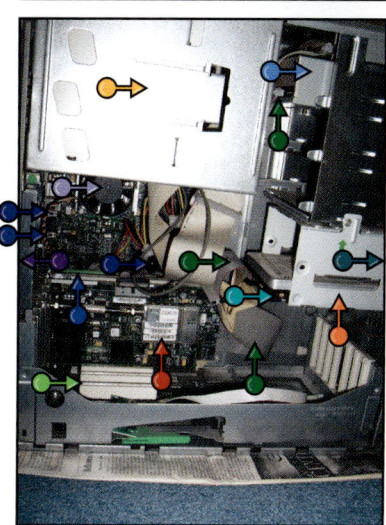

Warning!

Never, ever remove the cover from a PC that is both plugged in and turned on. Doing so is very risky both to you and the PC.

Can I not use an antistatic/grounding wrist strap, as long as I take great care in what I do?

No, even old pros at hardware make mistakes and do not ground themselves properly unless they use such antistatic wrist straps. All it takes is one wrong touch with static electricity, and you can at the very least damage the part you touch if not more components as well as get a real shock of your own. Get the wrist strap and use it whenever you go inside your PC.

continued

69

Determine What Is Inside *(continued)*

The only drawback to looking at an already-assembled PC to figure out the orientation for different parts before you put together your new one is that you may not be able to identify everything that is there. Look at the diagram shown here — that of a Pentium 4–grade Celeron midtower system with two hard disks and several integrated features — to see if you can determine what you see on your own system.

A Diagram of a Working PC

- **Power supply**
- **ATA/IDE drive ribbon cables running to motherboard**
- **Power cable connector**
- **Power supply connectors to case**
- **Power connectors from power supply to drives**
- **Motherboard**
- **Memory**
- **CPU, fan, and heatsink**
- **PCI slots**
- **Drive bays**
- **Hard disks**
- **Floppy drive**
- **CD-RW drive**
- **Video adapter**

The Back of the PC

You should also look at the back of the PC to understand how different connections are made. Most cases label the connections so that it becomes easier to identify where different connections should be made.

Power cord

Keyboard

Mouse

Printer port

USB port

On-motherboard video

Phone lines into/out of modem

Network connection

COM/serial port

Sound card connectors

Video port on back of video card

Game/MDI port

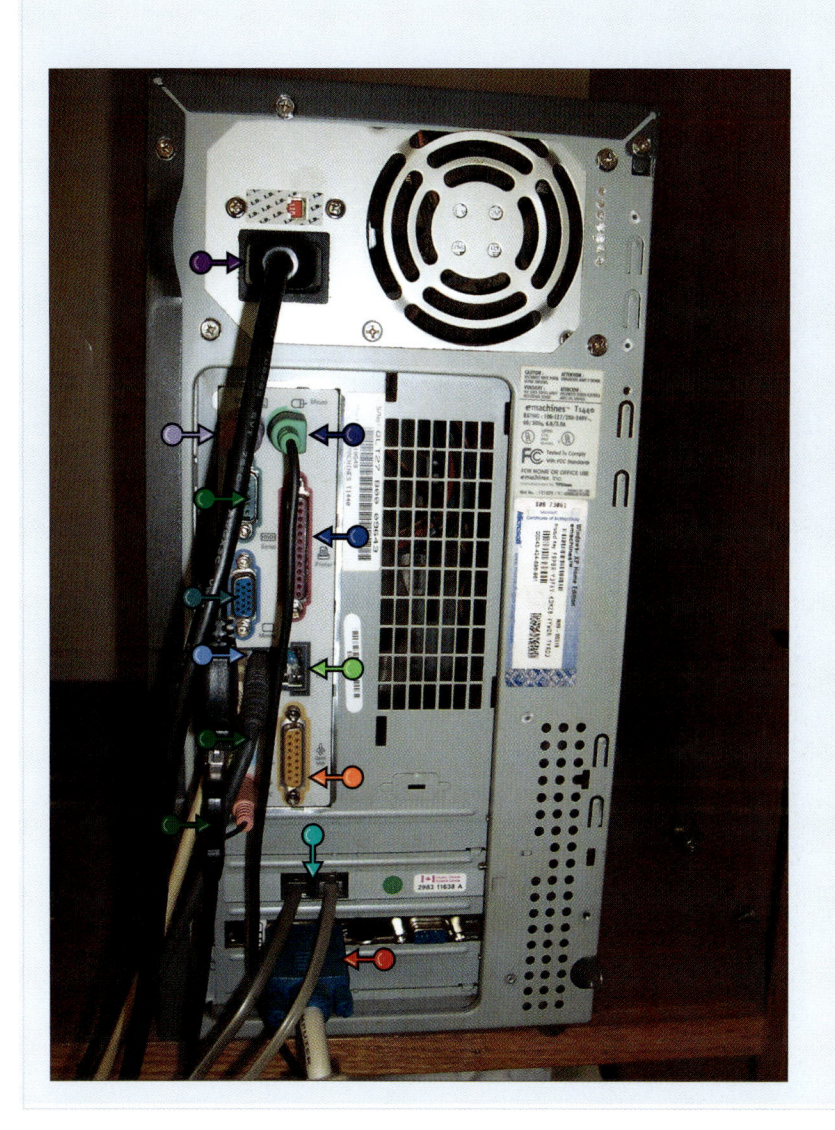

Chapter 5: Mapping Out the Case

71

Remove Faceplates

Most PC cases use faceplates to cover areas such as drive bays at the front of the PC and the slots at the back of the PC where expansion boards such as video and sound cards will later be installed. Often, the faceplates are pieces of metal, made from similar material as the case itself.

Remove Faceplates

Sometimes, the faceplates are merely stamped into the metal frame in such a way that they can be pushed or punched out. Others simply use a cover that can be taken off by removing a screw or other fastener that holds it in place.

① Determine which compartments you need access to where you need to remove the faceplates.

Note: You want to remove any faceplates that cover compartments that you will use to install components.

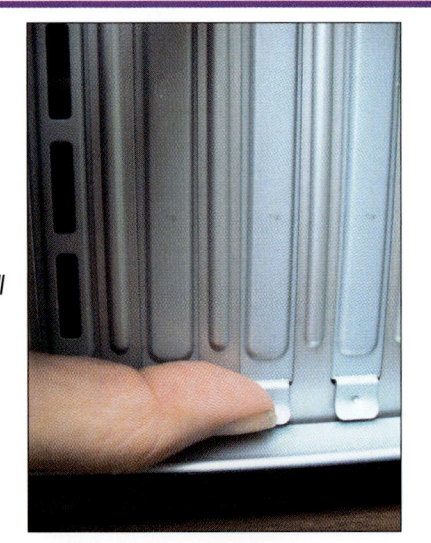

② Leave all of the other faceplates in place.

③ Uncover the faceplates corresponding to the following (for the target system designed for this book):

The AGP slot on the motherboard

One of the PCI slots on the motherboard

The drive bay to be used for the floppy disk drive

The drive bay used to hold the hard disk

The drive bay used to hold the DVD-RW drive

This is one of the faceplates covering one of the expansion board interfaces at the rear of the PC. Check the manual to see recommendations for removing faceplates and then use a screwdriver to remove any screws holding the faceplate in place.

Here is another faceplate, this one covering one of the drive bays at the front of the PC on the Antec Overture case. Again, consult the documentation and remove at least three faceplates – more if you plan to install more drives than in the target system design.

Why should I check which faceplates I am removing? Would it not be easier to just remove all the faceplates?

No, you should only remove the faceplates that cover compartments that you will use to install components. By leaving all the remaining faceplates, you reduce the dust and dirt that can get into the system over time because you are not leaving big holes in the case interface.

Also, cases are designed to move cooler air in and hotter air out in specific ways. If you remove extra faceplates, you may get more cooler air into and hotter air out of the PC, but you will also draw far more dust, smoke, grease, moisture, and other things into the system that you do not want.

Visualize Your Assembly

Look back at the digital photo or sketch with labels you created in the "Determine What Is Inside" section. Now look back inside your case and try to get a feel for how and where the different parts will fit into the PC.

Really examine the area inside and visualize how the motherboard will fit — usually on the opposite side of the case frame from where you are looking in — and then how everything else will go. Remember that almost everything connects to the motherboard.

Visualize Your Assembly

1. Pay particular attention to the far or bottom wall of the chassis because this is where the motherboard will be mounted.

② As you look between the case and the motherboard, try to visualize how you will insert the motherboard to line it up with the chassis and the housing in which the main board will be mounted.

③ Look at the motherboard documentation. Read what it suggests about mounting the board within the case, including special warnings.

④ Scan through your documentation and find the Web address of the manufacturers responsible for some – or all – of your parts.

⑤ Go online using another PC to locate more detail and help with your installation as well as the orientation of parts.

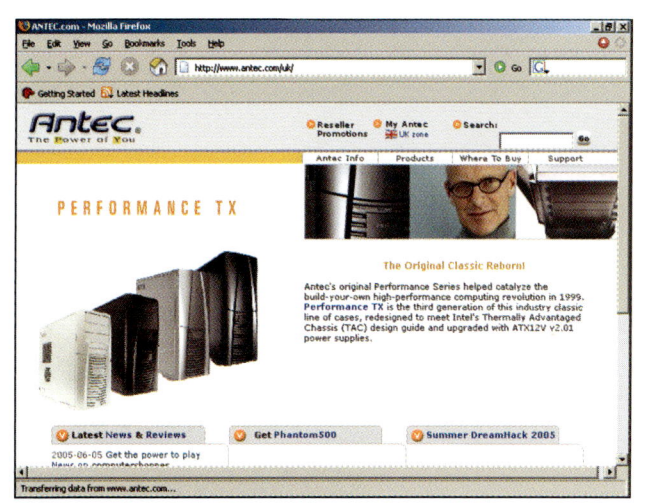

Q&A

What if, even after I buy new components, I really want to use an existing case or motherboard for the new system? Will this cause me much of a problem?

You can only press an existing motherboard or case into service if it is rated specifically to work with and fit the other components. For example, if the case and motherboard each fits a different type of form factor — or the style and size of the component — they will not be compatible. Check your documentation.

My Choice for the Power Supply

You want a strong and capable power supply for the energy demands of your new PC. From the previous chapter, "Mapping Out the Case," you know that a power supply is included in the case choice for the target system built in this book. This is an Antec SmartPower, 380 watts.

If you happened to choose another case and yours does not include a power supply, you can purchase the one that I have chosen separately. But you also have other options, covered on the next page.

The Antec SmartPower

The power supply included in the case selection for this book is 380 watts, which is reasonably capacious. Many budget already-assembled PCs today pack with a power supply rated between 200 and 250 watts. This is usually sufficient for a basic system, but does not leave you with much ability to upgrade or add components. Serious gamers may need at least 350 watts. If you anticipate adding a fair amount of extra hardware, you may want a power supply of 400 watts or higher.

Alternative Power Supply Choices

Be sure that a power supply does not automatically come with your case before you buy a separate one, especially if you chose a different case than the one selected for this book. Many cases do include a power supply but just as many do not. Also, remember to always double-check the wattage.

When shopping for a power supply, either for this system or as a replacement, there are several things to consider. See "Know Your Power Supply" for details.

Different Power Supplies

If you want to go with a different power supply than the recommended one, here are some alternatives available through CPU Solutions:

$

- Cooler Master eXtreme Power RS-380 380W for $32.79, rated as super quiet and with serial ATA power connections used for fast, new drives (shown here).
- Cooler Master Real Power 450W for $63.43, featuring intelligent fan speed control and green power design to conserve energy.

$$$$

- Antec TruePower 550W for $102.77, which works with most AMD and Intel processors, boasts low noise technology, and features two double ball-bearing fans for superior cooling plus two serial ATA connectors.
- Antec Phantom 350W for $159.51, the rare stylish power supply, which boasts a fanless design which — at least in theory — should prolong the life of the unit; this features a three-year warranty (shown here).

Know Your Power Supply

You need to understand how critical the power supply is in terms of PC operation. Obviously, it provides the "juice" to all the little parts; without the power supply, every tiny, little component would need to plug into an outlet.

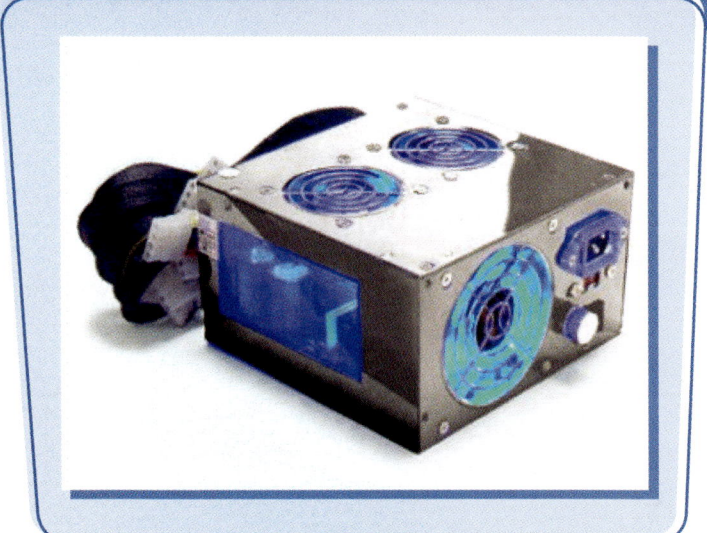

A Good Power Supply

But a good power supply does more than just supply power. It also does the following:

- Converts standard household current to the type used by the PC.
- Acts, at least minimally, as a sort of filter to try to prevent passing spikes or drops in household wiring from damaging components connected to the power supply.
- Tries to regulate power delivery so that even if one component is demanding a lot of power, other components are still getting all the power that they need.
- Provides an assortment of connectors so that you can connect the power supply to the motherboard, fans, drives, and specialty devices.
- Plays a big role in keeping the internal case cooler by using its one or more fans to force hot air out the rear vents.

What to Look for in a Power Supply

Whenever you buy a power supply, there are certain things that you should look for:

- Wattage, or how much power it can handle, as noted earlier in this chapter.

- Whether its form factor — or the particular design of the power supply — is compatible with the motherboard, the CPU type, and the case in use.

- How quiet it is; the more powerful a power supply is, the louder it can be. The power supply is often responsible for the overall level of noise associated with a PC in use.

- What type of cooling it uses; because power supplies factor both in producing a fair amount of heat as well as in pushing hot air out of the case, you need to see how it handles cooling. A good power supply usually uses at least one ball-bearing fan, whereas some of the best units use no fan at all, using other cooling technology.

- Whether it supports connections for recent hardware developments such as the ultrafast serial ATA hard disks. Although no serial ATA drives are installed in this system, you probably want to have the option of installing one at some point.

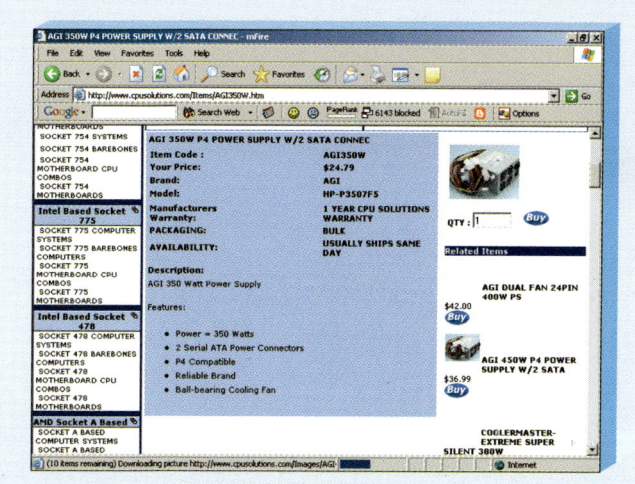

- The warranty period. Always look for a power supply with at least a one-year warranty. Some go as high as three years. Also look for information about MTBF (mean time between failures) in the product details: The more hours the power supply is rated to work before it fails, the better.

continued

79

Know Your Power Supply *(continued)*

Beyond the particulars, there is more for you to consider, like how much power your system demands. The rule with power supply wattage is that you want it to pack more power than you need. Although the Media Center PC built in this book could probably get away with less than a 300W power supply rather than the 380W that comes with the Antec case, you want to avoid taxing the power supply, especially if you add more hardware to the system.

Power Supply Label

Every power supply has a label attached to it that specifies its wattage, model number, and additional details that allow you to identify it which helps in obtaining a replacement later, as needed.

How the Power Supply Works

This diagram shows how power is delivered from the wall outlet to the various PC components via the PC power supply and its connectors.

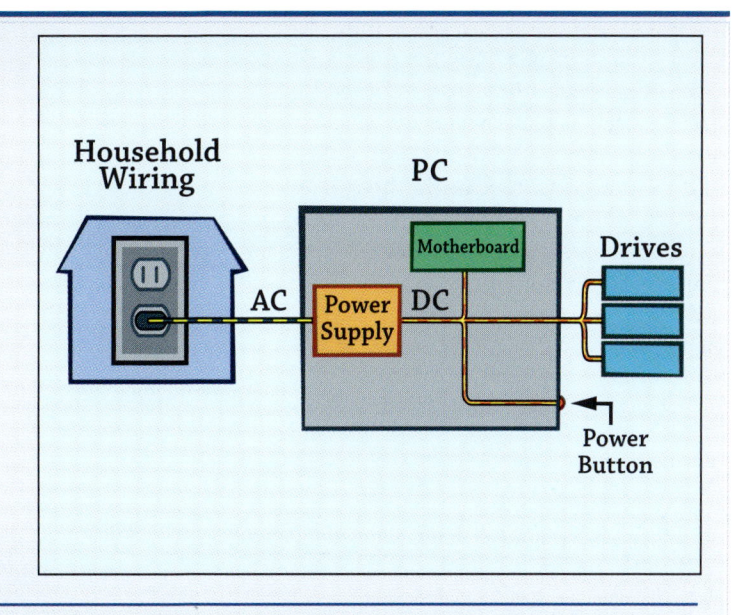

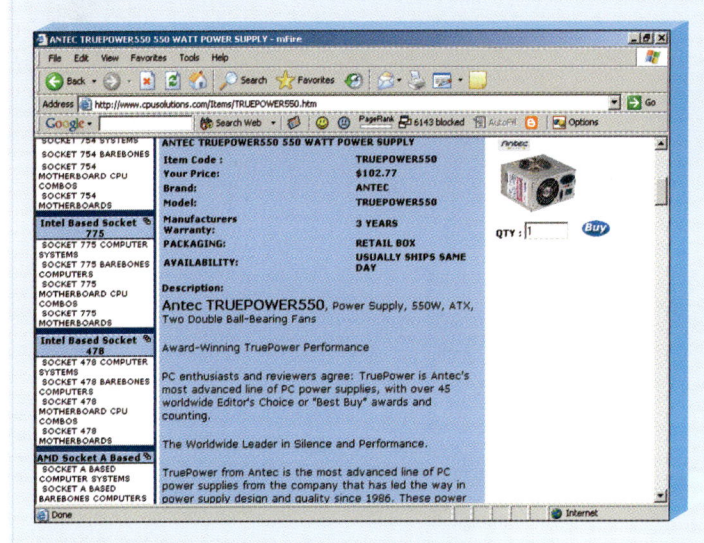

Find the Product Specs

You can click **More Info** from any CPU Solutions product listing to get additional technical information about the component.

Remember!

An underpowered power supply can drastically affect overall PC performance.

Chapter 6: Installing the Power Supply

81

Install the Power Supply

The very first thing that you should do is check the documentation for both the power supply and the case for any special instructions. Then, using the diagram or manual as a reference, follow these steps to install the power supply.

Install the Power Supply

1. Remove the power supply from its package.
2. Compare the power supply to the case to see how it should be installed.
3. Remove any temporary fasteners holding the wire bundles together.
4. Again referring to the documentation, look for information on setting the (usually red) voltage switch for use in the United States.

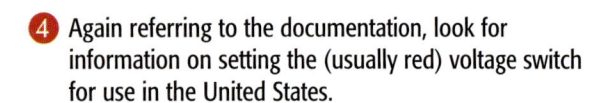

   Note: American units should be set to 115V rather than the 230V used for the European Union.

5. Locate the screws needed to mount the power supply into place.
6. Insert each screw into its mounting hole on the power supply.

   Follow the directions in the documentation to mount the power supply into place at the top or side of the case, as directed. Using a screwdriver, install the screws and make certain that they are secure.

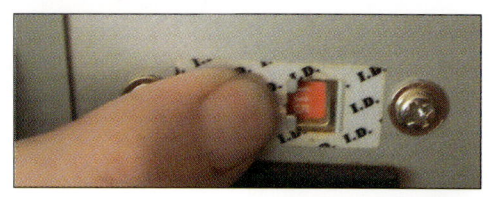

Check Your Power Cable

Remember the power cable that you located when you unpacked and opened the case in Chapter 5? If you want to test your new power supply to be certain that it powers up, you can do so after you complete the system.

Do not worry about the power supply connectors for now; you will connect those to different components as you add them, starting with the motherboard.

Check Your Power Cable

1. Remove the power cord from its bag and unfold it to its full length.
2. Plug the female end of the cord into the rear of the installed power supply.
3. Plug the male end of the cord into a wall outlet.
4. Press the power button.
5. Listen.

    Although there is nothing installed in the PC yet to boot it, you should hear the power supply fan begin to turn.

6. Place your hand at the rear of the PC near the grill covering the power supply and its fan.

    You should feel the fan producing a warm breeze.

7. After you verify that the power supply works, turn off the power and disconnect the power cable.

Warning: If you do not hear the power supply start up and do not see or feel the fan turning, there is something wrong. You may need to replace the unit. First, check to be sure that the outlet is working by plugging in another device.

Think Beyond: Protect Power

Do phrases such as "hard disk failure," "I had to replace my motherboard three different times," and "my PC will not boot again!" strike terror in your heart? They should. Even with grizzled veteran PC technicians, no one likes a system that does not work.

Although there is no "one size fits all" solution that will keep your PC operating no matter what, it is critical that you understand that the ways in which you can protect your power supply from an early death also serve to protect your entire system.

Dirty Power

One of the most common reasons that a PC becomes old before its time or one whose components you frequently have to replace is a phenomenon known as *dirty power*. No matter how wonderful and new your home and office wiring is, there is the chance that the power flowing through it may experience a fair amount of fluctuation. This fluctuation can damage your PC.

Chapter 6: Installing the Power Supply

Power Fluctuations

Power fluctuations can occur in — or be exacerbated by — any of the following situations:

- A nearby lightning strike
- Power surges and spikes
- Old or substandard wiring or wiring that has been damaged by mice or other rodents chewing
- A heavy-duty appliance on the same circuit or in the same power zone as your PC cycling on and off
- A defective or dying appliance sending fluctuations out through the rest of the wiring

continued

85

Think Beyond: Protect Power *(continued)*

Sometimes, there are common-sense measures you can take to reduce the risk that your PC may be hurt by power fluctuations. Here, I discuss how you can limit your power issues.

There are also special appliances designed to help absorb some of the power fluctuations before they can reach your PC. These can be an excellent investment, especially when you consider the costs of having to replace your PC or consumer electronics.

Ways to Reduce the Risk

- Shut down the PC and disconnect it from power — and from any other external sources such as a phone line or high-speed Internet connection — whenever there is a severe thunderstorm or storm threat.

- Set up your PC in an area in your home or office not shared by heavy-duty appliances; if that is not possible, shut down your PC whenever you have to run an old vacuum cleaner or some type of "big motor" appliance in the same area as your PC.

- Disconnect a misbehaving appliance until you can get it serviced.

- Do not plug your PC into the same outlet as any motorized appliances.

- Call in an electrician to check your household or office wiring and make any changes or upgrades, as needed.

Unfortunately, none of the previous measures are flawless. Many people leave their PCs running all the time. If a storm or power issue arises in the middle of the day when you are not home, you have no way to shut down the system.

Beware of Storms

Without adequate power protection, you should never operate your PC during a severe storm, particularly a thunderstorm or during a period of brownout conditions because of the electrical fluctuation risk.

Power-Protection Devices

Consider one or more of these protection methods:

- Special line conditioners that sit between your wall outlet and the plugs for your electronics to try to equalize fluctuations in power.

- An uninterruptible power supply (UPS, discussed in Chapter 2), which protects against surges and can provide a short period of battery power when you are experiencing a brownout or blackout; many UPSes include insurance to cover your equipment in case it is damaged in the event of a failure of the UPS to protect it.

- A surge suppressor is often built into quality power strips; it also serves to take the brunt of a power surge or spike rather than passing it along to your PC.

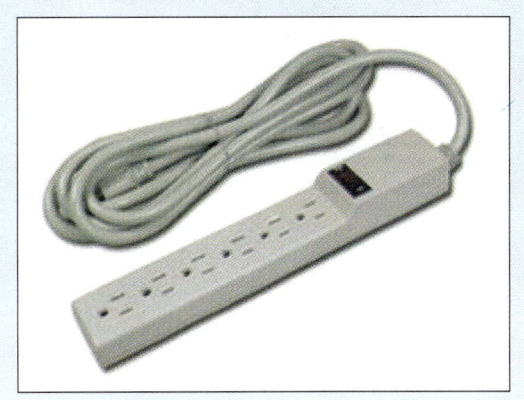

Part III

Installing Core Components

Now that you have the case set up for assembly and the power supply ready, you move swiftly along as you prepare the brain of the PC, called the *central processing unit,* or CPU. Special care is necessary here because the CPU — and its cooling features such as the fan and heatsink that you add to help remove excess heat from the delicate chips — can suffer damage from inexact mounting.

One thing to notice as you work is that you actually install the CPU and the memory to the motherboard *before* you mount the motherboard into the case. Of course, you could add these components after you install the motherboard, but it is usually much easier to work with these parts and get their installation just right with the motherboard still outside the case.

After the CPU, its fan, and the memory are in place on the motherboard, you focus your attention on the motherboard and the case as you mount the main system board into place. Special hardware, usually found within your new case, is there to assist you. Pay careful attention to the assembly instructions. This is necessary because it is not too difficult to damage the motherboard if you apply too much pressure or incorrectly seat it or screw it down too tightly.

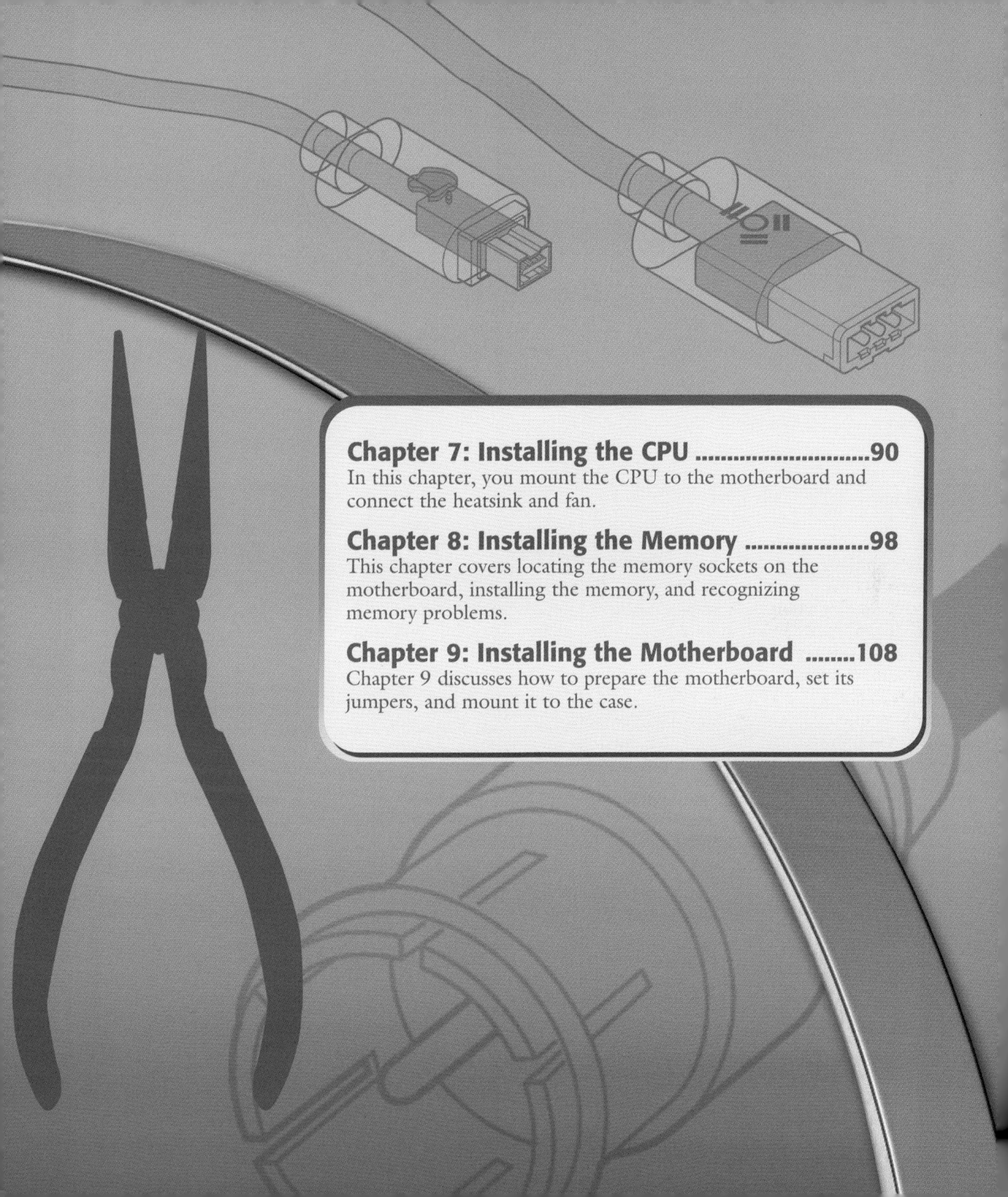

Chapter 7: Installing the CPU 90
In this chapter, you mount the CPU to the motherboard and connect the heatsink and fan.

Chapter 8: Installing the Memory 98
This chapter covers locating the memory sockets on the motherboard, installing the memory, and recognizing memory problems.

Chapter 9: Installing the Motherboard 108
Chapter 9 discusses how to prepare the motherboard, set its jumpers, and mount it to the case.

My Choice for the CPU

The AMD Sempron 2600 Socket 754 is a good choice for the CPU because AMD processors have earned their reputation as a serious alternative to Intel CPUs. Although this CPU is neither the fastest nor the cheapest one out there, it packs enough power and capability to handle the demands we place on it as the "brain" of this Media Center PC.

This Sempron comes with a three-year manufacturer warranty and the fan needed to cool it. It is also a good match for the motherboard I chose, a Biostar that you learn about in Chapter 9, which offers a similar warranty.

The CPU, Motherboard, and Memory

Remember that as you select a CPU and motherboard, the two must match one another. Whatever socket or slot the CPU uses must be available on the motherboard that you choose. This duo also factors into the memory the motherboard will use. In this case, the Sempron works well with double data rate (DDR) SDRAM, which this motherboard supports, and becomes our choice for memory for the new system.

90

Alternative CPU Choices

You have some other viable choices if you do not want to use the AMD Sempron. These range from the budget Intel Celeron with enough speed and power to handle a Media Center PC to the higher-end Intel Pentium 4 and AMD Athlon 64 Socket 954 CPU.

Different CPUs

Here are some alternative CPU selections:

$

- Intel Celeron D 325 with 2.53GHz clock speed, 533MHz front side bus (FSB), and 256KB L2 cache ($84.36) (shown here)
- AMD XP 3200+ with 2.167GHz clock speed, 333MHz FSB ($119.77)

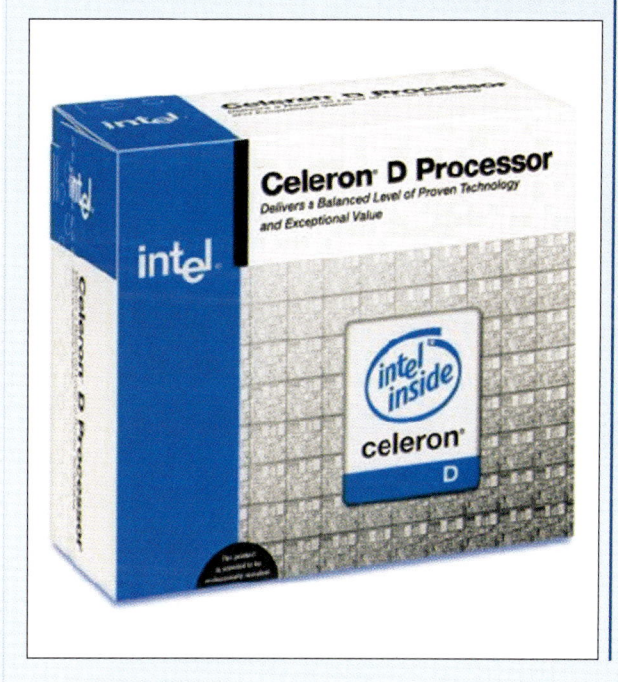

$$$$

- Intel Pentium 4 3.2GHz clock speed, 800MHz FSB, and 1024 L2 cache ($240.90)
- AMD Athlon 64 Socket 939 3500+ CPU with 2.2GHz clock speed and Newcastle Core, 64K + 64K L1 cache, and 512KB L2 cache ($294.08) (shown here)

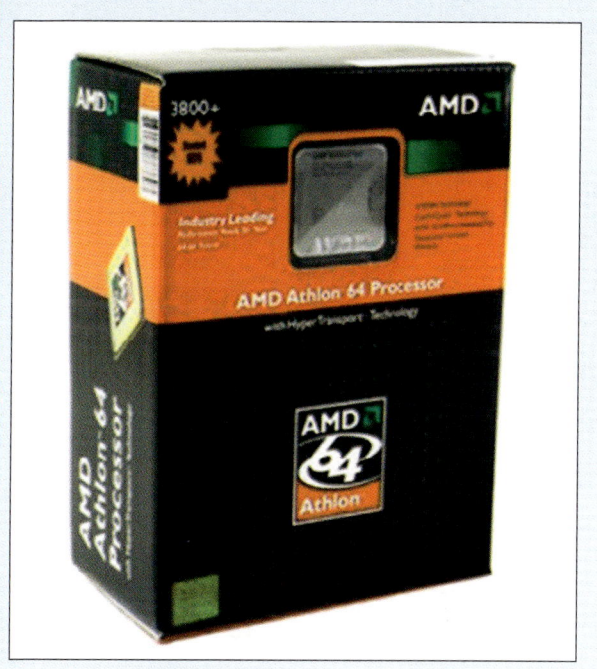

Mount the CPU into the Motherboard

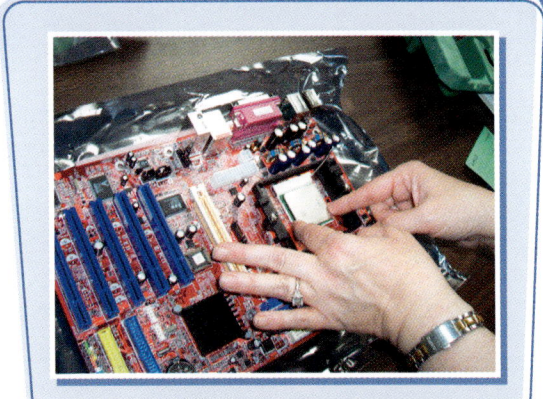

Because it is easier to mount the CPU — and the memory covered in Chapter 8 — onto the motherboard before the motherboard is installed into the case, this is how you will proceed here.

First, fully read the documentation that accompanies your motherboard and CPU. For example, the Biostar motherboard manual steps you through everything from the CPU and its fan to the memory. You also may want to consult your case and power supply documentation.

Mount the CPU into the Motherboard

❶ Place your toolkit and documentation on your worktable.

❷ Place your CPU, memory, and motherboard boxes on your worktable.

Note: Use extreme care when you have these parts out and unprotected. Be sure that your hands are clean and dry. Do not leave the parts lying out when you are not around. Also remember to use a grounding wrist strap.

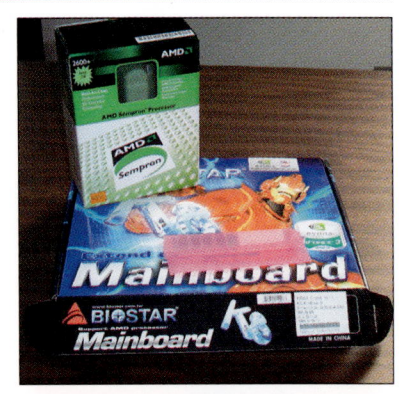

❸ Remove the plastic-encased CPU pack from the cardboard holder.

Note: Leave the fan temporarily in the package.

❹ Place the CPU pack on a clean, dry surface.

❺ Remove and unfold the documentation.

❻ Locate the certificate of authority on the documentation sheet and write in the serial number from the CPU – which can be seen through the transparent plastic – onto the certificate.

92

➐ Locate and gently lift the lever next to the CPU mount on the motherboard until the lever is raised to about a 90-degree angle.

➑ Remove the CPU from its plastic case and do not touch the pins.

➒ Note the triangle at one corner of the CPU and orient it to the triangle image on the CPU mount.

➓ Set the CPU down into the CPU housing on the motherboard.

⓫ Press the lever at the side of the CPU mount – use gentle but firm pressure – to install the CPU into place.

⓬ Be sure the lever returns to its original position.

⓭ Look closely to be certain that the CPU is level and seated correctly.

Note: If the lever does not go down evenly, do not force it. Recheck the way that the CPU seats — be sure that it is aligned with its triangle corner to the image of a triangle on the motherboard — and try again.

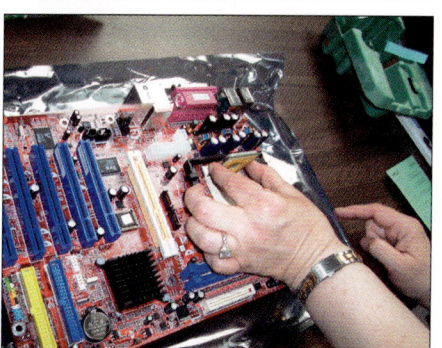

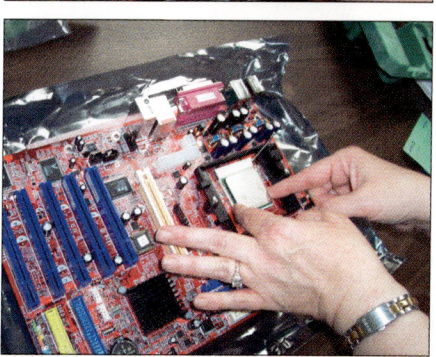

Chapter 7: Installing the CPU

93

Connect the Heatsink and Fan to the CPU

The AMD Sempron processor comes with a fan that already has the heatsink in place, along with the sticky thermal compound necessary to affix the heatsink to the CPU. Your job is to attach the fan, which then also automatically attaches the heatsink. The two of them together draw heat away from the CPU so that it is not damaged.

Connect the Heatsink and Fan to the CPU

1 Remove the plastic cover from the fan.

Note: Do not touch the sticky compound on the underside of the fan.

2 Look at the CPU mounting on the motherboard. Note the two sides with fixtures that correspond to the lever and latch on the fan's side. Orient the fan to these.

Note: For AMD CPUs, be sure that the cutaway portion of the heatsink on the fan is aligned to the raised portion of the CPU socket.

3 Hold the fan even as you press it into place over the CPU and begin to feel the lever/latches fit into position.

4 Press gently and firmly until the latches begin to grab the fan housing.

5 Press down on the lever until it is fully down.

Note: Make sure that you apply the fan/heatsink right the first time because pulling it off will damage the thermal heatsink compound. If you ever need to remove the fan/heatsink, you need to obtain and apply fresh compound from your CPU manufacturer.

94

Connect the Fan to the Motherboard

A fan needs electricity to turn, so you must now connect the fan to the motherboard, which will — in Chapter 9 when you install the motherboard — connect to the power supply to draw the power that it needs.

If you are using the designated Biostar motherboard, you can follow along with the details in the motherboard manual on page 9.

Connect the Fan to the Motherboard

1 Take the connector attached to the CPU fan by wire and set this down near the motherboard.

Note: Make certain that the wire is not twisted or kinked.

2 Look on the motherboard and locate the connector labeled JCFAN01.

This is the connector on the motherboard for the CPU fan.

3 Connect the wire-bound connector from the CPU fan to JCFAN01.

Note: Make certain that the connection is firm and secure.

4 Notice that there is extra wire. Gently fold the slack bit of cable together.

5 Locate a nonmetal twist-tie or piece of tape.

6 Gently tie or tape the slack wire together so that there is not so much loose cable.

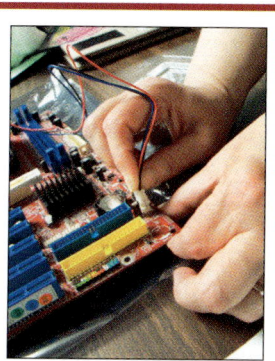

Chapter 7: Installing the CPU

95

Check the Insertion

At this point, and after virtually every connection you make and piece of hardware you install, you should stop and review everything that you have done. Glance back and forth between your documentation, this book, and the hardware that you have before you.

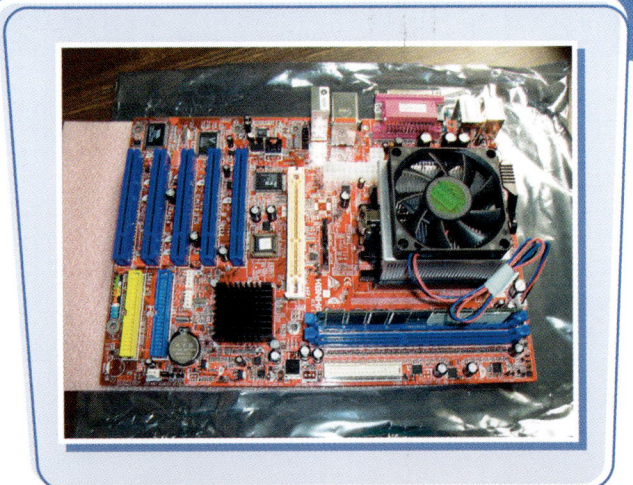

Check the Insertion

The idea here is to catch any problems now, while you still have the ability to see the motherboard because it is outside the case. Also, the deeper that you go into assembly, the more difficult it will be to spot smaller issues.

1. Review your documentation one more time to verify that you went through all the steps.

2. Get eye level with the CPU you mounted and be sure that everything appears level.

❸ Verify that the lever on one side of the CPU fan is fully engaged. Check the latch on the other side as well.

Note: There should be no looseness between the CPU and fan if you gently try to move the unit.

❹ Check that the CPU fan connector is firmly seated in the JCFAN01 connection on the motherboard.

Q&A

What should I do with my CPU booklet?

Make sure that you do not toss out your CPU booklet. This is where you recorded your CPU serial number. This should go into a master file folder you create or into a pocket in the PC journal you began in Chapter 4.

When do I install the motherboard into the case?

You have one more part to mount before you install the motherboard into the case in Chapter 9. This is the system memory. Go to Chapter 8 to learn how to do this.

Chapter 7: Installing the CPU

97

My Choice for the Memory

I chose 512MB of double data rate synchronized dynamic random access memory (DDR SDRAM) because it is compatible with the motherboard and CPU selection for the target system you build here and because this is a very adequate amount of memory for a media system.

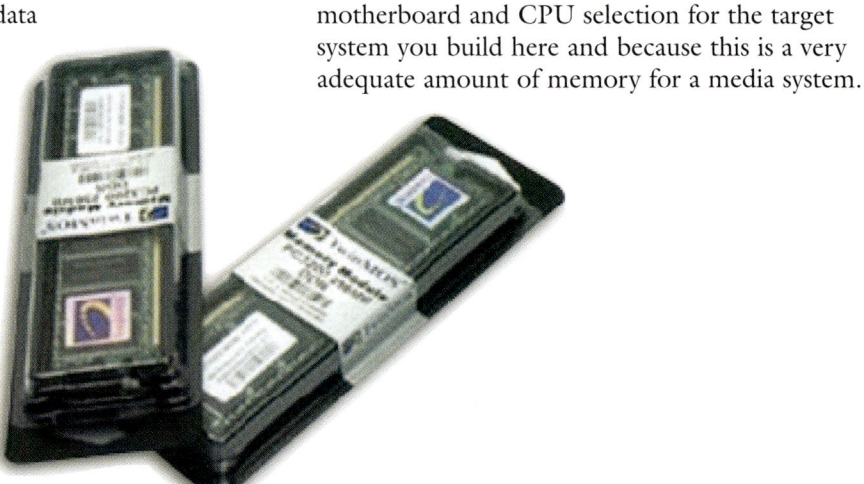

DDR SDRAM

DDR SDRAM is cost effective, fast, available in a number of different speeds to match varying PC requirements, and happens also to be used on the graphics board chosen for this Media Center PC. It is also abundantly available, so you can shop for it easily and not have to wait to receive your shipment.

Memory availability has been an issue with certain types of memory in the past. This is a sound reason to avoid building a system that requires more exotic memory types. If you choose DDR-SDRAM and a setup that supports it, you should have no worry that you will not be able to obtain upgrade or replacement memory at a later time.

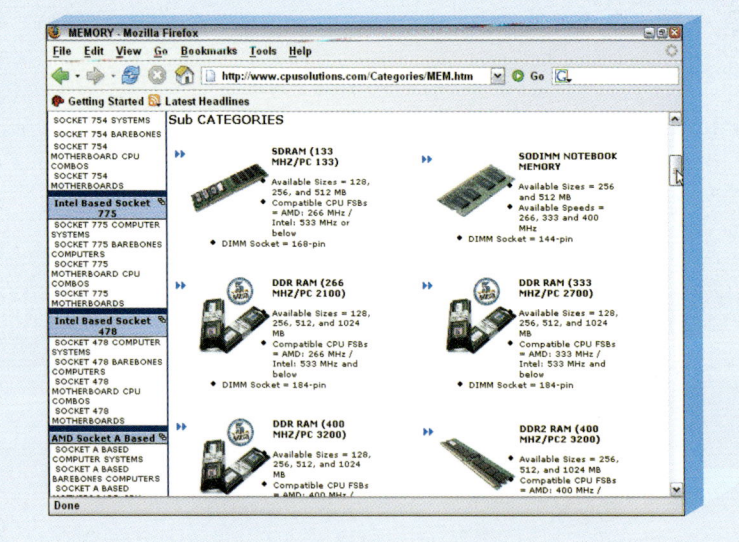

Alternative Memory Choices

Your chief concern when you shop for memory is that it is compatible with your motherboard selection. Most of the CPU and motherboard choices available enable you to use either DDR RAM — or the newer DDR2 SDRAM, which is quite a bit faster but not compatible with DDR SDRAM memory sockets because it is 240-pin–based whereas normal DDR RAM has 184 pins.

Options for Alternative Memory

You can either reduce the amount of memory, such as choosing 256MB rather than 512MB to save money, or take advantage of the relatively low prices of memory today to go up to 1GB, or 1,024MB, of memory. Do not attempt to install any less than 256MB, or you will experience lower performance. Your alternative choices include the following:

$

- DDR SDRAM 400MHz, 256MB, 184-pin ($25.99)
- DDR2 SDRAM 533MHz or 400MHz, 512MB, 240-pin ($67.85) (shown here)

$$$$

- Gamer Pro DDR SDRAM 400MHz, 512MB, 184-pin ($101.25) (shown here)
- DDR RAM 400MHz, 1024MB (1GB), 184-pin ($109.99)

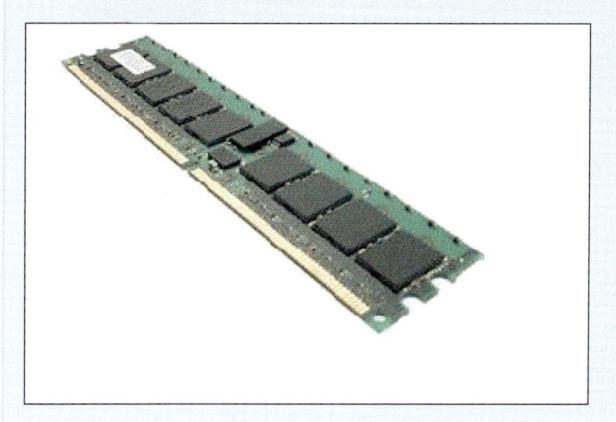

Chapter 8: Installing the Memory

99

Check Your Memory

When you receive your memory, it is extremely important that you check it to be sure that it is exactly what you ordered. Failure to do so could leave you without a system able to run. Worse, the wrong memory can potentially kill your motherboard.

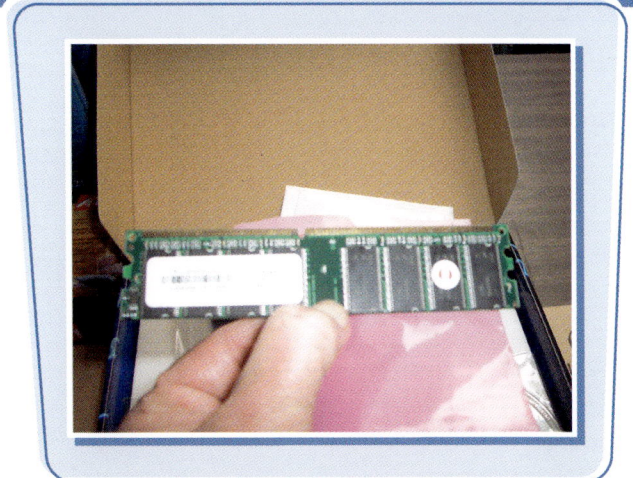

Check Your Memory

1. Remove your memory from its antistatic bag.

   Note: As you do this, be sure that you do not touch the gold connector edge or the black chips themselves. Hold the memory carefully by the edge of the circuit board.

2. Look at the label on the memory.

   Note: If there is no label, check to see if the type of memory and its capacity are printed somewhere on the board.

3. If there is any discrepancy between what you ordered and what you have, contact the vendor immediately for a replacement.

   Note: Do not use the memory to assemble your PC until you have the correct memory.

Know Your Memory Sockets

Your memory installs directly to the motherboard. It is your motherboard design that determines the maximum amount of memory you can install, the number of memory sockets you have available, and what types of memory are compatible with it.

There are at least two ways that you can check to determine what memory sockets your motherboard has available, if you did not resolve this when you placed your order.

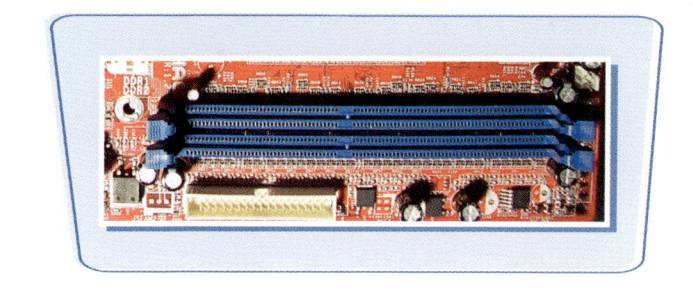

Know Your Memory Sockets

CHECK ONLINE

① Go to CPU Solutions and look up the details for your particular motherboard, which will specify the number of memory sockets/slots available and the maximum amount of memory that you can add.

CHECK THE MANUAL

① Consult your motherboard manual if you have received your order. This should spell out the same information as the CPU Solutions product details page.

Note: Remember to replace the memory in its antistatic bag until you are ready to install it.

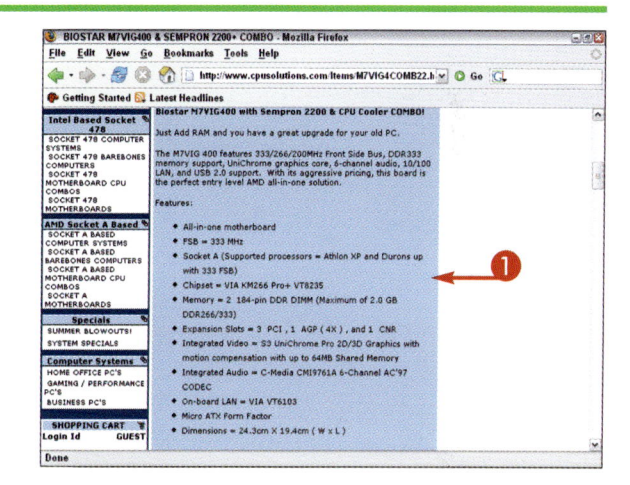

Install the Memory

You should install the memory before you mount the motherboard inside the case. This gives you both better visibility for the task at hand as well as more room to move about, which makes it more likely that you will get the memory in place correctly.

Install the Memory

① Locate the memory sockets on your motherboard.

Note: The memory sockets usually bear labels such as DDR1 and DDR2. You can find the memory sockets on the diagram earlier in this book (see Chapter 2) or in the motherboard manual.

② Push to release the latch at either end of the first memory socket – the one labeled 0 or 1.

If you plan to install more than one memory board, release the latches on the required number of consecutive sockets.

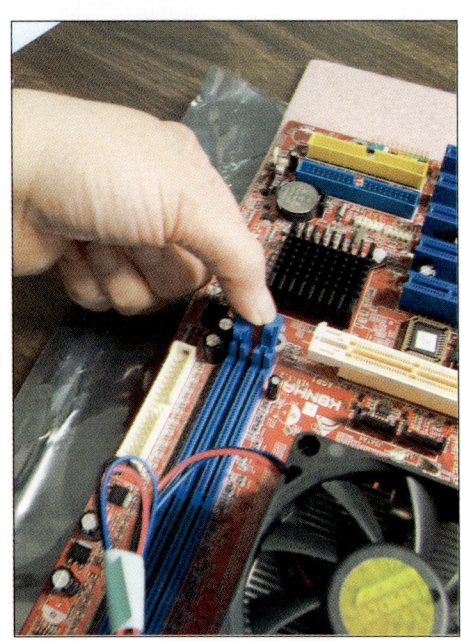

❸ Remove the memory from its antistatic bag.

❹ Orient the memory to the socket and begin to press it into place.

Note: Look at the notches on the memory board because these will help guide you in how the board must sit in the socket. The gold-connector edge is the side that goes into the actual socket on the motherboard.

❺ As you press, the latches may begin to engage themselves. If not, push the latches back into place.

Note: You must be careful not to exert too much pressure as you press the memory into place.

❻ Repeats steps **3** to **5** if you want to add any additional memory boards.

Note: Remember to add them to consecutively numbered sockets such as 0 or 1 for the first, 1 or 2 for the second, and so on.

What are *memory banks?*

After the sockets are filled, or *populated*, with memory, they are sometimes called *memory banks*.

What should I do to make sure that I do not damage my memory?

First, make sure that you are installing the memory with the correct side down (the gold-connector edge). There should be only one way that your memory installs so that it seats properly, but that is not always the case. Second, do not touch the gold connector edge or the black chips on the printed circuit board.

Chapter 8: Installing the Memory

103

Check the Seating

Verify your seating of the memory in its socket. This is imperative because — even though it should not happen — hardware pros will tell you that they constantly see memory that is installed upside down or only partially mounted.

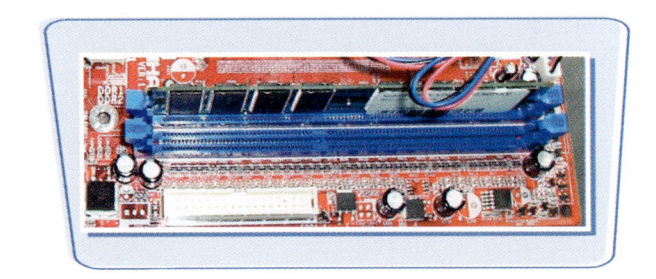

Check the Seating

① Bend down and try to look at the memory seating on the motherboard at eye level.

It should appear straight and even in the mounting.

② Make sure that the gold connector edge is the one installed into the socket.

③ Make certain that the latches are fully engaged. If not, reseat the memory until you can return the latches to the locked position.

④ Verify that you installed the first memory board to the first socket and so on.

If the first socket is empty, you may have a problem when you start your PC after assembly.

Add More Memory Later

Although you want to try to add all the memory that you want and need during the assembly process, if you need to, you can go back later and upgrade or replace your memory. It is only slightly more difficult to add memory after the PC is already in service.

Add More Memory Later

① Be sure to order the same overall type of memory that you installed the first time.

Note: If you choose to keep a PC journal, this detail should be recorded there.

② Before you add more memory, turn your PC off and disconnect the power.

③ Put on a grounding wrist strap.

④ Remove the PC cover.

⑤ Add memory consecutively. If you plan to keep your existing memory, add the new board to the next available socket. Do not skip sockets.

Note: Replace existing memory rather than keep it in place if you experience any problems with it, such as memory errors in Windows.

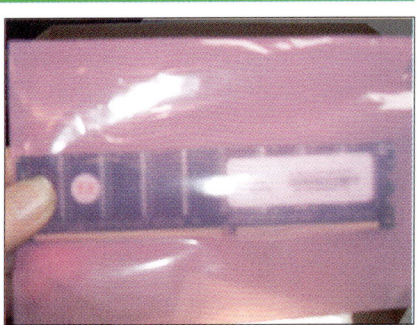

Recognize Memory Problems

Perhaps the most common reason for problems with memory goes right back to poor installation. So the first thing you should do is triple-check how you seated the memory and that you installed the first memory board to the first memory socket and so on.

Indications of Memory Problems

Understand that you will not see problems with memory until you start to use your new Media Center PC, after you finish the assembly. Then any trouble is apt to be seen either when you first turn on the PC — you may hear a series of beeps rather than the system boot up, which can indicate any number of problems from poor memory installation to another part not properly set up — or when Windows loads, in the form of a series of error messages when you try to install or use applications. If and when you can get into Windows, you should check the amount of memory you have installed and make sure that it matches the amount you physically added, as shown in the following section.

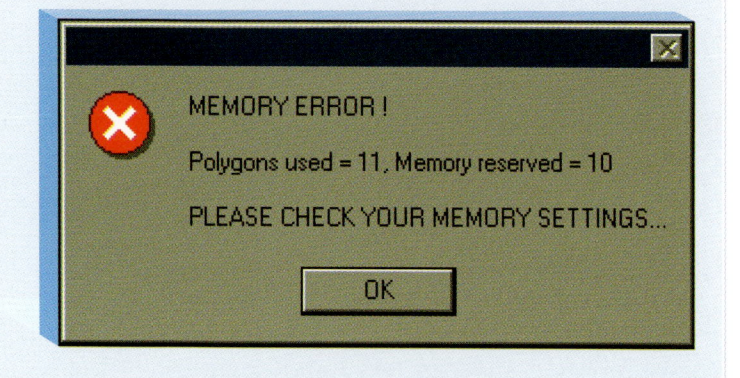

MEMORY ERROR!

Polygons used = 11, Memory reserved = 10

PLEASE CHECK YOUR MEMORY SETTINGS...

OK

Find Memory Information

To check the amount of memory that you have installed, you use the Control Panel.

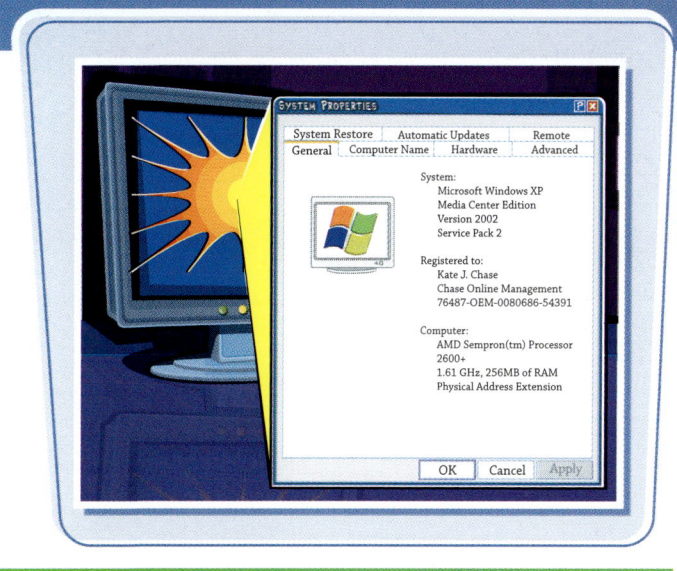

Find Memory Information

① Click **Start**.

② Click **Control Panel**.

③ Double-click **System**.

The System Properties dialog box appears.

④ Click the **General** tab.

⑤ Look for details on the memory near the bottom of the window.

⑥ Make sure that the amount of memory indicated matches the amount that you physically added.

Note: Chapters 25 and 26 explore tweaking and troubleshooting your fully assembled PC to overcome problems such as those related to memory.

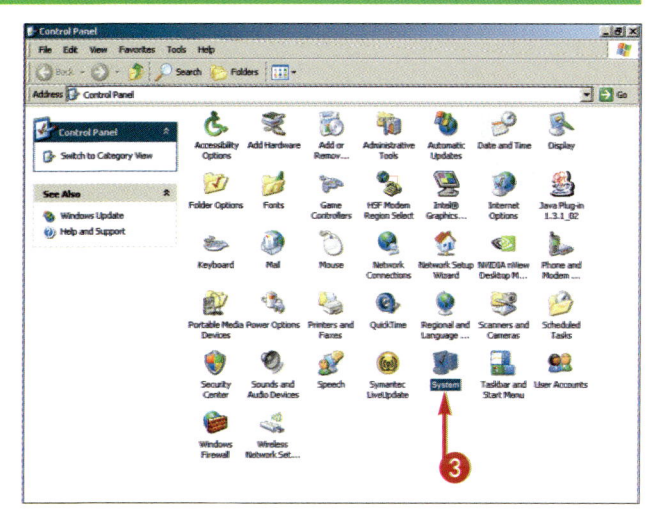

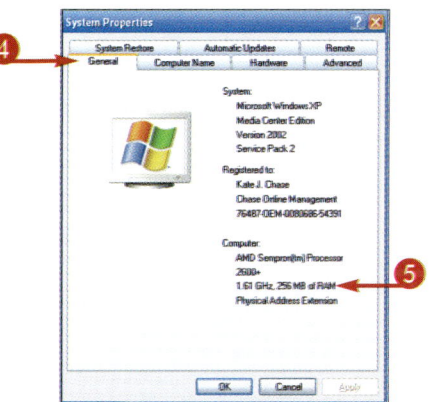

Chapter 8: Installing the Memory

107

My Choice for the Motherboard

When you choose a motherboard, you effectively determine the future of your PC: what types of hardware can be connected, what CPU and memory you can install, and how easily you can upgrade the system.

My choice of motherboard for the target Media Center PC is the Biostar K8NHA-G, which works with the AMD Sempron CPU also chosen (see Chapter 7), along with the memory (see Chapter 8).

Motherboard Features

You want to select a motherboard that is compatible with the CPU and memory you want to use, has enough expansion slots to accommodate more add-on adapters than you initially plan to install, and offers adequate support in case you run into problems.

This motherboard features five PCI expansion slots, plus an AGP port for the graphics card. It also comes with sound and network chips integrated into the motherboard, which means that you do not have to buy a separate sound card and network interface card.

If you decide later that you want to upgrade the integrated sound, all you need to do is purchase and install a sound card. The same holds true for the network card.

Alternative Motherboard Choices

You may want more or less from your motherboard than the one I chose for the target system. Through CPU Solutions, you have a number of other choices available, letting you opt for an Intel-based rather than AMD-based system, a motherboard with more or fewer expansion slots, or one with more or fewer features, including integration.

Different Motherboards

Your alternative motherboard choices include the following:

$

- Gigabyte 7VM400M-R AIO with integrated video (but with an AGP port to install a separate graphics card), six-channel sound, network capabilities, and compatibility with Athlon XP CPUs ($53.10) (shown here)
- Asus A7N8X-X NFORCE 8X with integrated video (again, with an AGP port to install a separate graphics card), six-channel sound, network capabilities, and compatibility with AMD Athlon XP and AMD Duron CPUs ($61.58)

$$$$

- Intel BLKD865GBFL 865 Chipset MB with integrated video, audio and LAN, and compatibility with Intel Pentium 4 and Celeron CPUs with 478-pin sockets ($106.99) (shown here)
- Asus A8NSLI NFORCE4 SLI ATX SKT939 Socket 939 motherboard with integrated video, sound, and LAN, and compatibility with AMD 64 and 64 FX CPUs but no independent AGP port ($164.45)

Check the Documentation

Because every motherboard is different, you need to refer to the documentation for yours to learn the specifics about installation and learn about any warnings or special steps that you need to take.

Start with the manual that came with your motherboard. Most such manuals give you all the basic information you need to know, with diagrams, details, required jumper settings, and even installation steps.

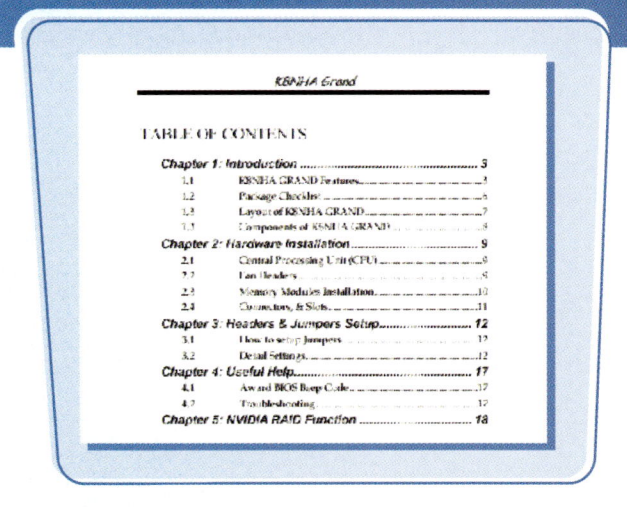

Check the Documentation

Note: Before you begin assembly — especially if you choose an alternative motherboard that may not come with as much documentation as the Biostar in use here — you may want to locate and consult the motherboard manufacturer's Web site.

① Navigate to the Biostar site at www.biostar.com.tw.

② Click **Motherboard.**

③ Click the socket – or slot – style of your motherboard. Here, it is **Socket 754**.

④ On the next page, click the closest match to your motherboard model. Here, it is **K8NHA Grand**.

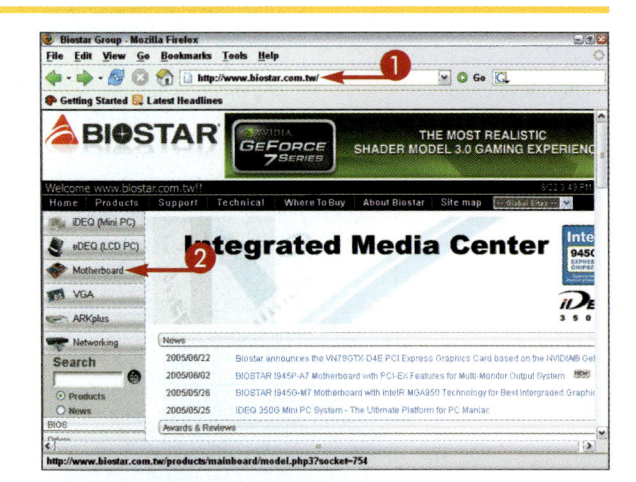

110

Chapter 9: Installing the Motherboard

❺ Read through the specifics.

● You can use the buttons at the top to open detail pages such as Manual and CPU Support.

❻ Look for details such as how to set jumpers and make connections and review them to understand what you need to do.

❼ Check for updated drivers or downloads that may be needed to get your motherboard to work with your new system and Windows Media Center PC.

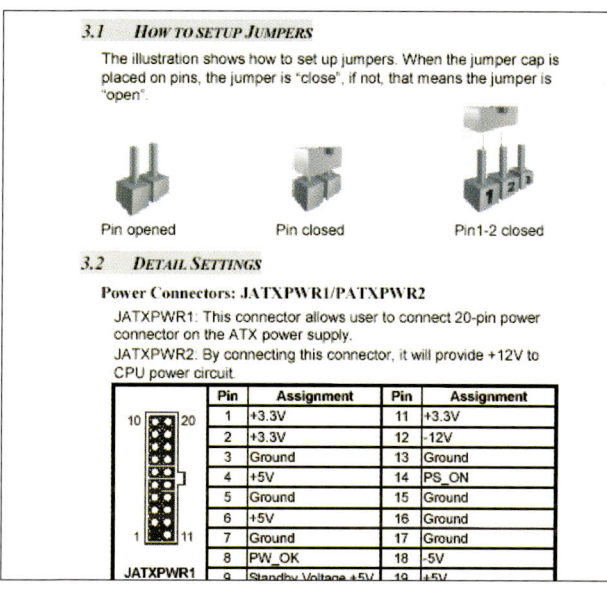

I find it difficult to go back and forth, consulting the Web site and going to my PC-building workspace. What do you suggest?

If you find something particularly helpful on the Web site, consider making a printout of the details so that you can bring it to your workspace as you assemble. You also may want to add the site to your Favorites list so that you can return to check more details later.

How can I best use my motherboard manual?

Read through it and, as needed, bookmark pages that seem particularly helpful. When done, lay the manual open within your sight in your workspace so that you can consult it again as you assemble.

111

Orient and Prepare the Motherboard for the Case

Ideally, there should be only one correct way to install the motherboard in your PC case. Unfortunately, this is not always true. Some manufacturers still make it possible to mount the motherboard upside down.

Orient and Prepare the Motherboard for the Case

① Refer to your documentation for both the case and the motherboard to see what these indicate.

② Pick up the motherboard and hold it near or within the open case.

③ Determine how the motherboard must go in. Use the screw holes on the motherboard and the case chassis as a reference point.

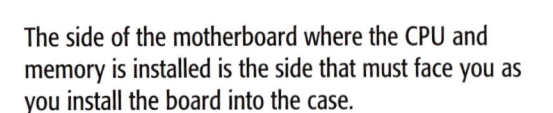

The side of the motherboard where the CPU and memory is installed is the side that must face you as you install the board into the case.

Note: If these are not yet installed, refer to the side where the expansion ports and other features such as the memory sockets and feature labels are located.

④ After you have a sense of the way you need to position the motherboard, gently lay it aside, back in or under its antistatic bag, until you are ready to physically mount it.

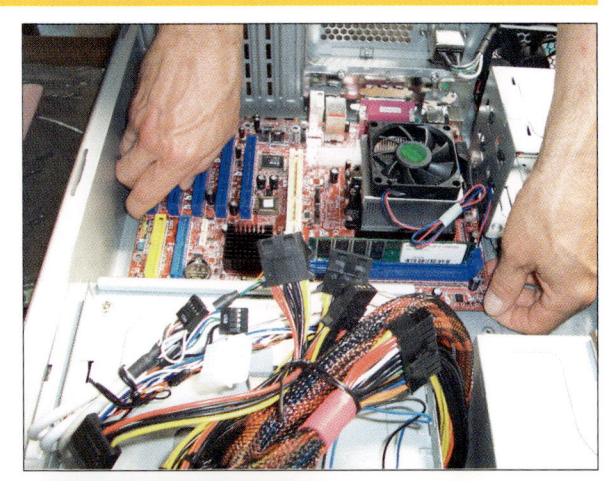

Set the Jumpers

Your motherboard usually requires that you set one or more jumpers, a step that you should do now before you install the motherboard. A *jumper* is a rudimentary form of switch that enables you to turn on or off a hardware feature based on whether a pin is open or closed. When a pin is closed, this means a tiny plastic cap, also called a *shunt*, is installed over the pin, which creates the jumper.

Set the Jumpers

With the Biostar motherboard chosen for the target system, as well as some if not all of the alternative motherboard selections, you may find that several jumpers are already preset for you to enable features such as the IEEE 1394 port — so you can install an IEEE 1394 external drive or a digital video camera.

But you should still go through your documentation to be certain which jumpers are required and that they are set properly.

① For example, to use the IEEE 1394 port, you would look for the set of pins labeled J1394A1 on the motherboard.

② After you consult your documentation, check to be sure that the plastic cap or shunt is positioned over pin 1 as the diagram directs.

③ If the shunt is not present, locate the cap and put it over pin 1.

Note: *Pins and jumpers are not unique to motherboard hardware. You will see them again when you configure drives for use.*

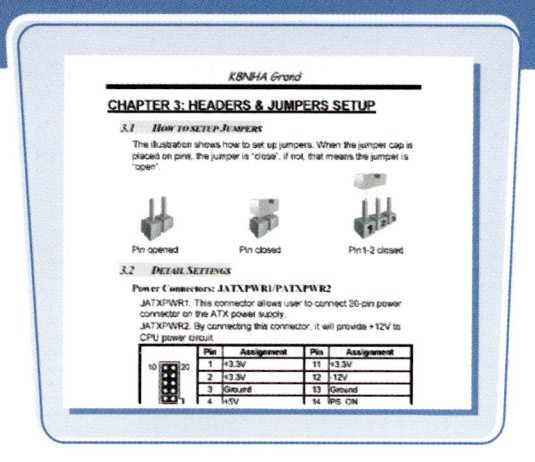

Chapter 9: Installing the Motherboard

113

Mount the Motherboard

In this section, you will install the motherboard into your case. But before you do that, you need to be sure all the work that should be done with the motherboard still unmounted is complete. Then you can begin by installing the standoffs.

Mount the Motherboard

CPU, MEMORY, AND JUMPERS

① If you have not installed the CPU and memory (see Chapters 7 and 8), do so now.

② If these are in place, check their installation to be sure that they are firmly inserted and will not fall out as you move the motherboard.

③ Adjust jumpers or switches on the motherboard as detailed in the motherboard manual or other documentation.

Note: See "Set the Jumpers" for more information.

BE CAREFUL

As you work, be patient, be calm, and exercise extreme care. It is all too easy to damage the motherboard if you apply too much pressure or try to force it into place.

You should not allow the board to drop or scrape up against another component.

INSTALL THE STANDOFFS

Note: The brass standoffs will sit on the bottom (with the piano style) or the back wall (of a tower design) of the case.

① Look inside the case and locate the seven holes near the left side — as seen from the front — of the rear of the case.

② Remove the first standoff from your container and screw this into one of the standoff holes in the case with your fingers.

③ Continue until all the standoffs are in place.

Warning: Insert all seven standoffs. Each one is there for a reason; you increase the chance of damage to your board if you install only a few.

Q&A

Where can I find the standoffs?

The brass metal or plastic standoffs and short screws that you need to mount the motherboard are in the hardware bag that came inside your case. There you will find seven of each. Before you insert them, you may want to place them temporarily in one of the cups or containers you got as part of your toolkit in Chapter 4.

What are the standoffs for?

The screws — just as you may think — fasten the motherboard into its mounting. These standoffs keep the circuit board from coming into direct contact with the metal case, which could cause an electrical short.

Chapter 9: Installing the Motherboard

continued

115

Mount the Motherboard (continued)

Your motherboard should be out on your worktable, at rest on its antistatic bag, with your CPU and memory in place. Now you will install it into the case, atop the standoffs. Then you will replace the back panel of the case with an alternative back panel.

After you apply the alternative back panel, you will screw the motherboard into place to secure its mount inside the case.

Mount the Motherboard (continued)

INSERT THE MOTHERBOARD

1 Lift the motherboard with both hands, but be careful to touch only the sides.

2 Bring the motherboard to the case and judge how best to place it down to line it up with the standoffs.

3 Rest the motherboard in place above the standoffs.

4 Look at the motherboard and determine what else needs to be done before you screw it in place.

APPLY AN ALTERNATIVE BACK PANEL

With the piano style case, there is a problem because not all of the motherboard connectors fit with the current back panel. You must be able to access ports and connectors through the back panel so that you can install additional hardware.

Therefore, the piano case comes with an alternative back panel that you can apply in place of the existing one.

① Lift and remove the motherboard from the case back to its spot on top of the antistatic bag.

② Place your hand just inside the case at the back panel and pull the back panel off.

③ Locate and apply the alternative back panel.

④ Push it into place securely.

⑤ Reinsert the motherboard back on the standoffs and see whether the back port and connector holes are available.

⑥ As needed, push in and up on any light metal parts that block the port and connector holes.

INSTALL SCREWS

① Locate the first of the short screws and place it in the first available screw hole on the motherboard.

② Repeat step **1** to install the remaining six screws.

Warning: Do not screw too fast or too hard. You want the screws to be just tight enough to keep the motherboard in place but not so tight that you flex or damage the board.

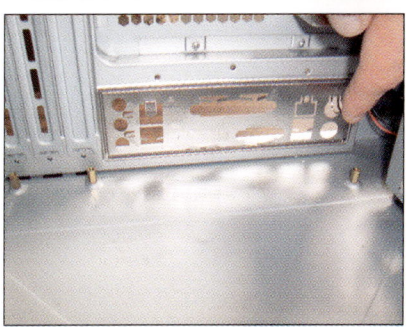

Connect the Power

You need to install the two power connectors from the power supply to the motherboard. These connectors, through the wires attached to them, will provide electricity to the motherboard and what is installed to it.

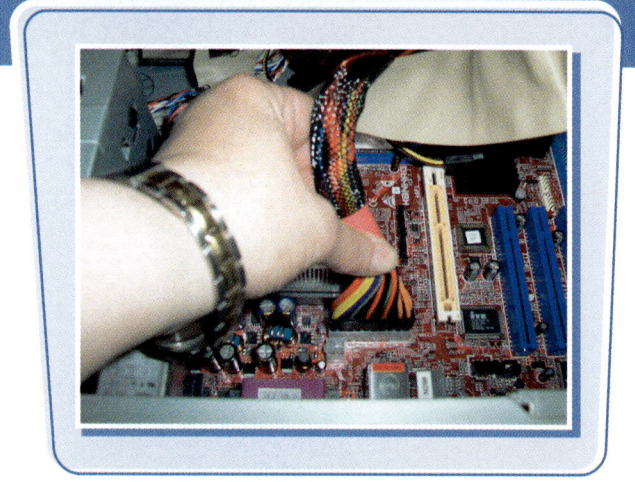

Connect the Power

1. Consult your motherboard manual to determine the position of your motherboard connectors from the power supply.

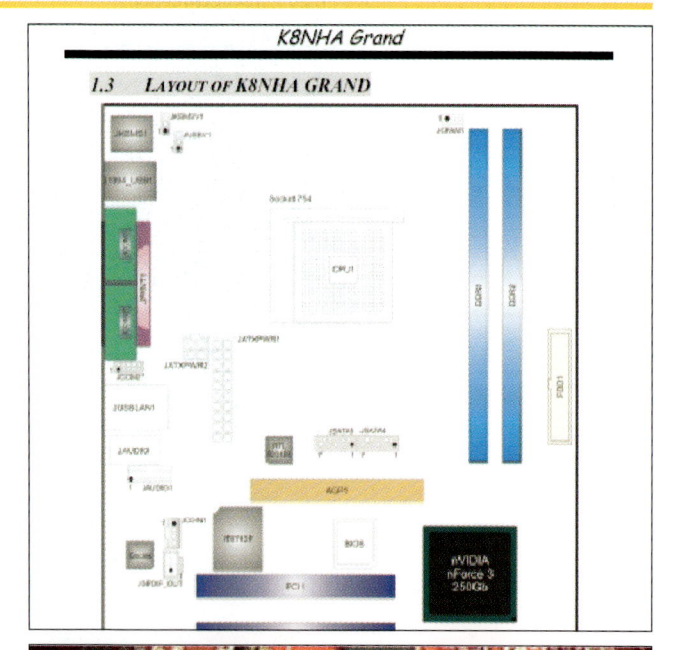

2. Locate the power connectors on the motherboard.

    These are labeled JATXPWR1 and JATXPWR2 if you use the Biostar motherboard selected for this system.

118

❸ Locate the 20-pin JATXPWR1 connector wires coming from the power supply.

❹ Insert the white connector plug in the JATXPWR1 connection on the motherboard.

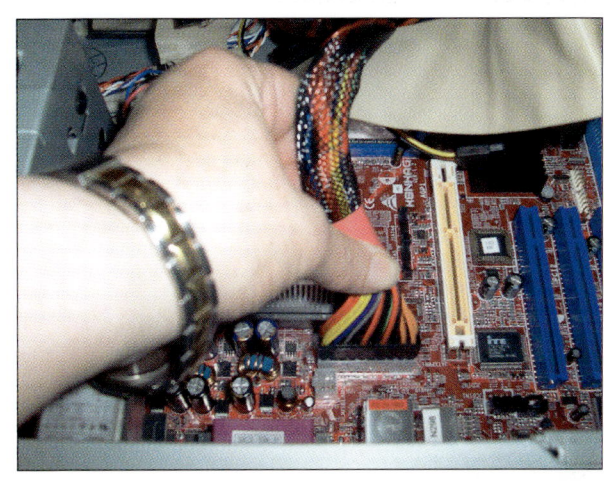

❺ Locate the square 4-pin JATXPWR2 connector wires from the power supply.

❻ Insert its white connector end into the JATXPWR2 connection on the motherboard.

Chapter 9: Installing the Motherboard

Q&A

I am working with a different motherboard that I chose, and I see a bunch more connections on the motherboard. What should I do?

Regardless of which motherboard you use, you need to read through your motherboard manual and see what additional connections from the power supply to the motherboard are needed, connectors from fans, and other hardware that is already installed in the case. All of these connections must be made before you try to start the PC when fully assembled.

The little square plug that provides the second connection from the power supply to the motherboard appeared damaged and will not connect properly. What should I do?

If you notice a damaged connector — and this one is very important — you need to get the part replaced. In this case, this is the power supply, so contact CPU Solutions (or other vendor) and tell them what is wrong and that you need a replacement as soon as possible.

119

Make Other Connections and Double-Check the Installation

Before you move on in your assembly, you should make certain that everything you have done so far is complete and that each item is firmly and securely installed in the exact right place.

First, check through your motherboard manual and power supply documentation. Locate all additional connections that must be made between the motherboard and the power supply. After complete, then double-check your installation thoroughly.

Make Other Connections and Double-Check the Installation

1. Bend down so that you are at eye level with the case edge and look to be sure that the motherboard appears to lie straight and correctly on the standoffs.

2. Touch the edge of the motherboard to be sure that there is no looseness.

3. If there is, check each screw and secure any slack ones.

120

④ Check the back panel at the rear of the PC to be sure that none of the motherboard ports or jacks is blocked by the panel.

⑤ If so, bend the light metal out of the way so that you can reach the ports and jacks.

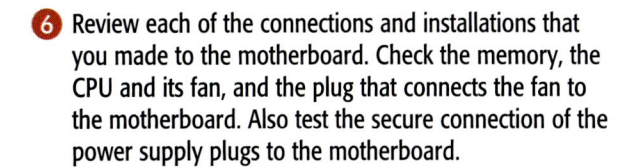

⑥ Review each of the connections and installations that you made to the motherboard. Check the memory, the CPU and its fan, and the plug that connects the fan to the motherboard. Also test the secure connection of the power supply plugs to the motherboard.

Q&A

What will happen if I do not take the time to make sure that all the connections are made?

This step is very important. For example, you may need to connect wires leading from the front of the PC, where the power button is located, to the motherboard, and if you do not, the first time you try to turn on the PC, nothing will happen. Unfortunately, because every setup will be different, you will need to determine these connections based on your documentation and what you see before you.

What if I cannot figure out where a particular connector goes?

First, try to determine where the connection comes from — such as a fan or the power supply or a button — and then scour the motherboard and other hardware documentation to seek out a reference for it. If all else fails, contact CPU Solutions or other vendor for assistance.

Chapter 9: Installing the Motherboard

121

Part IV

Setting Up Your Drives

If you have ever avoided installing a brand new hard disk because you were sure that the job is impossibly difficult, you are in for a surprise. If you follow the steps in this part, you will become a drive master in no time at all.

Again, your pre-planning comes in handy because this is another process that requires a fair amount of attention to key details. For example, you have to know how you want to use your drives and then configure them correctly so that the system recognizes the drives and their connections. Without this configuration, your drives may not operate properly, or Windows may not see them as available. After you master these steps, you will be able to easily go on to add or replace drives at any time in the future.

In the target system built here, you will mount three different drives: a hard disk, a DVD player/recorder, and a floppy disk drive. Later, in Part VI, you will see how simple it is to add external drives that connect through the USB/IEEE 1394 ports located at the back and/or front of your PC case.

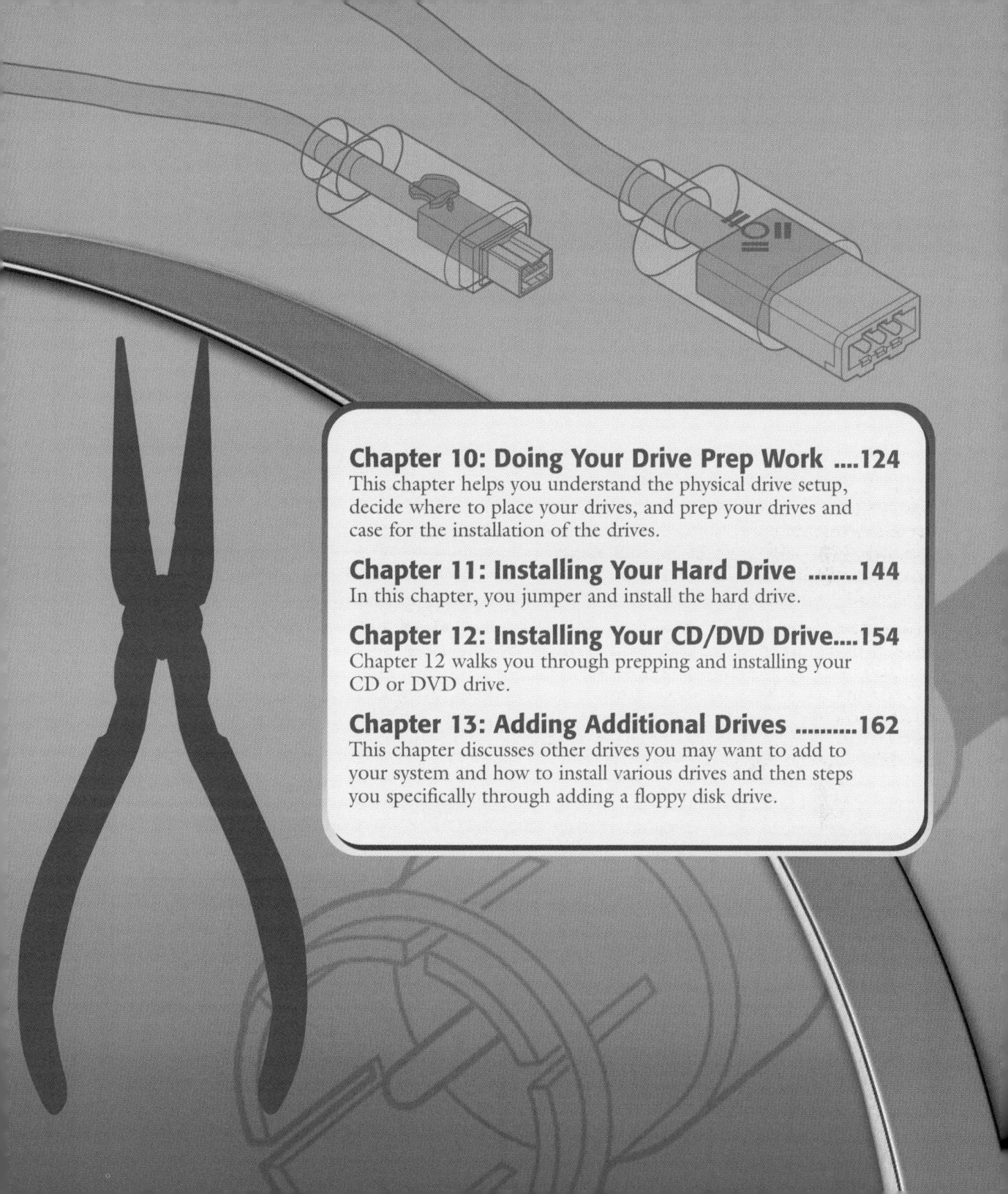

Chapter 10: Doing Your Drive Prep Work 124
This chapter helps you understand the physical drive setup, decide where to place your drives, and prep your drives and case for the installation of the drives.

Chapter 11: Installing Your Hard Drive 144
In this chapter, you jumper and install the hard drive.

Chapter 12: Installing Your CD/DVD Drive....154
Chapter 12 walks you through prepping and installing your CD or DVD drive.

Chapter 13: Adding Additional Drives 162
This chapter discusses other drives you may want to add to your system and how to install various drives and then steps you specifically through adding a floppy disk drive.

Understanding the Physical Drive Setup

When you plan a new system, you must consider more than the question of what kind of drives you want to include. You also need to decide what drive platform you will use, such as internal versus external and IDE versus SCSI. This matters because the configuration and setup of each varies a bit.

In this chapter, you will learn everything you need to know to configure your drives before you install them into your PC.

External versus Internal

The primary hard disk in any PC is usually internal. This means that drive is mounted in one of the drive bays contained within the PC case.

Increasingly, however, high-speed external drives of all types are in demand for a number of reasons, not the least of which is that external drive prices are becoming competitive with internal drives.

See the section "Know the Difference between External and Internal Drives" later in this chapter for specific points of difference between these two drive types.

IDE versus SCSI

Internal drives have two major types: integrated drive electronics (IDE) — also called ATA — and small computer system interface (SCSI, pronounced "scuzzy"). Hard disks, CD drives, and DVD drives can all be either IDE or SCSI.

The price differences between SCSI and IDE drives are less obvious now. Also, IDE drives have become much faster and can be used in ways that formerly required only SCSI drives before.

IDE

IDE drives are the best-selling drives available. By and large, IDE drives are the kind most frequently seen in consumer PCs such as the Windows Media Center PC you are building now.

SCSI

SCSI drives have traditionally been used in more professional-type systems rather than consumer-style systems such as this Windows Media Center PC. SCSI drives are favored in professional settings because they allow more devices such as drives to be attached than an IDE setup, which usually offers a maximum of four IDE drives; SCSI drives tend to cost more, and they can be a bit more difficult to set up.

IDE Controllers versus SCSI Controllers

Here you see the two IDE controllers on the motherboard. IDE1, the blue controller, is the primary IDE controller, and IDE2, the yellow one, is the secondary IDE controller.

Whereas IDE drives connect to one of the two IDE controllers on the motherboard, SCSI drives connect via SCSI cable to an adapter — called either the *SCSI host adapter, SCSI card,* or *SCSI controller* — that installs to an expansion slot on the motherboard. Sometimes, SCSI controllers are integrated into the motherboard directly. Special software with the controller helps you configure SCSI drives for use.

continued

125

Understanding the Physical Drive Setup *(continued)*

IDE-Based versus SCSI-Based

Understand, too, that a PC system is usually either IDE-based or SCSI-based. This means that all or most of the drives contained in the PC are either one form or another rather than a mix of types. It is, however, possible to have both IDE and SCSI drives in the same system as long as you have a SCSI host controller, but this mixing is not usually done.

Serial ATA Drives

A new type of faster hard disk, called serial ATA or SATA, is beginning to replace both traditional IDE and SCSI drives. Whereas a regular IDE drive transfers data at a maximum of a bit over 130MBps, a SATA drive transfers 150MBps in the same second.

About the only reason you do not see SATA drives replace IDE drives completely is that not every motherboard supports SATA because the connectors are not physically present.

Add a SATA Drive Later

The target system in this book uses a motherboard with SATA built-in. Although no SATA drive is part of the PC as assembled here, you can choose to add one either during the initial build or upgrade to a SATA drive at a later time.

SATA Adapter

Even without a SATA-capable motherboard, you can install a SATA adapter to one of the motherboard's expansion slots and then connect the SATA drive through a SATA cable to the adapter that you add. You lose a bit of the speed when you use an adapter over a fully SATA setup.

126

SATA II Drives

This holds true for SATA II, the faster and more recently released version of the drives. Instead of 150MBps, SATA II drives transfer at up to 300MBps, or more than twice as fast IDE drives.

SATA and SATA II drives are considered high performance because of the speed boost. They are also usually some of the most capacious, with many models able to hold 300GB or more. Many SATA drives advertise as running much cooler than their IDE counterparts because of an advanced design that allows optimized power consumption — the less power generated translates into less heat.

The Drive Setup for the Media Center PC: Piano Case versus Tower Case

Because I chose a piano-style PC case for the Windows Media Center PC rather than a standard tower-type design, we are faced with a unique situation. This situation has some different possible solutions.

In a tower design, you would just install the different drives into stacked drive bays so that it would be easy to connect the hard disk and the DVD-RW drive via the same ribbon cable to the same IDE controller on the motherboard. In this relationship, the hard disk — which is normally always the designated first drive in a PC with the drive letter of C: — is referred to as the *master* and the DVD-RW drive the *slave*.

continued

127

Understanding the Physical Drive Setup (continued)

The Drive Setup for the Media Center PC: Issues with the Piano Case Drive Setup

The piano design, however, presents a slight challenge. There are drive bays in two separate locations, plus room for up to two additional drives on a platform that sits above the power supply installed in Chapter 6.

The set of drive bays located at the right front of the case allows you to add two drives, each with an opening to the front of the case once the faceplates discussed in Chapter 5 are removed. Here, you could add both the hard disk and the DVD-RW drive and connect them to the same IDE drive ribbon cable to the same IDE controller on the motherboard.

The problem with adding both the hard drive and DVD-RW drive in the right front set of drive bays, however, is that the DVD-RW drive — at full height — is too large to be placed on the platform over the power supply, which only has room for a half-height drive. To resolve this, you could place the hard drive in the front drive bay directly below where you install the DVD-RW drive, but this also will not work because the drive bay is larger than the hard disk.

No Stacked Drives

You also may not want to stack a high-capacity hard disk right next to another drive that can get quite warm. A common reason for this may be concern for heat build-up, which you can have when drives are nested very closely together.

So — while you will also learn how to configure two drives for use on the same controller in this chapter — you will see now how you can set your hard disk up in one location and the DVD-RW up in another, with each having its own IDE ribbon cable that connects to each of the two IDE controllers on the motherboard. Chapters 11 and 12 show you that installation. Later, you can add other drives as slaves onto these drives.

When You Want to Connect Two Drives to the Same IDE Controller

Each IDE controller can accept up to two IDE drives, regardless of the type. Normally, the hard disk is connected first and then any other drive type, such as a second hard disk or a CD or DVD drive.

Dual Drive Cable

To make it possible for two drives to connect to just one IDE controller, you need a dual drive IDE ribbon cable that enables you to connect the drives together before you connect them both to the same IDE controller.

Jumpers

You also need to set jumpers found at the back of the drive to specify the role each drive has. You learn how to do this in the section "Prep Your IDE Drives for Use."

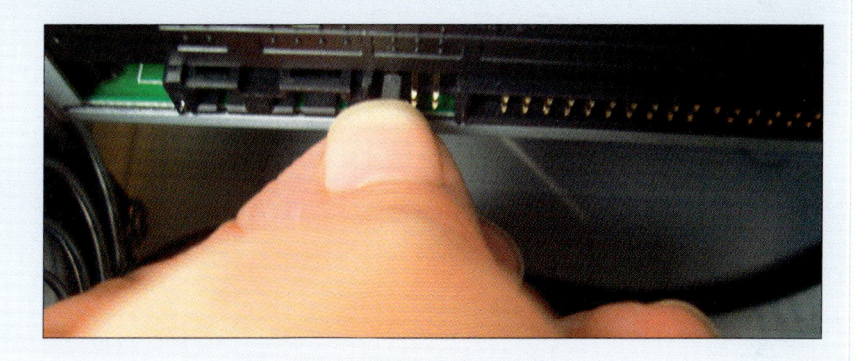

Determine Where Each Drive Goes

Before you can install the drives, you must configure them for use. To do this, you need to know how you plan to install the drives.

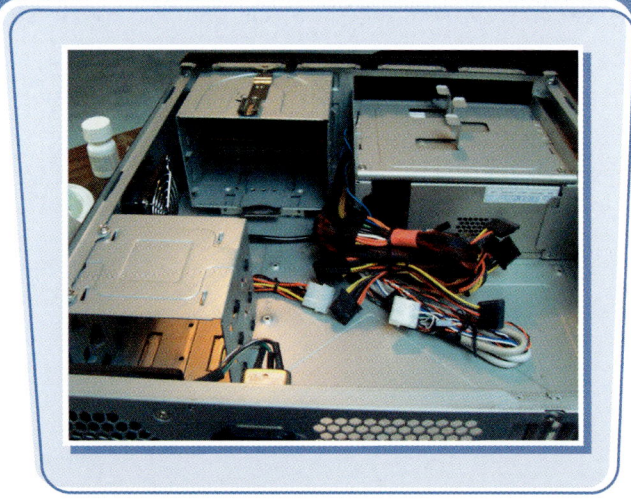

Determine Where Each Drive Goes

The floppy disk drive goes on its own special cable, which is connected to a unique floppy controller on the motherboard. Chapter 13 shows you how to do this, so you do not have to worry about this right now.

Instead, focus on the other drives such as the hard disk(s) and CD/DVD drives that you have for your new system.

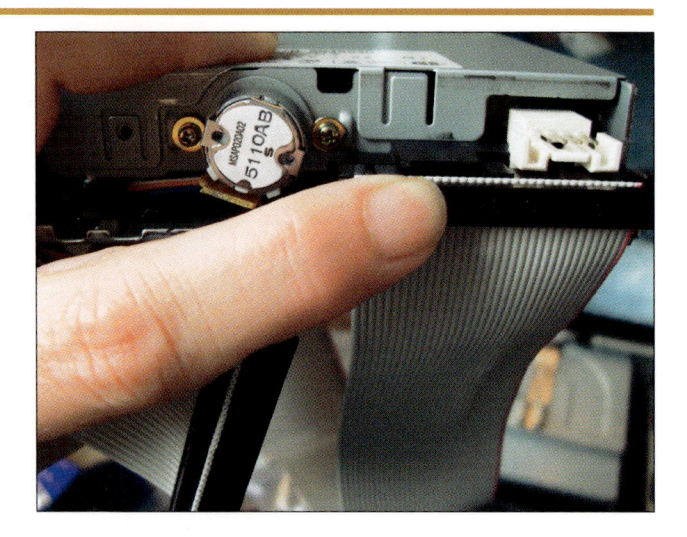

130

① Decide where to mount the drives.

Note: Your primary hard drive should go into a front drive bay (above the power supply). Mount others close by, such as the CD/DVD drive in the top-right drive bay and the floppy disk to the left of the hard drive.

② Determine whether the drives are close enough to share a ribbon cable.

Note: They are not for the target system; each needs to be connected directly to an IDE controller on the motherboard by its own ribbon cable.

③ Based on your drive placement, choose how you want to connect the drives to the motherboard.

Note: Be sure that you do not need to stretch the drive ribbon cable to reach between the drive and the IDE controller.

If they are close enough, you can connect two drives together with the same dual disk ribbon cable. If they are not close enough, you need two IDE drive cables, with each connecting to one of the two motherboard IDE controllers.

Q&A

I plan to install two hard drives. One is a 10,000 RPM drive and very speedy, whereas the other is 7,400 RPM and not quite as fast. I plan to connect these together, but which goes first?

Whenever you connect two drives on the same ribbon cable and IDE controller, the fastest drive should always go first. When you pair a hard disk with a CD/DVD drive, the hard disk is the master.

I want to pair up drives to share an IDE controller, but my drive ribbon cable only has connections for one drive. What should I do?

Get a dual drive IDE/ATA ribbon cable. You can get this through CPU Solutions or at any store that carries PC hardware, especially hard disks. When you connect both drives, the master drive should be attached at the far end of the cable, and the slave drive needs the middle drive connector.

Chapter 10: Doing Your Drive Prep Work

131

Prep Your IDE Drives for Use

IDE drives configure through a set of pins and jumpers at the rear of the drive, in the same area where the ribbon cable and the power supply connector attach.

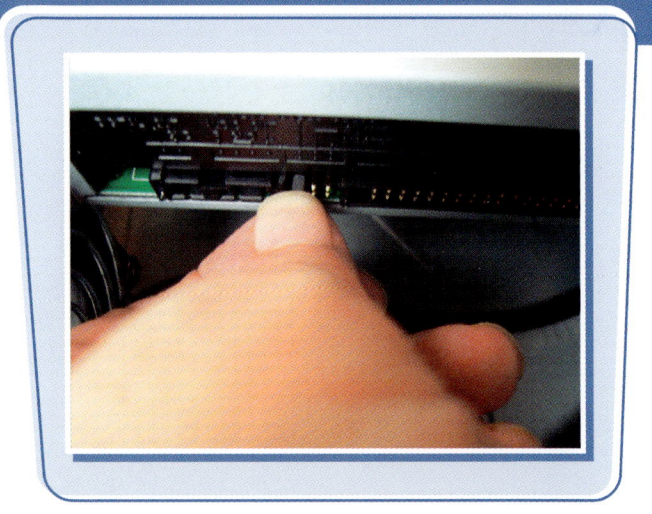

The Label on the Drive

Often, a label on the top of the drive not only tells you what the drive is, but also tells you about the pin-jumper assignment and provides a diagram to guide you through the setting. Make sure that you read this label.

If your drive does not contain a label, read the section "Using Online Help Guides and Documents" to learn about your drive.

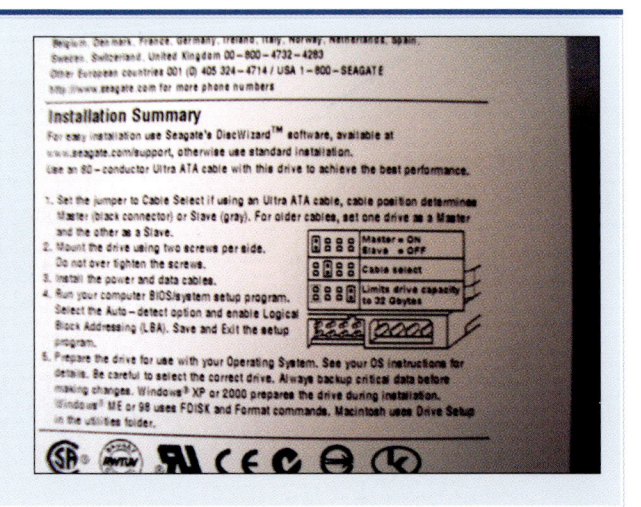

About Drive Jumpers

There are three standard pin settings on every IDE drive. A jumper or plastic shunt is placed over the row of pins that correlates to the drive assignment that you need.

These assignments are as follows:

- Master or primary: This is the one to use for the first of two drives that will connect via the same dual-drive ribbon cable to the same IDE controller on the motherboard.

- Slave or secondary: Use this when you configure the second of two drives that will connect via the same dual-drive ribbon cable to the same IDE controller on the motherboard.

- Cable select: Set this jumper when a drive will function as a single connection on a ribbon cable that connects to an IDE controller on the motherboard. If you want two drives to each have its own IDE controller and cable, set the jumper on both drives to Cable Select.

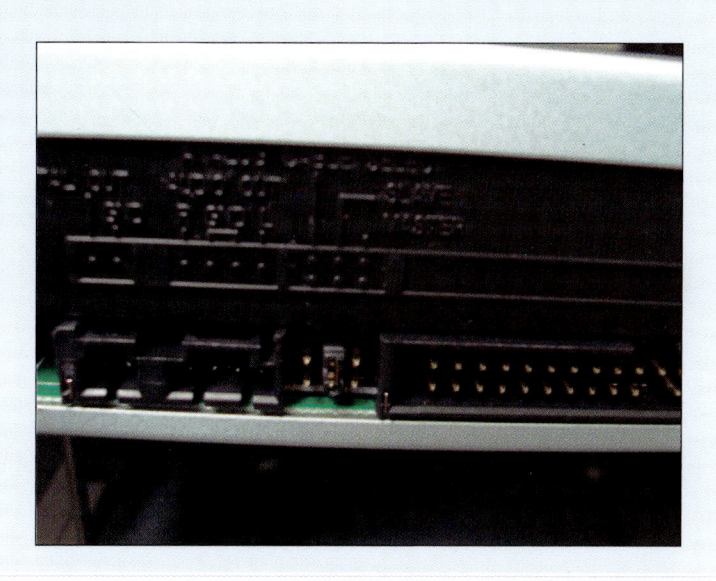

Prep Your IDE Drives for Use *(continued)*

When you have two drives you want to share the same drive ribbon cable and the same IDE controller, you now know that you need to set these drives up through jumper placement to be master and slave drives.

Most drives, by default, come with the jumpers automatically set to Cable Select. This is the correct setting for drives that operate independently of each other and will not share the same ribbon cable or IDE controller.

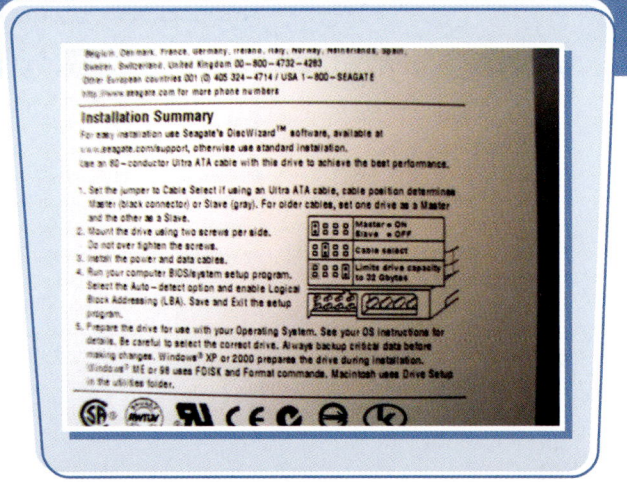

Prep Your IDE Drives for Use *(continued)*

SET UP TWO DRIVES AS MASTER AND SLAVE

1 Determine which drive should be first — the master — and which should be second — the slave.

Note: Because the first drive that you connect sets the speed for the drives, you want your fastest drive as the master, which is usually your hard disk.

2 Look at the back of the first drive to see where the jumper is — usually on Cable Select — and then pull the jumper off and place it on the Master pins.

3 Repeat step **2** for the second drive, but set the jumper and pins to Slave or Secondary.

SET UP TWO DRIVES AS INDEPENDENT DRIVES

1 Check the drive label or documentation for each drive to see how it designates the jumpers.

There may be small differences between drives and manufacturers.

2 Verify that the jumper at the back of each drive is set to Cable Select. If not, move the jumper so that it is set this way.

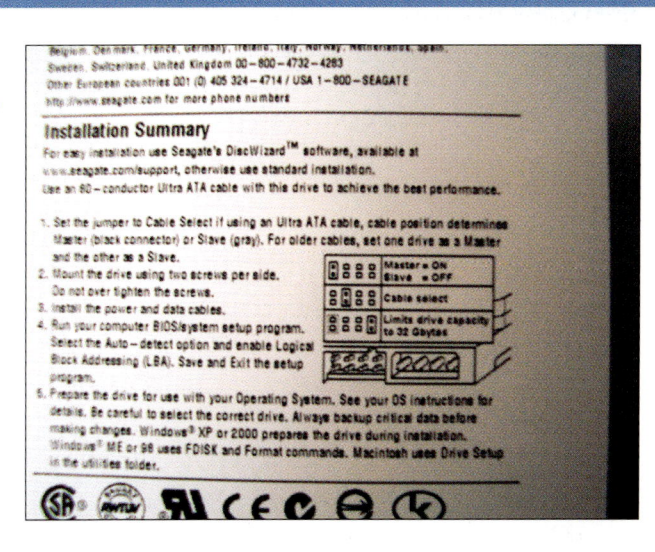

Chapter 10: Doing Your Drive Prep Work

Q&A

How do I set the jumpers for my floppy disk drive?

You do not need to set jumpers on the floppy disk drive.

What will happen to my jumper settings if I need to change my drives later?

If you change drives later, you need to reset the jumpers based on how you plan to use the new drives.

135

Know the Difference between External and Internal Drives

There is more to understand about the differences between external and internal drives other than one type mounts inside the case whereas the other does not.

Internal drives are typically put to use as primary storage drives where your Windows operating system and applications are installed and run and where your always-needed files are located. External drives, by comparison, often are put to work as backup drives where you can store copies of files and setups from the internal drives.

External Drives

External drives today usually connect via high-speed external ports, such as the USB 2.0 or IEEE 1394 ports that are found at either or both the front and back of the PC. They are also portable, which means that you can disconnect and reconnect them at will and move them to other systems you may have. You also may be able to share an external drive between different PCs on a network in your home or office.

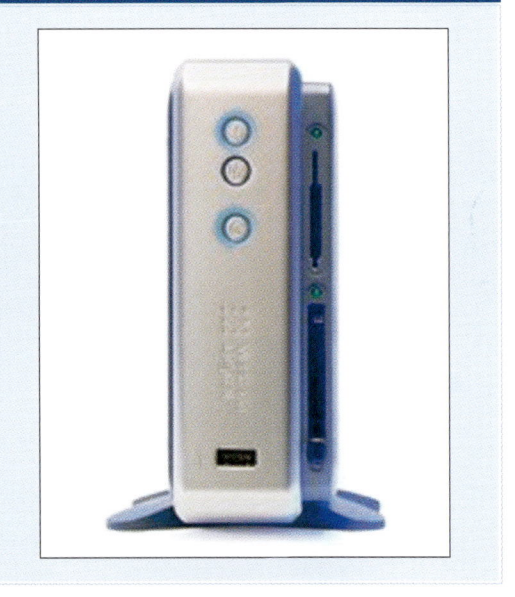

Add an External Drive

Although no external drives are part of this Windows Media PC setup, you can easily obtain and add one to your system. They are available in a number of different storage capacities from a few gigabytes all the way up to 300GB and beyond.

How You Can Use an External Drive

You can acquire an external drive to use it as the following:

- As a backup drive where you store a copy off all files from your main hard disk.
- As storage for all the images you shoot with your digital still camera or movies you create through a digital movie camera; you can also use it as storage for all your music files.
- As a shared device that you can connect to via many PCs on a network or physically move between different PCs in your home or network.
- As an easy way to transport files from your home and office or to copy files from your laptop that you can later transfer to your desktop PC.
- As offline storage for files you use rarely but need to access from time to time.

Chapter 13 discusses how to add extra drives, and Chapter 22 covers how to install USB and IEEE 1394 devices.

Using Online Help Guides and Documents

All too often, you find that drives you buy pack with very little in terms of manuals or other documentation. This is not only frustrating but also can make it fairly difficult to know how to proceed.

Forget the frustration. There is a way to get where you want to go from here. The answers and details that you need are available online, which is one of the reasons a second PC with an available Internet connection becomes invaluable as your build your new system.

Drive Manufacturer Web Sites

In this section, you learn how to take advantage of drive manufacturer Web sites to learn more about your drives and any special details that you need to know to set them up. Even if you have never before visited such a site, you will be amazed at the wealth of support you can find there and put to use.

Find Manufacturer Sites

First, you need to find the Web site address of your drive manufacturer. This can be found on the drive package or in the often-limited documentation that you receive with your drive. You can also try, in the address bar of your browser, to type in the name of the company followed by **.com**. If that does not work, you need to search for the address using a Web search engine such as Google, Yahoo!, or Ask Jeeves.

Different Manufacturer Sites

Although every Web site tends to differ a bit in how you use it and browse through it, there are some similarities as well. Most you discover have two primary areas, one that lists all their products and one specifically for support.

To help you along, here is a list of some of the most popular drive manufacturers, along with their Web site addresses:

- Fujitsu at www.fcpa.com
- HP at www.hp.com
- IBM at www.ibm.com
- Maxtor at www.maxtor.com
- Samsung at www.samsung.com
- Seagate at www.seagate.com
- Toshiba at www.toshiba.com
- Western Digital at www.westerndigital.com

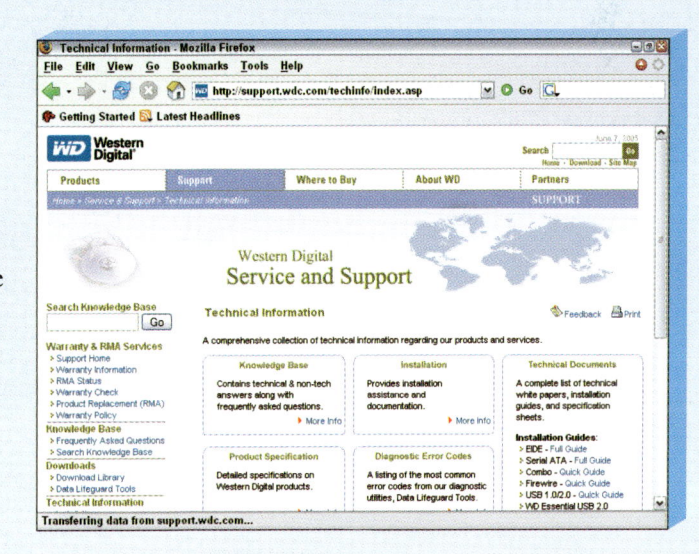

Chapter 10: Doing Your Drive Prep Work

continued

139

Using Online Help Guides and Documents *(continued)*

One of the most helpful pieces of information you can find online is complete installation instructions, often with special videos that you can download and watch through your browser, showing you each step of the process.

Different manufacturers may use slightly varied wording to identify jumpers and settings on your disk. You should check the manufacturer site to learn about the specifics for your drive setup.

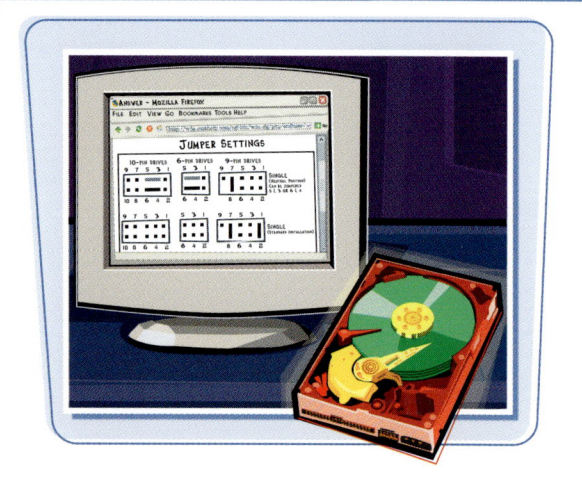

Using Online Help Guides and Documents *(continued)*

FIND DRIVE INSTALLATION INSTRUCTIONS

1. Navigate to the Web site of your drive's manufacturer.
2. Click **Support**.
3. Locate your drive type and select it.
4. Click to open specific pages about different aspects of your drive, such as Installation.

    You can download any specifics or print the pages that you need.

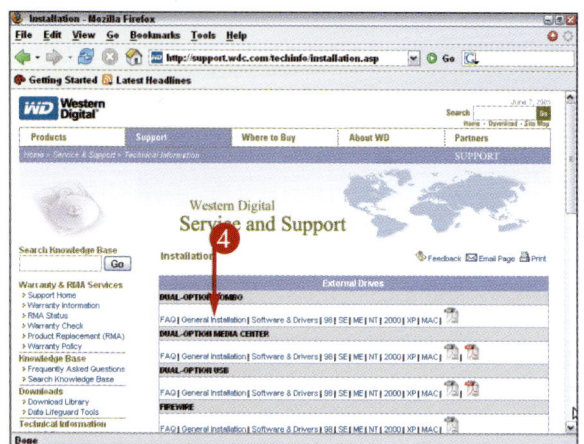

140

FIND JUMPER DETAILS

1. Follow the preceding steps **1** to **3**.
2. Browse through the listing to find details about your drive setup.

3. Open and read any pages that cover jumpers.

   Take notes or print the pages for later reference.

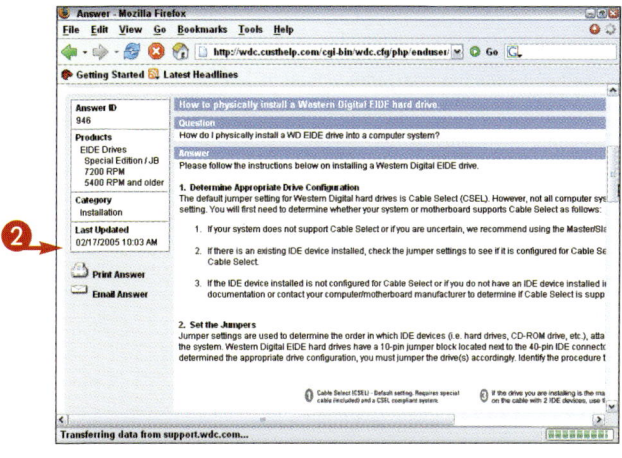

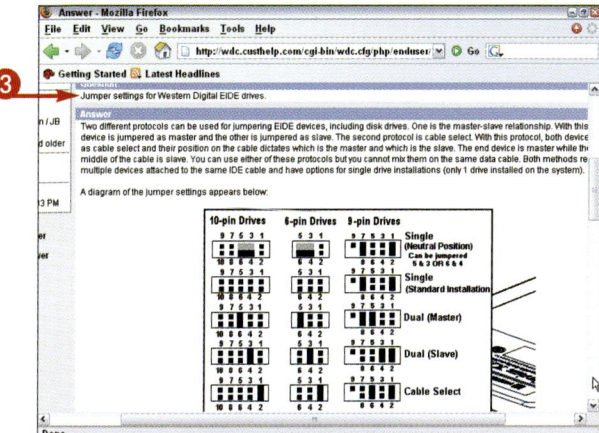

Aside from installation and jumper instructions, what other information can I find on the manufacturer's Web site?

One other thing that you should check is what it says about any software that arrives with your drive; this software is usually available to help you after you have installed the drive and want to prepare it for use with Windows.

Can I buy only external drives, and not install internal drives?

No, you should have at least one internal hard drive where your operating system is installed. But you are free to make any additional hard drives that you add external, which connect through the USB and/or IEEE 1394 ports at the back as well as the front of your case.

Chapter 10: Doing Your Drive Prep Work

141

Check Your Cables

Verify that you have all the drive cables you need to install your drives. CPU Solutions normally provides exactly what you need, based on what you order.

Check Your Cables

How many ribbon cables you need varies by how you intend to install your drives. If you follow the drives selected for the target system built here, you have a floppy disk drive, a hard disk, and a DVD-RW drive. The floppy drive has its own separate drive cable. If you plan to install the other two drives together to use the same IDE controller, you need one dual-drive ribbon cable.

If instead, you plan to install each drive separately to each of the two IDE controllers, you need two single-drive ribbon cables.

However, you can use a dual-disk ribbon cable to install a single drive; you just leave the secondary connector unconnected. If you need another cable, order or buy it now before you assemble the PC.

Note: *In the next two chapters, you will learn how to physically install the drives and connect the cables.*

Remove Screws and Retainers

Did you remove the drive faceplates when you prepared the case back in Chapter 5? If not, you need to remove them now.

Remove Screws and Retainers

1. Look at the drive bays inside your PC case.

2. If there are screws or retainers attached to the mounting holes at either side of the drive bays you plan to use, remove these with a screwdriver and place them in your toolkit containers.

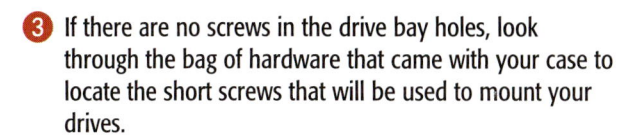

3. If there are no screws in the drive bay holes, look through the bag of hardware that came with your case to locate the short screws that will be used to mount your drives.

Note: Most drives require at least two screws, one for each side.

Chapter 10: Doing Your Drive Prep Work

143

My Choice for the Hard Drive

A media center PC tends to require a fair amount of drive space because music and video take up a good deal of room. Because you also need room to install media applications, you want a capacious and fast drive.

For this reason, I chose the Seagate Barracuda 120GB 7200 RPM IDE drive. This is about three times the hard disk real estate of a common consumer 40GB hard disk, so it allows you space to grow.

Seagate Drives

Another factor in the choice is that Seagate is a reputable name in hard disk technology. I have used Seagate drives successfully for many years on dozens of different systems. Seagate's online support also is quite robust, so I know that you can find answers to any questions that may arise about the installation or use of its hardware.

Alternative Hard Drive Choices

Perhaps you want more — or less — hard disk space or want a hard disk from another manufacturer such as Western Digital, another big name in drives.

Different Hard Drives

CPU Solutions offers a number of alternative choices:

$

- Western Digital IDE 80GB Caviar 7200 RPM hard disk ($58.51)
- Western Digital IDE JB 200GB Caviar 7200 RPM hard disk ($107.21)

$$$$

- Western Digital IDE JB 250GB Caviar 7200 RPM hard disk with 8MB cache ($139.99)
- Western Digital SATA 2500 JD 350GB hard disk ($139.99)

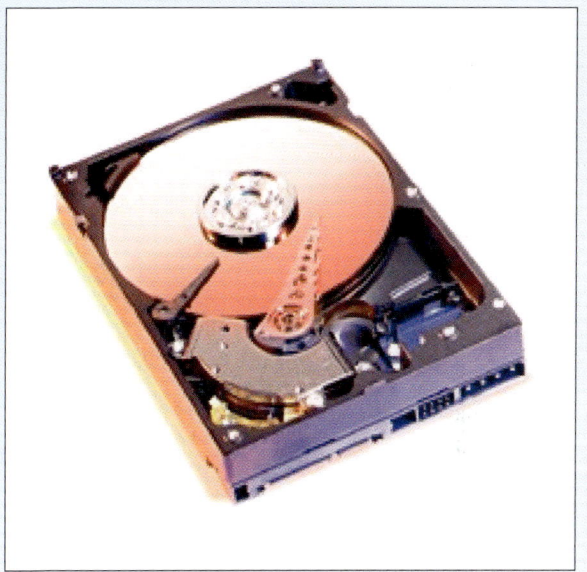

If you choose the SATA drive and select a motherboard other than the Biostar picked for this system, you want to be sure that your motherboard choice has SATA ports — the Biostar has two — or you must purchase a separate SATA adapter to install to your expansion port. Chapter 10 has more details about SATA drives.

Jumper and Prep the Drive

Before you mount the drive, you must make certain the jumper located at the rear of the drive where you make your drive configuration is set properly.

Jumper and Prep the Drive

Chapter 10 details how to set jumpers based on how you want to install the hard disk in conjunction with your other drives. It also discusses the placement of the drives. With this system, you will install the hard disk over the platform for the power supply in the piano-style horizontal case and attach it to the first IDE controller on the motherboard using a separate drive ribbon cable from the CD/DVD drive you install in Chapter 12.

① Check the jumper at the rear of the drive.

② Consult the label on the drive, as needed, to check the jumper settings.

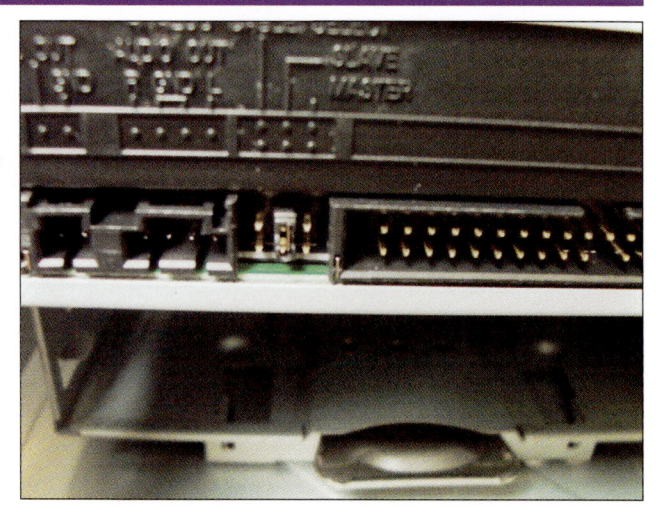

③ Also consult the drive documentation, Chapter 10, and online help resources to be sure that you have the right configuration.

④ Change the jumper, as needed, so that the plastic cap is installed over Cable Select.

⑤ Double-check your work.

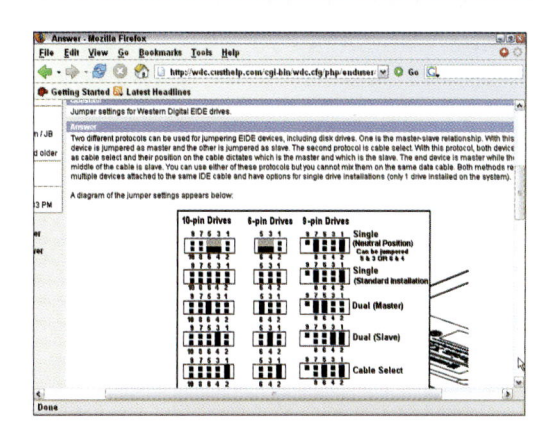

Q&A

If I chose a different drive setup, will my jumper settings be the same as those shown here?

No, not necessarily. If you decide to set up your drives differently, be certain that your drives are then jumpered accordingly. Review Chapter 10 and the manufacturer Web site.

I am having trouble changing the jumper. What can I do?

You may want to use the cushioned-tip tweezers suggested for the toolkit that you put together in Chapter 4 to remove and replace the jumper or cap.

147

Install the Drive

Because the hard disk will be mounted in the platform over the power supply in the piano-style case, you must remove the metal platform first to do this. Then you will mount the drive to the platform and return the platform with the drive to the case.

Install the Drive

① Locate the two screws that hold the platform in place over the power supply.

② Remove these screws and place them into a container.

③ Lift the platform out and place it on your work table.

Note: To install the floppy disk drive on the same platform, to the left of the hard disk, consult Chapter 13 before you replace the platform.

④ Place the hard disk on the right of the platform.

⑤ Line up the holes on the hard disk with the holes on the right of the platform.

The hard disk should be set slightly back from the front edge of the platform.

⑥ Place the first screw in place from the outer edge of the platform so that it goes into the side of the hard disk as it sits against the platform edge.

⑦ Use your screwdriver to secure the screw in place.

⑧ Repeat steps **6** and **7** to add the second screw in the second hole.

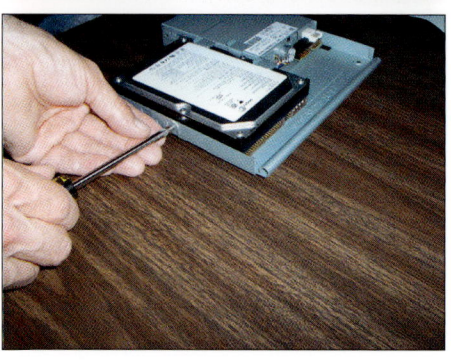

9 If you intend to add the floppy drive here (see Chapter 13), add this to the platform to the left of the hard disk.

10 Adjust the drive placement so that the front of the floppy drive lines up with the front edge of the platform.

11 Use two screws to secure the floppy drive to the left side of the platform.

Note: If you choose a different placement of the floppy drive, you can skip steps 9 to 12.

12 Check the front faceplates on the left side of the case as it faces you. Be sure the faceplate that covers the floppy disk drive bay is removed as discussed in Chapter 5.

Optionally, you can also remove the faceplate for the drive bay just to the right of the left-most drive bay so that you can see the hard disk access light.

13 Replace the platform — now with the one or two drives added — in the case.

14 Screw the platform into place.

Attach the Cable

You now need to attach the drive ribbon cable. There are two connections that you must make: one to the drive itself and another to the IDE controller on the motherboard.

Attach the Cable

TO THE DRIVE

Note: Most drive cables have a color code: a red or sometimes blue stripe appears along the edge of one side of the cable, which corresponds to pin 1 on the back of the drive and pin 1 of the IDE controller on the motherboard.

1. With the color-coded edge as your guide, insert the drive connection end of the cable into the back of the drive so that the color-coded edge inserts at the right of the cable connector.

2. Make certain that the connection is secure.

150

TO THE MOTHERBOARD

Note: You now need to plug the other end of the drive ribbon cable into the first IDE controller — usually labeled IDE1 or IDE0 — on the motherboard. This will complete the cable connection.

① Locate IDE1 or IDE0 on your motherboard. Consult your documentation, as needed.

② Attach the other end of the drive ribbon cable to the IDE0 or IDE1 controller.

③ Check to be sure that the connection is secure.

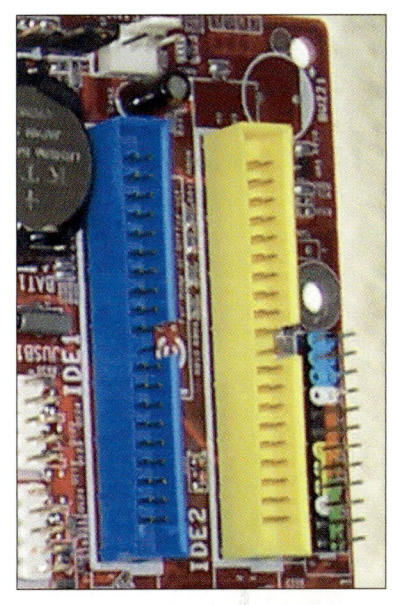

Q&A

If I am installing two drives to the same cable, using a dual-disk ribbon cable, is there anything different that I do here?

Yes, insert the second of the three total connectors into the rear of the second drive just as you did the first.

I added the floppy disk to the platform with the hard disk. How do I attach its cable?

If you installed the floppy disk at the same time as the hard disk, go to Chapter 13 to see how to make your connections.

Chapter 11: Installing Your Hard Drive

151

Connect the Power Supply to the Hard Drive

Your final step in the physical mounting of the hard disk is to attach one of the power plugs that connect via wires to the power supply to your hard disk. This connection will — when the PC is powered up — send electricity to the drive to operate it.

Connect the Power Supply to the Hard Drive

1. Locate one of the four hole connectors from the power supply that fits the power plug just to the right of the drive ribbon cable at the back of the drive.

2. Insert the connector firmly into the power plug at the rear of the drive.

3. Test the connection.

   You may need to apply a bit of extra pressure to get the plug securely seated.

Check the Drive Mounting

Before you simply assume that your hard drive is successfully installed, you want to go over everything you have changed or connected to be certain.

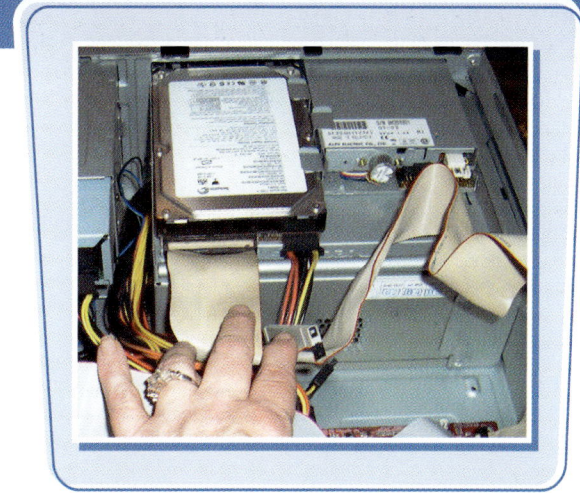

Check the Drive Mounting

① Look at the drive itself to make certain that it sits evenly and not at any angle.

② Check the screws that hold the drive in place to be certain that both screws are firm and in place.

③ Verify all your connections both at the rear of the drive and on the motherboard.

④ Look again at your jumper settings.

My Choice for the CD/DVD Drive

My choice of media player drive for the Windows Media Center PC was a simple one. Because I anticipate both playing DVDs as well as recording my own, I decided on the Benq IDE 16x DVD recorder.

This unit enables me to play all types of CDs and DVDs, as well as record my own DVD-Rs and DVD-RWs. It is the most flexible choice and comes with a changeable cover so that it works in both beige and black setups.

Recordable DVDs as Storage

Consider, too, the size of the hard disk you add. To make backups of 80 or 120 or more gigabytes of files on the hard disk needs a capacious drive. Because far less than 1GB of data stores on a recordable CD, you will be overwhelmed if you try to record enough CDs to back up all of your hard disk. A recordable DVD, by comparison, stores nearly 5GB, so you may need only eight to ten DVD-Rs to store a backup that would otherwise take over 100 CD-Rs. However, backing up a full 120GB hard disk would take more than 150 recordable CDs or more than 20 recordable DVDs.

Alternative CD/DVD Drive Choices

Although I strongly recommend that you consider the Benq DVD-RW drive selected for this system, you can also explore some alternatives.

Different CD/DVD Drives

If you need to save money and you are certain that you will neither play nor record DVDs on your Windows Media Center PC, you can get away with something as inexpensive as a CD-RW drive, which will play all types of CDs and record to both CD-R and CD-RW media. Or, if you think you want to play DVDs but see no reason to record them, you can get a dual drive that will play DVDs but still lets you record CD-R and CD-RW discs.

Your IDE drive choices are as follows:

$

- Samsung TSH352ABEWP 16x DVD player and CD-RW drive ($24.95)
- AOpen 52x32x CD-RW drive with changeable faceplates to match your case color ($26.96) (shown here)

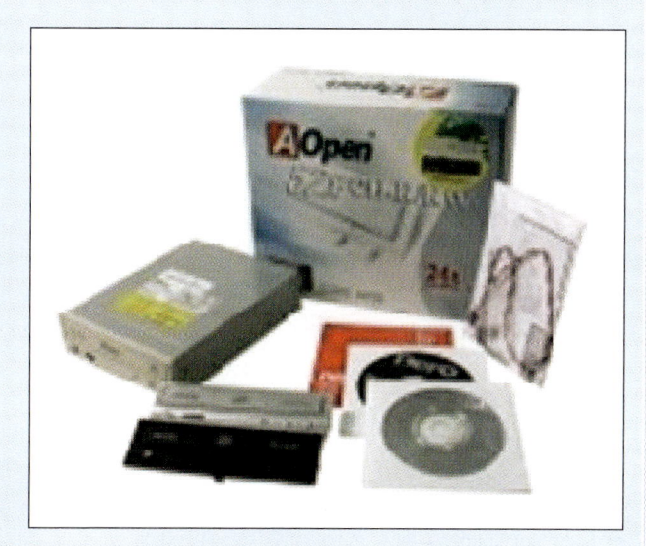

$$$$

- Lite-On 52X Combo Drive, which records CD-Rs at 52x speed, records CD-RW disks at 32x speed, and plays recorded DVD-ROM discs at 16x speed ($40.47) (shown here)
- Lite-on DVD-RW, which plays and records DVDs of all types and reads all types of CDs ($63.39)

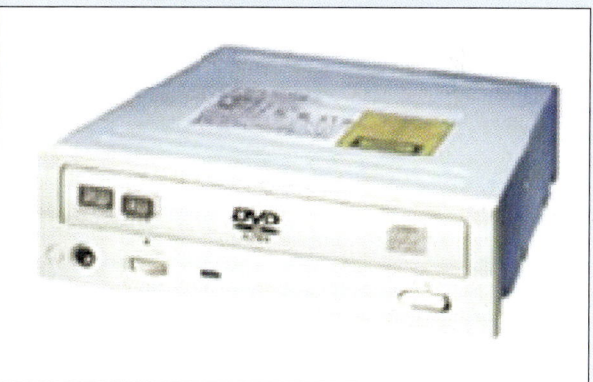

Chapter 12: Installing Your CD/DVD Drive

155

Prepare the Drive

Just as you have done successfully with your hard disk, you need to prep the CD or DVD drive and the case for the installation.

Note that an IDE CD or DVD drive requires the setting of a jumper (see Chapters 10 and 11).

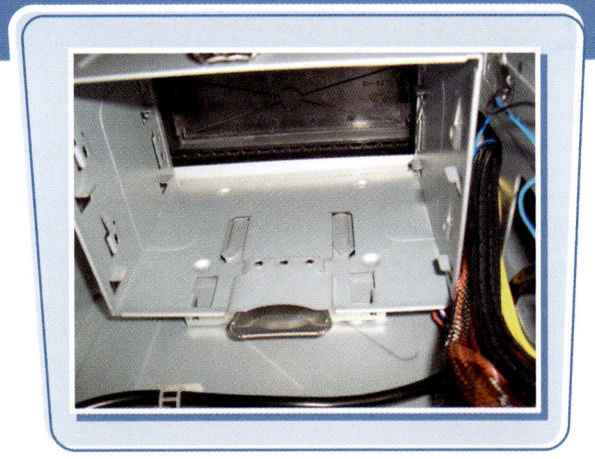

Prepare the Drive

① Consult your drive documentation for any special information about installing your drive.

② Check the drive manufacturer Web site to see if any details or help is available.

③ Jumper the drive for **Cable Select** if the drive will be on its own cable and IDE drive controller, as **Slave** if the drive will connect via the same ribbon cable as the master hard disk, or as **Master** if you plan to add another drive to the CD/DVD drive on the second IDE controller on the motherboard.

Note: I suggest that you jumper the drive as Cable Select because it is the only drive connected to the motherboard IDE controller.

④ Determine which drive bay you will insert the CD/DVD drive into.

⑤ Make sure that the faceplate for the drive bay is removed. If not, remove it.

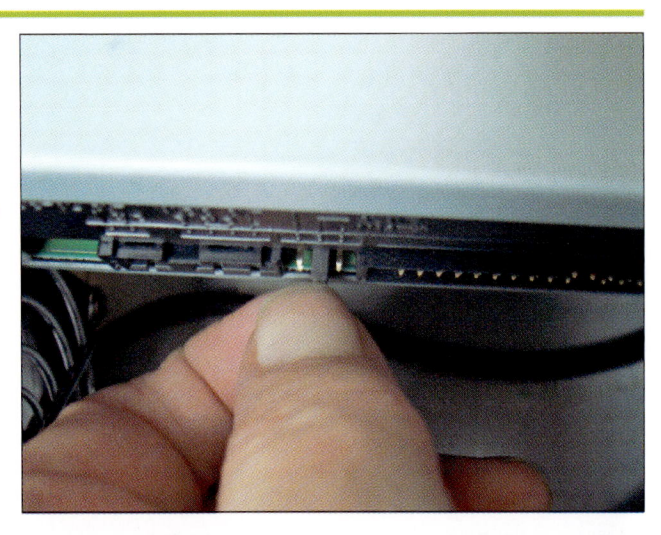

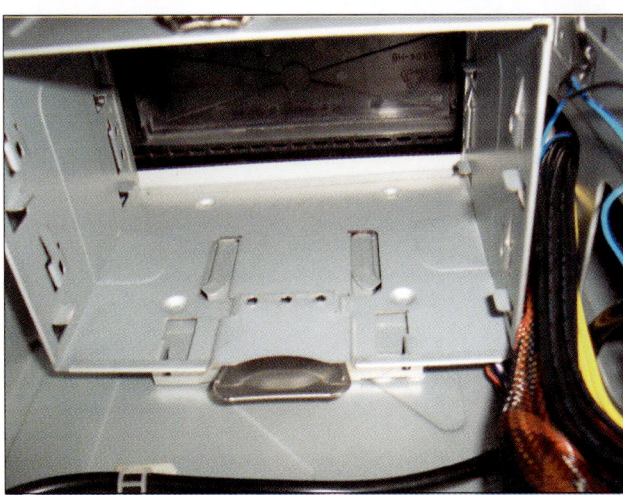

Install the Drive

Ready to install your CD/DVD drive? Here, you will use the top drive bay on the right side of the case opposite the power supply and the platform where the hard drive is mounted.

Install the Drive

1. Remove the screws and/or retainers already present on the mount holes for the designated drive bay and place them in your toolkit containers.

2. Slide the CD/DVD drive into place in the drive bay.

3. Line the drive up so that it interfaces with the front of the case where the faceplate was.

4. Now line the drive up with the mounting holes so that you can install the screws.

5. Insert the first screw into one of the mounting holes on the outside of the drive bay and use your screwdriver to secure the screw.

6. Insert the second screw into one of the mount holes on the other side of the drive bay and use the screwdriver to secure it in place.

7. Repeat steps **5** and **6** to add one more screw to each side of the exterior drive bay.

8. Check the drive from both the front and back to be sure that it is seated evenly and secure in place.

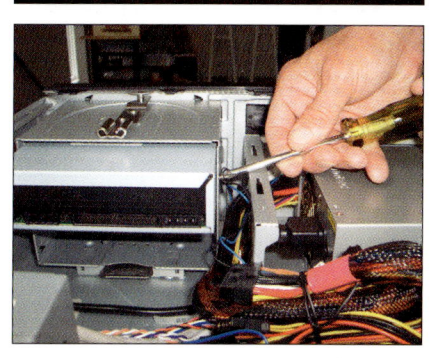

Chapter 12: Installing Your CD/DVD Drive

157

Attach the Cable

Use the same basic type of IDE drive ribbon cable that you used for your hard disk to connect one end to your new CD/DVD drive and the other end to the second IDE controller on the motherboard.

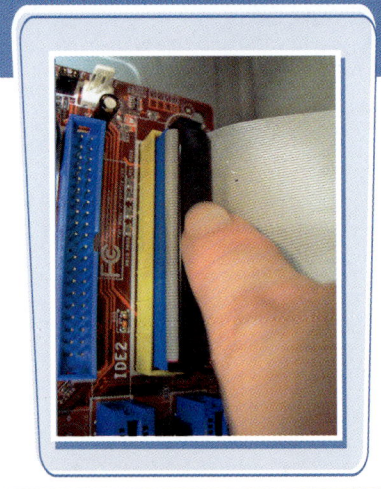

Attach the Cable

The only variation to these steps is if you plan to make your CD/DVD drive the secondary drive on the same drive ribbon cable to which you attach your hard drive as the master — or if you plan to make the CD/DVD drive the master and install another drive as the slave or secondary drive. These instructions show you how to attach the drive as a single drive.

① Find the color-coded edge of the drive ribbon cable.

② Install the drive ribbon cable to the back of the CD/DVD drive so that the color-coded edge appears on the right side.

③ Extend the drive ribbon cable.

④ Locate the second IDE controller on your motherboard — labeled either IDE1 or IDE2.

Note: *This is IDE2 on the motherboard chosen for the target system.*

⑤ Insert the free connector end of the drive ribbon cable into the second IDE controller.

⑥ Verify your connections to be sure that they are secure.

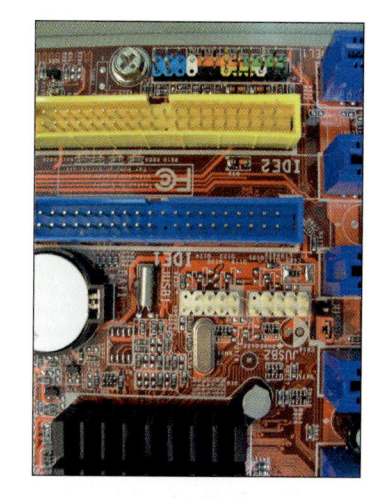

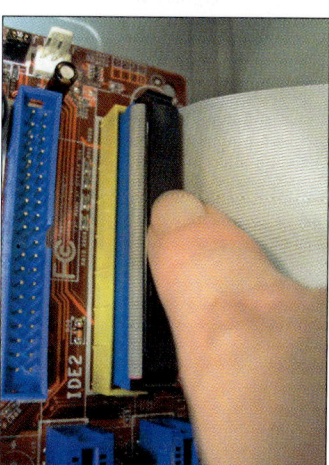

Q&A

What do I use to attach my CD/DVD drive to the sound card?

A special audio cable may need to attach between the CD/DVD drive and the sound card or sound chipset integrated into the motherboard. Chapter 15 shows you how to do this. However, strictly speaking, Windows XP does not usually require this cable because sound is emulated through the software and built-in chipset sound. But if you use fancy surround sound or other elaborate speaker setups, you may still require this cable.

159

Connect the Power

Finally, you must connect the power supply to the new CD/DVD drive to power that drive after you finish your assembly of the PC, plug it in, and turn it on.

Connect the Power

1. Check through the bundle of wire connectors on the power supply to find the same type that you used to connect to the hard disk in Chapter 11.

2. Gently pull this wire connector around to the rear of the installed CD/DVD drive.

3. Firmly press the power supply connector into the power socket at the back of the drive.

4. Test the connection to make sure that it is firm and secure.

Verify Your Installation

Now go through the installation and its connections to be sure that you did everything completely and correctly. This extra measure makes it far less likely that you will experience problems when you start the PC after you finish building.

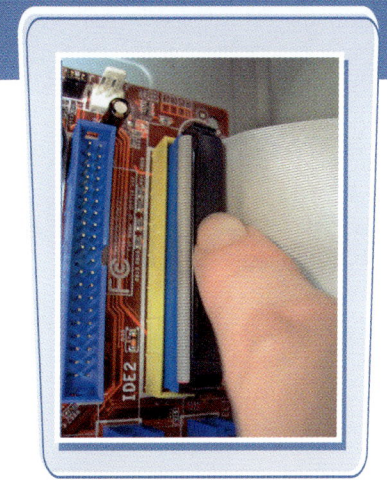

Verify Your Installation

① Check again to be certain that the drive appears even and correctly seated in its drive bay.

② Look at the screws and make sure that each is firmly in place.

③ Verify the drive ribbon cable connections at both the drive and the IDE controllers on the motherboard.

④ Test the connection from the power supply to be sure that it is not loose and is fully seated.

Chapter 12: Installing Your CD/DVD Drive

My Choice for the Additional Drives

You may want to be able to easily transfer documents to and from the office, so I chose to add a floppy disk drive to the target system — an Alps black one. Such a drive is not only inexpensive but also remains useful for moving smaller files such as documents.

However, floppy disk drives are no longer quite as standard as they once were. In fact, a few manufacturers have followed Apple's lead with their iMac computers and no longer offer a floppy drive unless a customer requests it.

A Floppy Disk Drive

Granted, a floppy disk has very little capacity: just a bit over 1MB. Although this is plenty enough room for a few spreadsheets, several documents, and even smaller media files, it is not the right medium to back up or transfer larger files. Also, fewer manufacturers use floppy disks to store software such as that which comes with your new hardware purchases.

Alternative Additional Drive Choices

Consider thoughtfully what other drives you may need or want on your system. Perhaps you want a second hard drive or some type of removable media drive — where you can pop a disk out and take it with you — that can serve as a backup disk.

Different Additional Drives

With the internal drives that you have in place, you still have room for up to two more internal drives. But you may also want to think about external drives, such as those that connect through your USB or IEEE 1394 ports on the outside of the PC.

Other suitable drive choices include the following:

$

- Soyo Internal/External 9-in-1 card reader drive that reads Flash memory and provides extra USB ports ($16.99)
- SanDisk 1GB Cruzer Mini portable drive ($54.05)

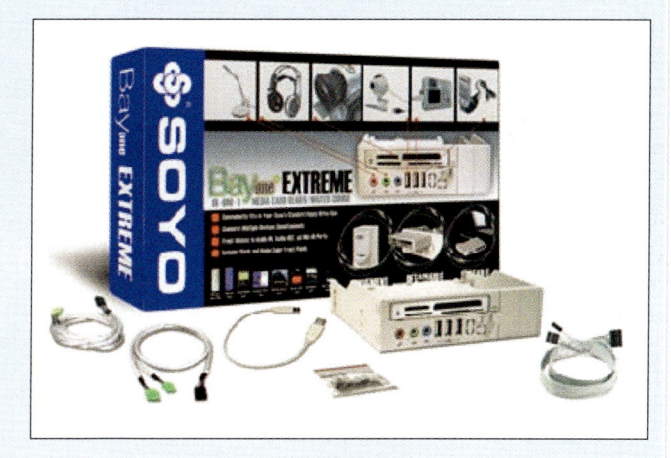

$$$$

- External USB 2.0 or IEEE 1394 hard drives ($60 to $350, depending on GB capacity)
- One of the internal hard drive choices noted in Chapter 11, such as a SATA hard disk ($88 to $335)

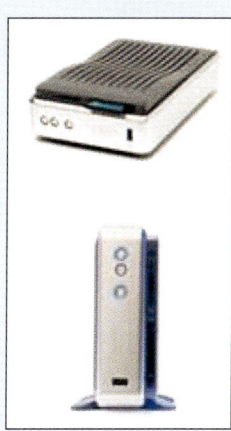

Add the Basics

How you install and configure your additional drive depends on the type of drive. External drives set up much differently — and easily — than internal drives because you do not have to worry about jumpers, master and slave drive assignments, or even opening the case.

Other internal drives install very much like the hard disk and CD/DVD drive that you added in Chapters 11 and 12 — except for SATA drives. See Chapter 10 for more information about SATA drives.

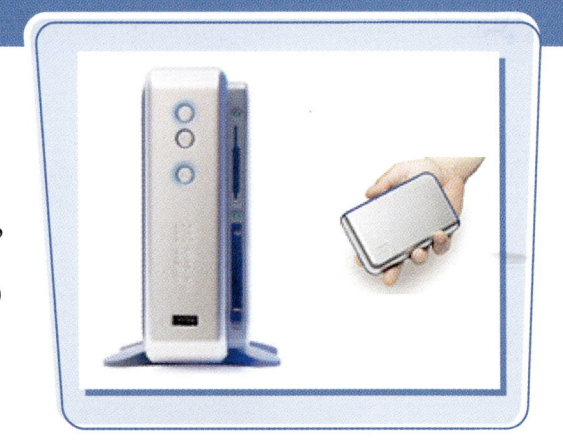

Add the Basics

ADD AN INTERNAL DRIVE

1. Map out the drive bay that you will install the drive into.
2. Install the drive.
3. Attach any needed cables.
4. Connect the power.

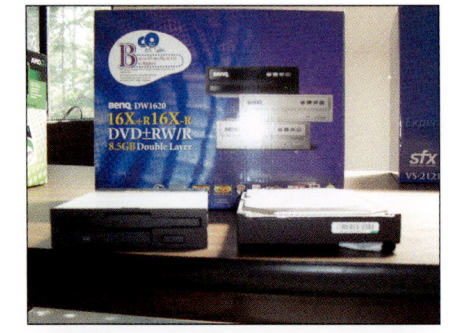

ADD AN INTERNAL ATA/IDE DRIVE

1. Jumper the drive according to how you will install it (see Chapter 10).
2. Set the drive up around existing drives so that no more than two drives connect to the same IDE controller on the motherboard, for a maximum of four.
3. Install a connector from the power supply to the back of the internal drive.

ADD A SATA DRIVE

1. Check to see if your motherboard has SATA connectors built in, as the Biostar K8NHA-G does.

    If so, you have what you need to install SATA drives.

2. If your motherboard does not have SATA connectors, install a SATA controller into a PCI slot and then connect the SATA drives via SATA cables to it.

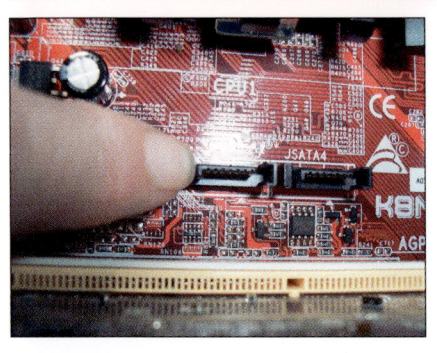

ADD AN EXTERNAL DRIVE

An external drive can serve as a backup drive to store copies of important files on the primary hard disk; a portable backup drive that goes back and forth to different PCs to back up various critical files on each to make a kind of centralized file store; an easy way to transport big files to and from the office; or a repository for special programs that you can install only to an external drive, such as games you do not want on your hard disk.

① Unpack the drive from its box.

② Read the accompanying documentation.

③ Set the drive in place near the PC case.

④ If there is a power cord for the drive, plug this in and turn on the drive.

Note: External drives connect either via the USB port or the IEEE 1394 port typically found at the rear or front of the case. Some drives, called combos, can connect through either USB or IEEE 1394 ports.

⑤ Attach the USB or IEEE 1394 cable to the drive and then to the appropriate port on the PC itself.

⑥ Run the accompanying software to prepare the drives for use.

Note: To learn more about what you do as you set up USB and IEEE 1394 hardware, refer to Chapter 22, "Installing USB and IEEE 1394 Devices."

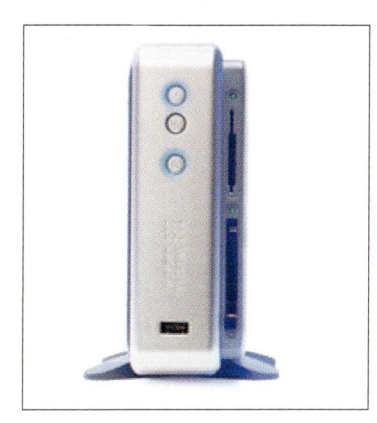

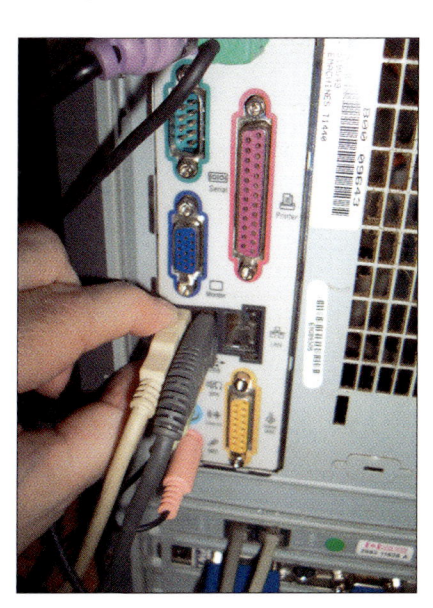

Install the Drive

Here, you install the floppy disk drive into the Windows Media Center PC. Follow along even if you plan to install a different drive because you will find that you will perform many of the same steps with other internal drives.

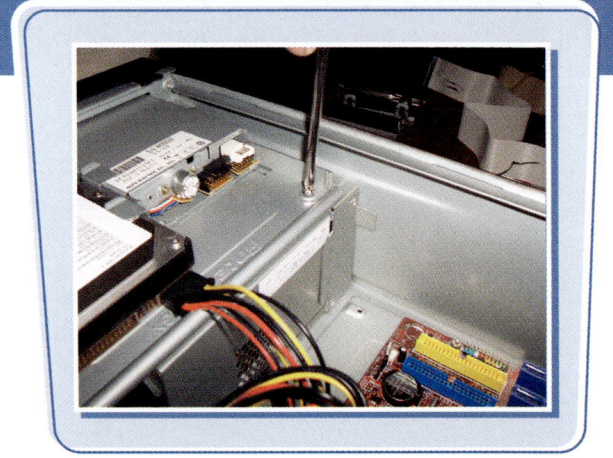

Install the Drive

1. Determine which drive bay you want to use to install the floppy disk drive.

   The bay that you select needs to have a faceplate that you remove so that you can access the front of the drive.

   Note: *I suggest that instead of installing the floppy drive to one of the standard drive bays, you install it to the platform over the power supply in the piano case, just to the side of the hard disk.*

2. Remove the faceplate from the selected drive bay.
3. Take the floppy disk drive out of its package.
4. Consult the floppy disk drive's accompanying documentation, if there is any.

❺ Remove any screws or retainers for the chosen drive bay and set them aside.

❻ Insert the floppy disk drive in the drive bay.

❼ Apply the screws or retainers to firmly mount the floppy disk drive in place.

❽ Review the installation. Make sure that it is balanced and even and that the front of the drive is accessible.

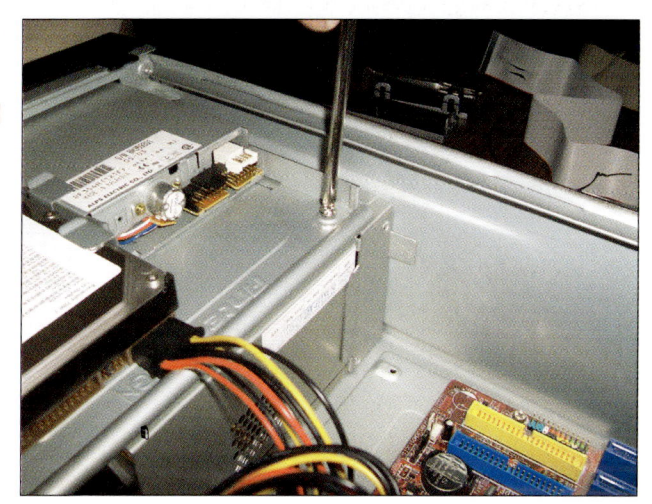

Chapter 13: Adding Additional Drives

Do I set jumpers for the floppy disk drive?

No, the floppy disk drive does not need to have jumpers set at all.

Can I place the floppy disk drive next to the hard drive on the platform over the power supply?

Yes, to do so, follow the instructions in Chapter 11 for how the hard disk is set up there.

167

Affix the Cable

You now must connect the newly added floppy disk drive to the floppy disk controller available on the motherboard. A floppy ribbon cable makes the connection.

Affix the Cable

1. If your floppy ribbon cable is folded, unfold it and extend it to its full length.

2. Insert one end of the ribbon cable into the cable connector located at the rear of the floppy disk drive.

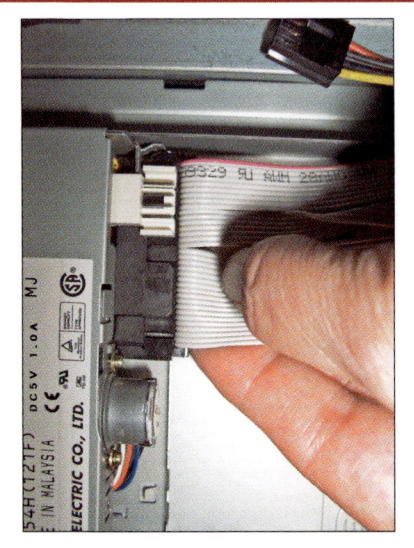

3. Locate the floppy disk drive — sometimes labeled FDD — controller on the motherboard.

4. Insert the other end of the drive ribbon cable into the floppy disk controller.

5. Verify that both ends of the cable are firmly and securely in place.

Connect the Power

Because the drive requires power to operate, you need to install a connector from the PC power supply to the power connection at the very back of the floppy disk drive.

Connect the Power

1. Find the power connector at the back of the drive.

2. Check through the connectors located at the end of the bundled wires to locate one that is either labeled for the floppy disk drive – or FDD – or one that matches the drive connection type.

3. Push the power connector securely into the power connection at the drive rear.

4. Check to be certain that the power connector is firmly in place.

   It should not pull out easily if it is inserted fully.

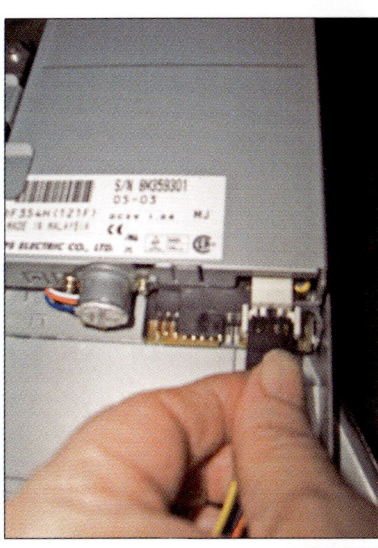

Chapter 13: Adding Additional Drives

169

Part V

Installing Add-on Adapters

Add-on adapters give you the ability to include all sorts of essential as well as advanced functionality in your PC through the installation of printed circuit boards that fit in the expansion slots on your motherboard. These expansion slots on current model PCs are usually either peripheral connection interface (PCI) or accelerated graphics port (AGP), which is used exclusively for video adapters.

Common add-on adapters include a video adapter (or graphics card), an audio adapter (or sound card), a modem to allow you to connect to the Internet, and a network interface card (NIC) to help you connect multiple PCs together to share both data and a high-speed Internet connection. There are also many specialty add-on adapters that enable you to add a feature to your system that you would otherwise have to buy an all-new motherboard or even a whole PC to have, such as when new types of hardware are released to the market.

As you will learn in this part, many systems today integrate chips from individual adapters directly into the motherboard, so separate adapters are optional. Integrated chips, however, are not always as robust, so you may want to replace an integrated component with a separate adapter. The target system built here includes integrated sound and network capability, but you also learn how to install such adapters separately if you choose different components.

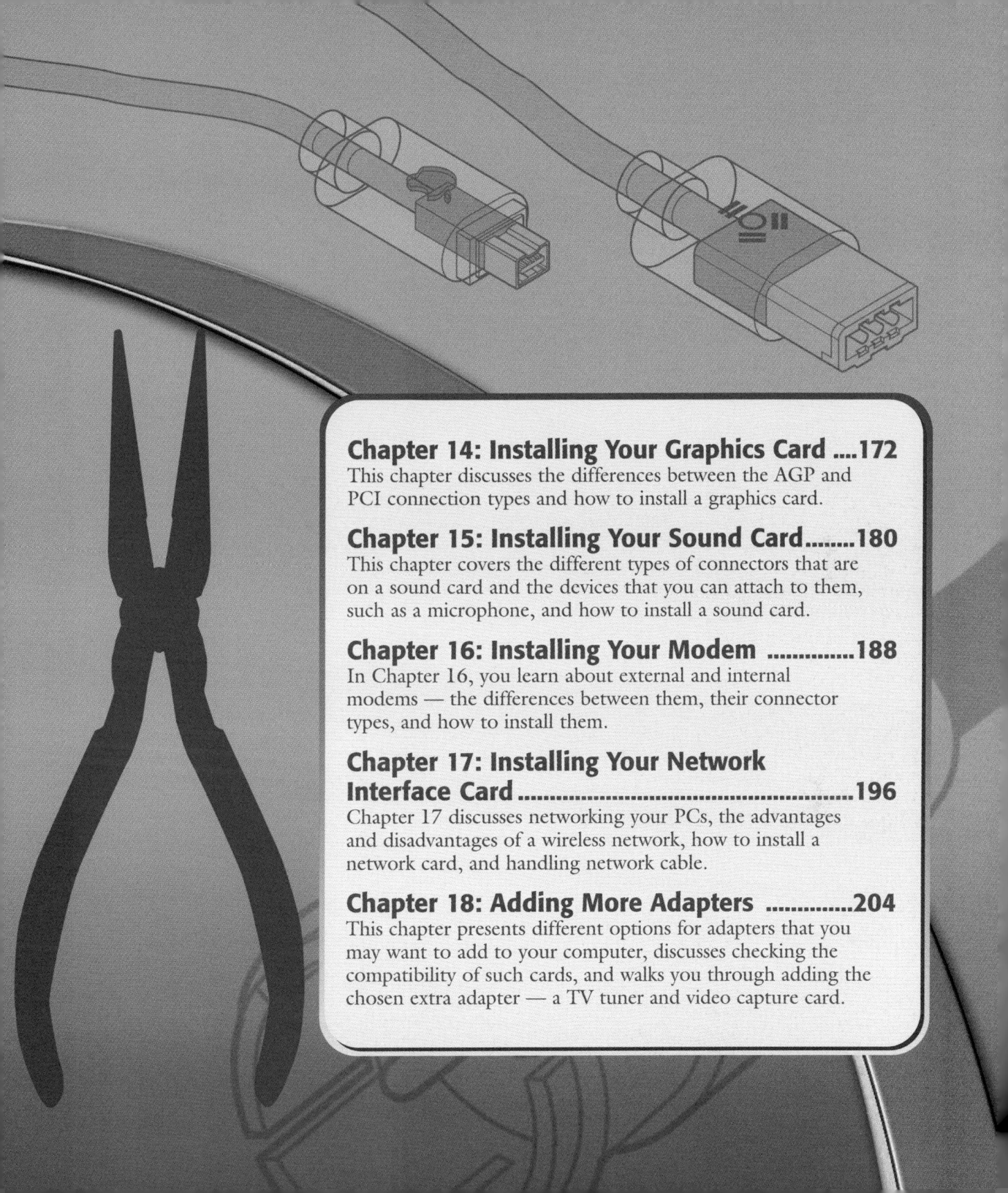

Chapter 14: Installing Your Graphics Card 172
This chapter discusses the differences between the AGP and PCI connection types and how to install a graphics card.

Chapter 15: Installing Your Sound Card 180
This chapter covers the different types of connectors that are on a sound card and the devices that you can attach to them, such as a microphone, and how to install a sound card.

Chapter 16: Installing Your Modem 188
In Chapter 16, you learn about external and internal modems — the differences between them, their connector types, and how to install them.

Chapter 17: Installing Your Network Interface Card 196
Chapter 17 discusses networking your PCs, the advantages and disadvantages of a wireless network, how to install a network card, and handling network cable.

Chapter 18: Adding More Adapters 204
This chapter presents different options for adapters that you may want to add to your computer, discusses checking the compatibility of such cards, and walks you through adding the chosen extra adapter — a TV tuner and video capture card.

My Choice for the Graphics Card

With a Windows Media Center PC, you must include a strong video adapter, also called a *graphics card*, which features a powerful video processor and plenty of onboard video memory to take some of the work off the main CPU so that you do not have to wait for images to draw on your screen.

The graphics card needs to work and play well with a DVD player, downloaded movies, and extras such as a TV tuner so that you can enjoy your new PC for viewing. You want your display crisp, clear, and ready to dazzle you.

The Gigabyte Radeon Graphics Card

Because of all these considerations, I chose the Gigabyte Radeon 9250 128MB graphics card for $47.40. Gigabyte is an established manufacturer, and the Radeon chipset is one of the big standards in video chipsets. A Radeon card that I previously had made all the difference in the enjoyment of graphics-intensive video games and movie watching. However, the most serious of extremely high-end 3D gamers may want one of the higher-end alternative graphics cards.

Alternative Graphics Card Choices

Do you want a graphics card with more memory than the chosen Radeon or one that uses the NVIDIA chipset — such as a GeForce card? Or one that includes some TV ability right within the card?

Different Graphics Cards

You may want to choose from one of these alternative recommendations that are either in the same price range or run to quite a bit more because of their added features and functions:

$

- EVGA GeForce FX 5200 128MB AGP graphics card ($50.39)
- ATI All-in-Wonder 9600 128MB AGP graphics card with TV functions ($175.56) (shown here)

$$$$

- EVGA 6800 GT 256MB DVI+DVI+TV PCIx graphics card ($423.04) (shown here)
- EVGA GF 7800 GTX 256MB PCIx graphics card ($629.99)

Chapter 14: Installing Your Graphics Card

Understand Your Adapter Type

There can be some very big differences between graphics cards that may not always be easily understood, even if you take the time to read the product details before you buy. These differences can account, at least in part, for the broad price range.

AGP versus PCI

Besides the motherboards that integrate video directly into them so that they do not require a separate graphics card, there are two card connection types:

- AGP (accelerated graphics port), which is used exclusively for video hardware such as a graphics card.

- PCI (peripheral component interconnect), which uses one of the usually multiple PCI slots available on the motherboard that are used by other cards such as the network card and sound card; most cards and slots today, however, are PCI Express, also called PCIx or PCIE.

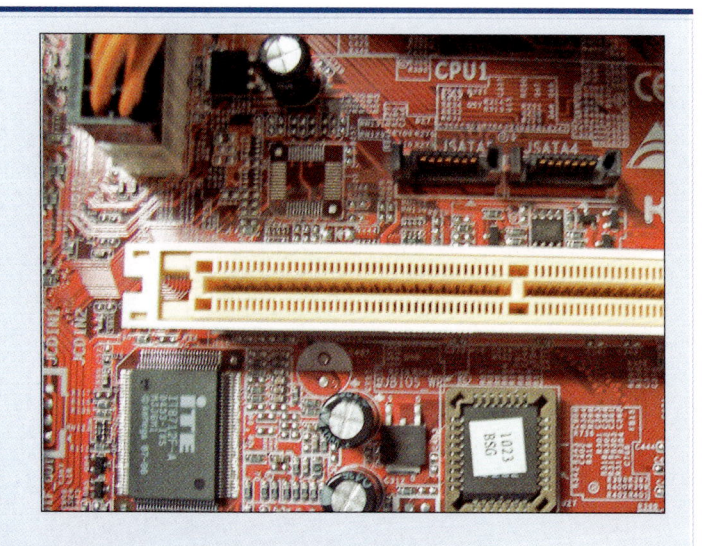

Choose AGP When Possible

You should always, whenever possible, buy an AGP graphics card because AGP cards operate faster than those that install to a PCI slot. Most major release graphics card offer an AGP version but not always a PCI type.

When AGP Is Not Possible

There are times, however, where you may not be able to use an AGP card. For example, some motherboards with integrated video do not offer an AGP port. If you decide to replace the integrated video with a separate graphics card, your only choice is to buy and install a PCI-connect graphics card.

```
(ALL-IN-WONDER® 9800 PRO Chipset)

Unleash THE BEAST Within

Banding digital mediums of Gaming, TV and Video together in a virtual
world of multimedia wonderment, THE BEAST RADEON 9800 PRO, with
features such as: TV-ON-DEMAND™, THRUVIEW™, VIDEOSOAP™, support
for DirectX® 9.0 and OpenGL, will liberate your creative BEAST within!

Features:

Powered by the RADEON™ 9800 PRO visual processing unit
Unparalleled TV and DVD features: TV-ON-DEMAND™, Gemstar GUIDE
Plus+™, mulTView™, VIDEOSOAP™, THRUVIEW™ and much more
Easily edit video into your own creations: Video CD and DVD Authoring
*Optional*Radio frequency wireless remote for your PC provides a hand
held 30-foot user interface. Control your mouse and PC applications at
the click of a button.
Stereo TV tuner with 125 channels
Intelligent Teletext on your PC
Zoom & pan - zoom in on the action on-screen and choose your own
close-ups
128MB DDR memory accelerates the latest 3D games
256-bit memory interface removes hardware performance bottleneck and
provides end users with faster 3D graphics
```

Other Notable Graphics Card Features

Other features that can distinguish one graphics card from another include the following:

- The amount of video memory: You want at least 128MB for a Media Center PC — although 256MB is much better.

- The type of chipset: Most graphics cards use either the Radeon chipset from ATI or the NVIDIA GeForce chipset; if you play lots of games, consider which chipset is most often recommended by those games.

- The additional hardware: Read the product details to see what additional hardware is included or supported, such as the ATI TV cards that add TV functionality to a basic graphics card or features to support high-definition (HD) TV viewing or video capture.

Chapter 14: Installing Your Graphics Card

175

Install the Graphics Card

Because of the strategic differences between graphics cards — even between various versions of the same type — your first step always should be to review your documentation carefully. Specifically look for any switches or jumpers that must be set, as well as how the driver must be installed. Then follow the steps here.

Install the Graphics Card

1) Remove the graphics card from its box and set it on its antistatic bag.

2) If the documentation mentions the change of a switch or jumper, take care of this now, before you install the card.

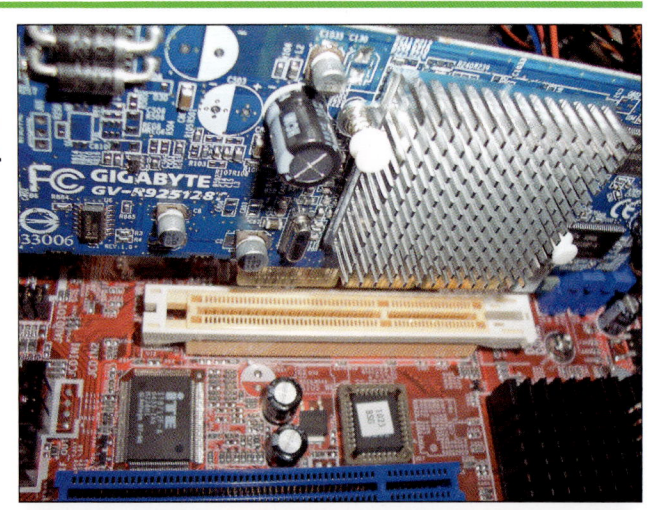

3) Locate the AGP slot on your motherboard.

Note: *This is usually found directly above the PCI slots and may be brown, gold, or gray in color.*

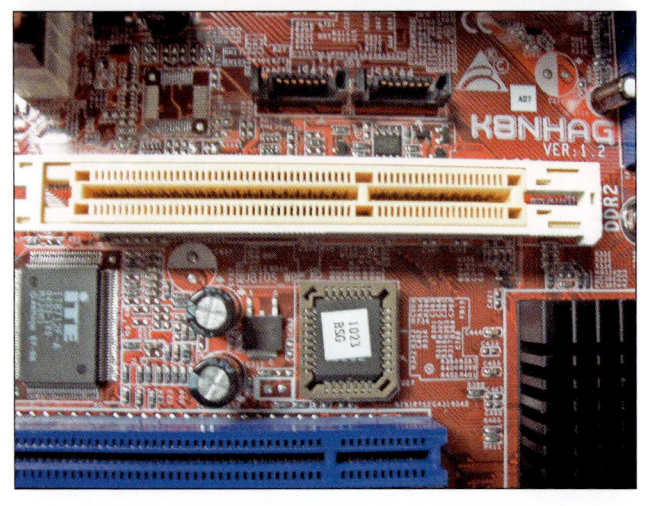

④ Remove the screw or retainer at the lower end of the slot and set it aside.

⑤ If present, remove the faceplate that corresponds to where the card will interface with the rear of the PC.

⑥ Orient the graphics card for insertion into the AGP slot.

⑦ Install it into place and make sure that it is firmly and properly seated.

⑧ Replace the retainer or screw to secure the graphics card in place.

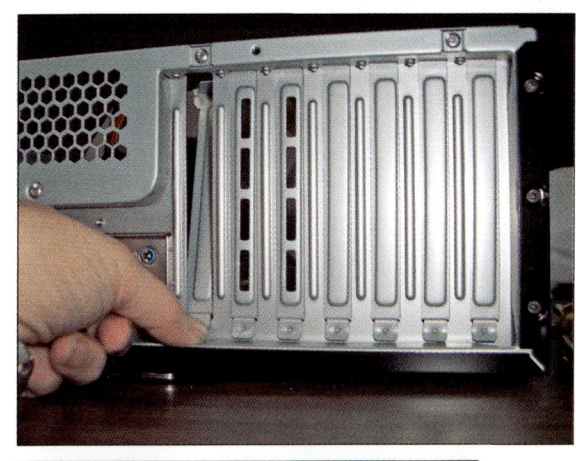

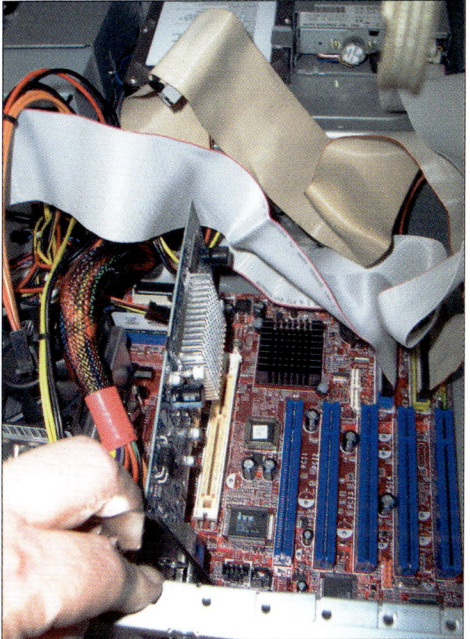

I am having trouble finding the AGP slot. What can help me find it?

To help you find the AGP slot, you can consult your motherboard manual. Also, a silk-screened label on the motherboard should help you identify it.

I have a PCI graphics card, not an AGP one. How do I install my card?

Follow the instructions found in Chapter 18 to install the card to a PCI slot. Note that some PCI graphics card need to be inserted in the first PCI slot on the motherboard.

Check the Seating of the Graphics Card

Verify that the graphics card is thoroughly and properly seated. This is important because the failure to do so can halt the newly assembled PC in the bootup process and sound a number of beeps to alert you to the problem.

Check the Seating of the Graphics Card

Note: First and foremost, you want to be certain that you placed the graphics card in the AGP slot rather than a PCI slot. If you happen to switch them, the graphics card cannot seat fully.

① Check that the card sits evenly within the slot.

② Check the back of the PC where the connection edge of the graphics card shows.

You must be able to access the video port later, when you connect your monitor to this port. Any unevenness or distance between the rear of the PC and the card edge indicates that the card is not properly installed.

Identify any Extra Cables

Check the graphics card box. Do you see any extra cables there? If so, you need to identify them. For example, some high-end graphics cards require a special power connection that you need to install.

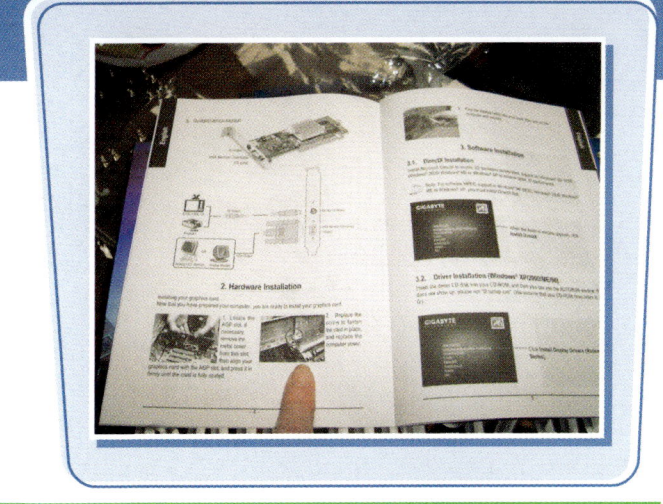

Identify any Extra Cables

The video cable necessary to connect the monitor to the graphics card is almost always packaged with the monitor rather than the card itself. Thus, any additional cables that come with your graphics card may be accessory cables for a special purpose, such as those to connect a nondigital camera or even a TV.

Refer to the documentation that comes with your graphics card if the cables do not have clear labels.

If the graphics card has little or nothing in the way of a manual, you can go online to the manufacturer's Web site to determine what the cables are. You also may be able to find what they are if you go back to the site where you purchased the card – such as CPU Solutions – which should list any accessory under the product details.

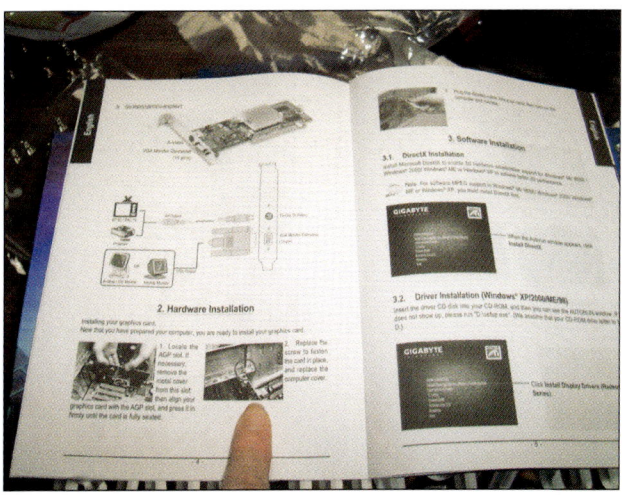

My Choice for the Sound Card

When you need to be budget conscious as you design a new custom system as you are here, one of the ways you can shave some cost is if you use a motherboard that integrates some of the components normally found in add-on adapters, such as sound, graphics, network, and modem.

The Motherboard's Sound Capabilities

The Biostar motherboard chosen for this Windows Media Center PC includes integrated sound and network capabilities. The audio functions integrated onto this board seem as if they will fit the sound demands for what will be done with this system. So you do not need to add a sound card separately.

If you are unsure of whether you need a separate sound card, you may want to follow what is done here. Try the integrated sound on the motherboard; only if you decide that you do not like the quality of the built-in audio should you invest in a separate sound card.

Alternative Sound Card Choices

When audio is very important to you — as it is likely to be when you build a Media Center PC — you want to make the right choice of sound card so that the quality is good and the playback pure.

Different Sound Cards

If you want to add a full sound card to your Windows Media Center PC rather than depend on the integrated sound available on the Biostar motherboard chosen for this system, you may want to consider one of these alternative choices:

$

- Creative Labs SB 2.1 OEM PCI Dolby Digital Surround sound card with support for up to four speakers ($29.99)
- Creative Labs Audigy ES with game port ($46.16) (shown here)

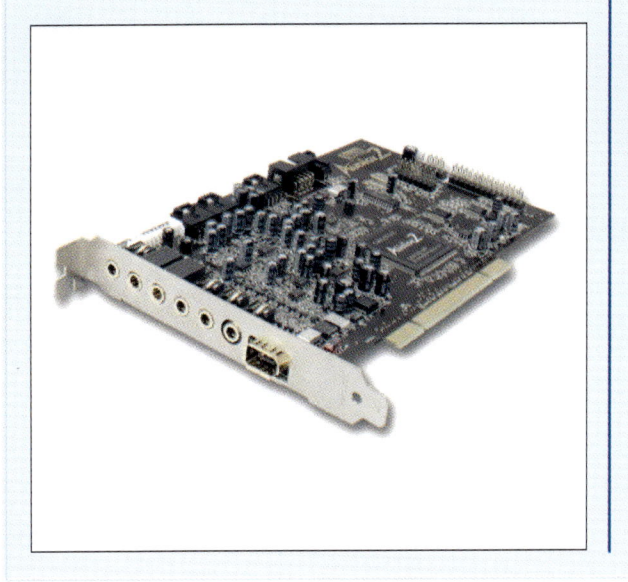

$$$$

- SoundBlaster Audigy 2 ZS 24-bit high definition sound card with IEEE 1394 port ($94.77)
- SoundBlaster 5.1 Audigy 2 ZS Platinum with advanced DVD playback ($187.98) (shown here)

Note the Connectors

Before you install your sound card, examine the connectors — also called *plugs* or *jacks* — along its connector edge. The connector edge is the part that interfaces with the very back of the PC after you install the card into a PCI slot on your motherboard.

These connectors enable you to install various audio devices to the sound card. The card actually performs multiple jobs, such as recording, playback, and some of the work of the CPU of putting together the sound that you hear.

Sound Connectors

The connectors include plugs for a microphone and speakers. Your sound card may also have a connection to plug in a MIDI device such as a digital music keyboard or a drumpad, for headphones, and even for some older-model game hardware such as non-USB joysticks and game controllers.

Speakers

Speakers are the hardware most frequently connected to the sound card or the audio connectors from a sound-integrated motherboard. You can control the volume both from physical dials or switches available on the speakers or through the sound icon available in the system tray through which you can adjust audio playback.

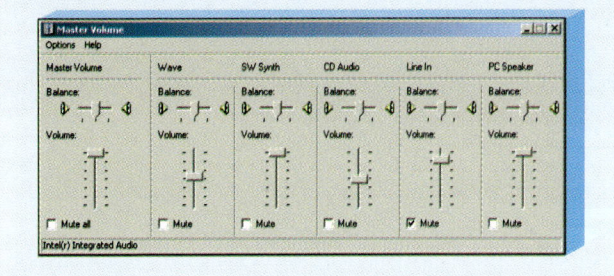

A Microphone

A microphone (mic) is a popular addition to a sound card. Through it, you can record your own sound files using Sound Recorder, add narrative to PowerPoint presentations, and dictate using the Speech Recognition function in Windows XP and Windows Media Center PC to "talk" to programs such as Microsoft Word.

Other Devices

Add something such as a MIDI-compatible keyboard or a drumpad — which often connects through a USB port as do special sound mixing devices that give you something of a small digital sound production studio — and you can also make your own music with your new Windows Media Center PC.

Install Your Adapter

Your first job is to physically install the sound card into a PCI expansion slot on the motherboard, which has already been mounted in the case.

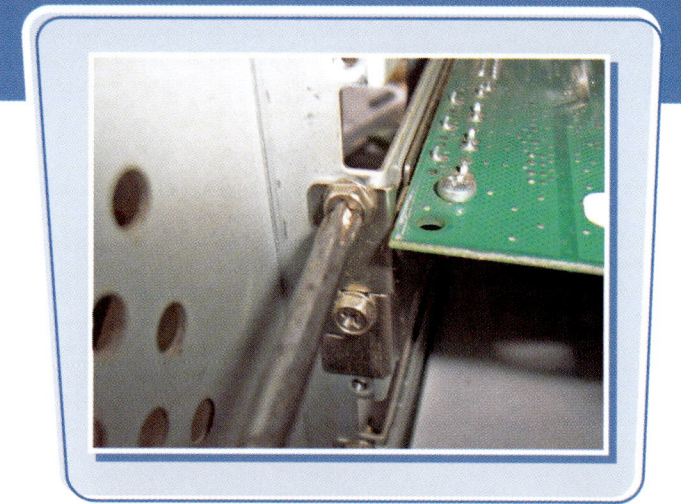

Install Your Adapter

On most motherboards, the PCI slots are colored a deep blue as they are on the selected Biostar motherboard. Others may use white, beige, or another color.

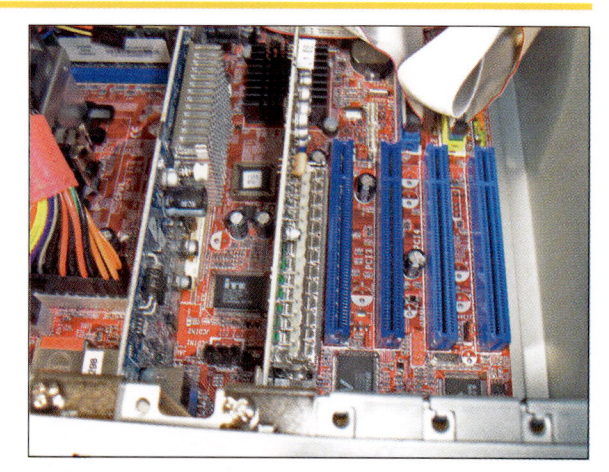

① Locate the PCI slot where you want to add the sound card.

② Remove the screw or other retainer that may be located at the bottom of the slot and set it aside.

184

③ If a faceplate is in place at the rear of the case that corresponds to the slot, remove it.

④ Remove the sound card from its package.

⑤ Orient the sound card to the motherboard's PCI slot.

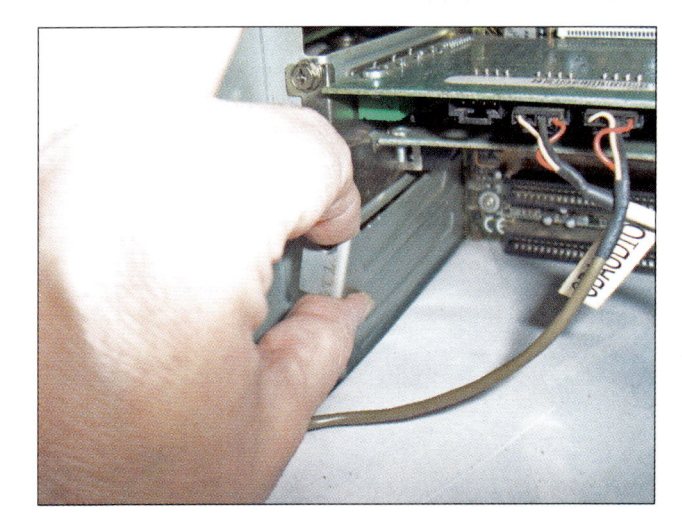

⑥ Insert the sound card into the PCI slot where the connector side sits fully into the slot itself.

⑦ Replace the retainer or screw at the bottom of the slot to secure the sound card in place.

⑧ Check the seating to be sure that it is fully and firmly in place.

Q&A

I am happy with the sound capabilities of the Biostar motherboard, so I am not installing a separate sound card. Can I skip reading this chapter?

No, but you can skip most of it. The only part of this chapter that you need to follow is the next section, in which you connect a cable from your CD/DVD drive to the audio-integrated motherboard.

I am not using the chosen Biostar motherboard. How do I find my PCI slots?

Check your documentation if you are using a different motherboard to determine where the PCI slots are located. There should be many of these slots, such as three or five.

Connect the CD/DVD Drive to the Sound Card

You usually need to connect a cable between the CD/DVD drive to the sound card (or to the appropriate connection on the motherboard for integrated sound). Check your sound card documentation to see whether this is necessary under Windows XP.

This connection lets the sound portion of CD or DVDs being played to be handled by the sound card. Without the connection, you usually will not have sound from a CD or DVD drive.

Connect the CD/DVD Drive to the Sound Card

1 Check the package in which your CD/DVD drive came and find the necessary cable.

Note: The documentation should spell out exactly how the cable should be connected. Also check the manual for the motherboard or sound card to determine where the cable needs to be installed.

2 Locate the connector on the CD/DVD drive.

3 Install the first end of the cable to the appropriate spot on the installed CD/DVD drive.

4 Take the other end of the cable and attach it to the appropriate spot on the motherboard – for an integrated audio chipset – or on the sound card.

5 Check the connections to be certain that they are correct.

Note: If, when you finish the assembly and start the PC, you get no sound from the CD or DVD drive, check this cable first because a loose connection is the likely cause for no sound.

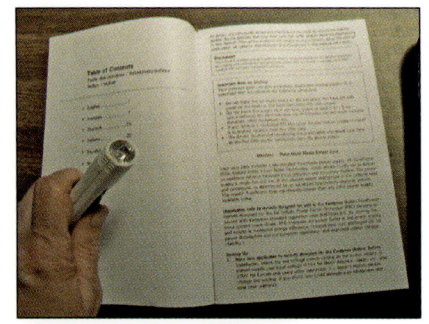

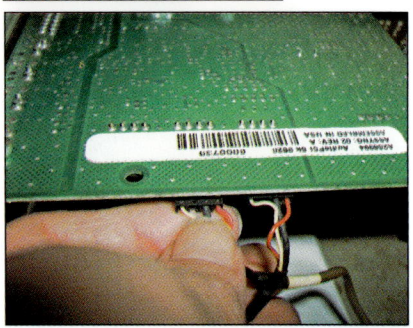

Check the Installation

Before you consider the sound card installation complete, it is important that you check through what you did, how the sound card is seated, and how the cable between the CD/DVD drive is connected. Failure to do so will make problems harder to troubleshoot later, when more is assembled into the case.

Check the Installation

1. Make sure that the sound card is fully and properly seated.

2. Make certain that you have the correct side inserted into the slot.

   If any part of the connector side of the card rides up above the slot, you may need to remove the card and reseat it.

3. Recheck the documentation that came with the motherboard, the CD/DVD drive, and the sound card.

4. Make sure that you have installed the cable between the CD/DVD drive and the sound card or motherboard properly.

5. Verify that the rear of the card, at the back of the PC, is accessible so that you can connect speakers and other components.

6. With integrated sound, check the rear of the PC to be sure that you can locate the connections for the speaker, microphone, and similar components.

Note: If you have a digital camera, take a shot or two of your installation, when finished, so you can refer back to it later.

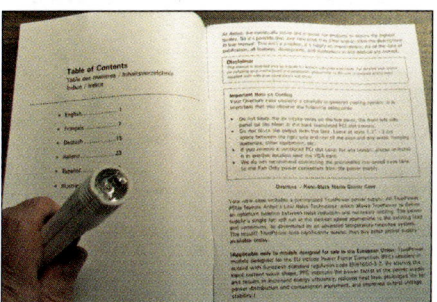

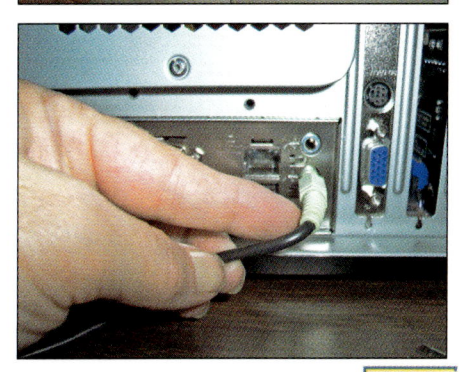

My Choice for the Modem

Because the Windows Media Center PC built in this book will probably be connected to a network where high-speed Internet access comes into a different computer and is then shared out to other PCs on the network (or perhaps will just be connected itself directly to a broadband connection, if it is not on a network), I chose not to include a modem in this setup.

Your Internet Access

You must consider exactly how you will access the Internet with the new system that you assemble here. If you already have some type of broadband Internet access, such as a cable modem, DSL, or satellite, you want to use the type of modem or adapter that your service provider requires.

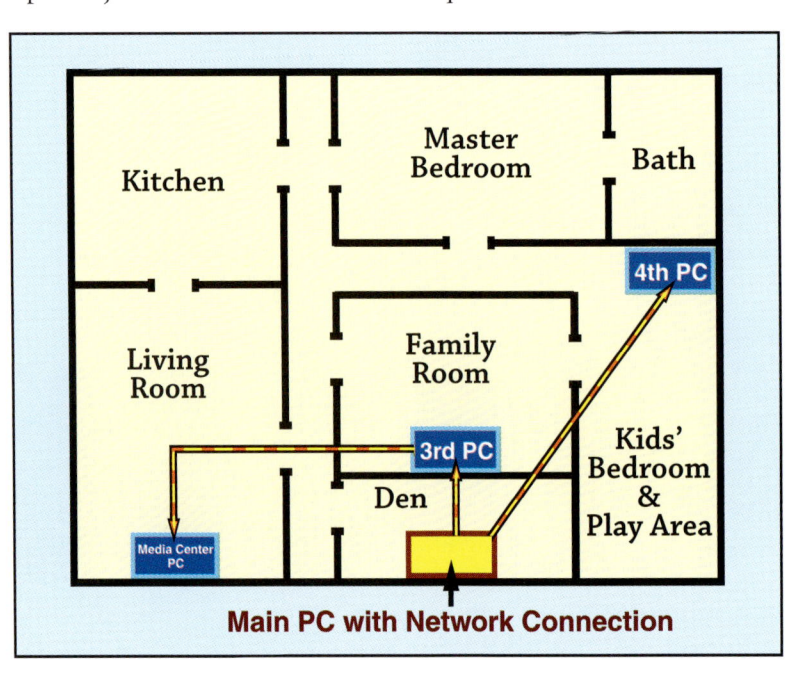

If you choose to share Internet access among multiple PCs on a network, you need the modem or other device required by the service provider in one PC and then have a network card in each additional PC that connects the Internet access to them.

Main PC with Network Connection

Alternative Modem Choices

To take full advantage of the services a Windows Media Center PC offers, you want high-speed or broadband access. This usually requires that you use the specific type of modem or other device the service provider specifies. Check into this.

Different Modems

You may want to install a standard modem, the type that uses a phone line, as a backup for when your high-speed Internet access is unavailable. Such a setup helps you to be able to check e-mail and do at least some Web surfing if your regular service is down for a day or two. Many standard modems also include the capability to send and receive faxes right from your PC desktop.

Some of your alternative choices for a backup modem — or even a high-speed modem — include the following:

$

- Diamond SupraMax USB external modem ($19.89) (shown here)
- Conexant USB external modem ($25.62)

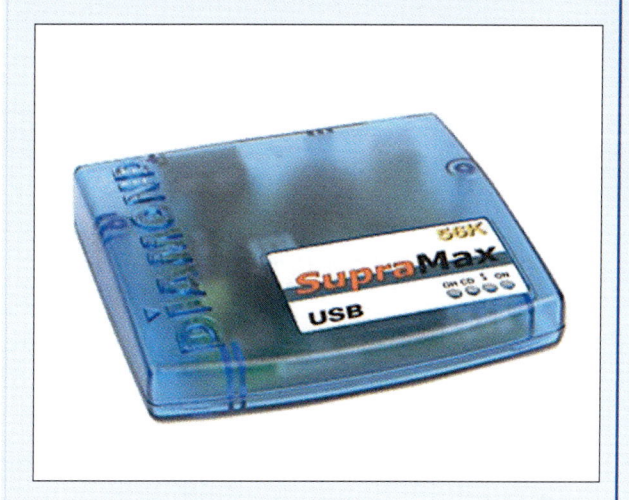

$$$$

- US Robotics 2973 PCI-connected hardware modem ($43.29)
- D-Link USB Cable modem ($69.99) (shown here)

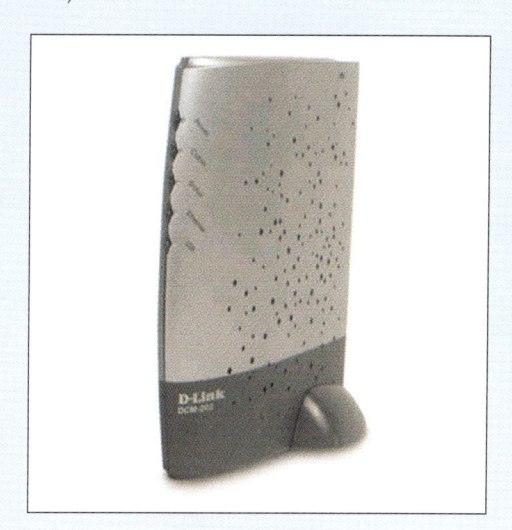

Identify the Modem Type

The type of modem that you get determines how it will install to your PC. There are two basic categories: broadband for high-speed Internet connections and analog for dial-up phone line access. But here, concern yourself with whether your modem is external or internal.

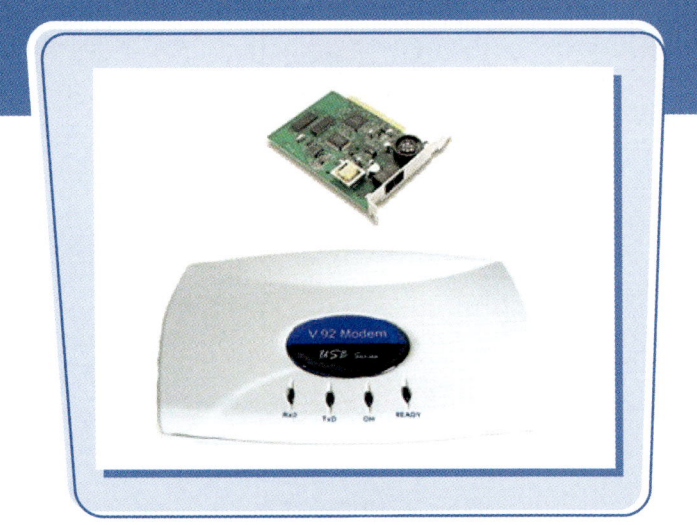

Identify the Modem Type

An internal modem connects through a PCI slot in your motherboard, so you must install it as part of the in-case assembly.

Note: *This is done similarly to the way that you set up the sound card in Chapter 15.*

By comparison, an external modem sits outside the case.

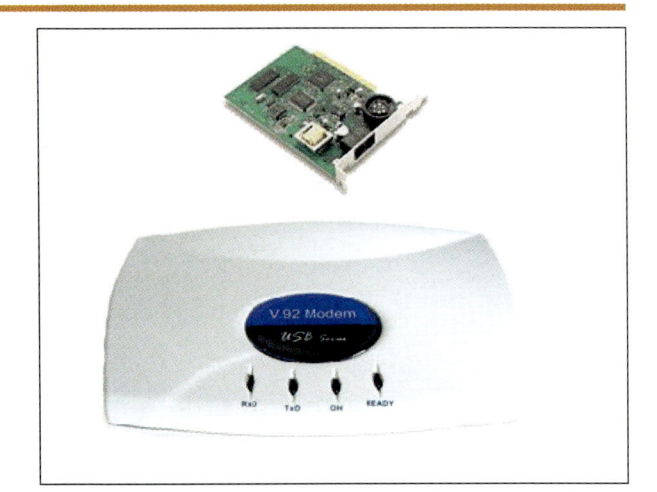

An external modem connects through a USB port at the front or rear of the PC or through a USB hub, which enables you to connect multiple USB devices to a single USB port.

Note: *A bonus advantage of an external modem is that its onboard lights help you see what the modem is doing, such as whether it is connected or sending or receiving data.*

Recognize the Connectors

Whether you choose an external or internal modem, you will find that it includes some basic connections, usually found at the rear of the unit.

Recognize the Connectors

At the rear of a standard, phone line–based modem, you will find jacks usually labeled as "line in" and "line out" or "phone" and "wall." These enable you to connect the phone line into the modem and then connect, through an additional phone line, a phone set to it.

Thus, you need a phone jack located close to where you will place the PC so that you can connect it to the telephone line.

With a broadband modem, such as cable, DSL, or satellite, the jacks or connectors at the back enable you to connect the cable, DSL line, or cable running from the satellite dish.

Follow directions from your Internet service provider to connect your cables properly.

Chapter 16: Installing Your Modem

191

Install Your Modem

How you install your modem depends on whether you have an external or internal modem. They connect quite differently, with external modems always being easiest to set up.

Note that after you have your PC assembled and before you start it up, you need to turn on an external modem. There is usually a power switch or flip switch located on the front or side of the modem.

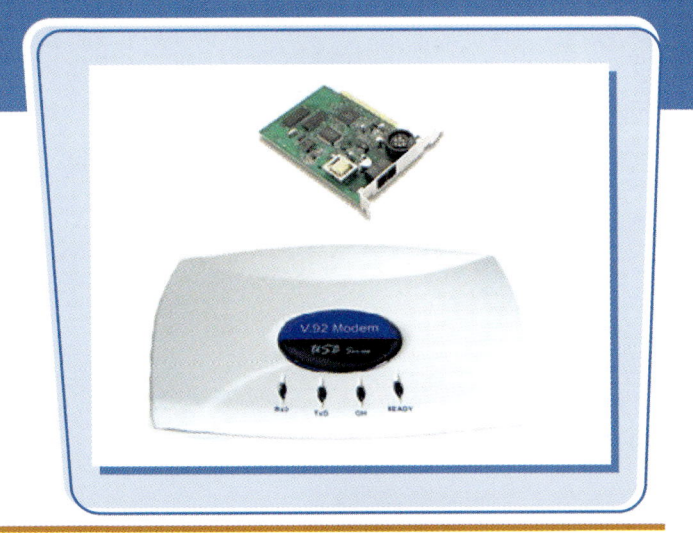

| Install Your Modem |

INSTALL AN EXTERNAL MODEM

1. Place the modem near your PC.
2. Connect the power cord to a wall outlet.
3. Insert the USB cable into the modem's USB jack.
4. Insert the other end of the USB cable into the USB port on the PC.

INSTALL AN INTERNAL MODEM

1. Locate the PCI slot where you want to install the modem.
2. Remove the screw or retainer in place at the bottom of the PCI slot.
3. Remove the faceplate that was held in place by the screw or retainer.
4. Remove the modem from its package.
5. Orient the insertion edge of the modem to the PCI slot.
6. Insert the modem fully and firmly into the PCI slot.
7. Replace the screw or retainer to hold the modem card in place.

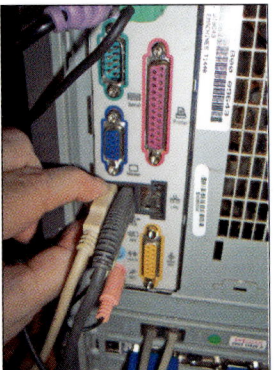

Connect the Modem's Phone Line or Cable

Exactly how you connect your newly installed modem depends entirely on what type of Internet connection method you use. To install a phone line–based modem, follow the steps here.

Connect the Modem's Phone Line or Cable

① Connect a standard phone wire to the closest available phone jack.

② Insert the other end of the phone wire into the "line in" or "wall" jack at the rear of the modem or where the rear of the modem card appears at the rear of the PC.

③ If desired, attach a separate phone wire to the "line out" or "phone" jack at the rear of the modem.

④ Connect the other end of this wire to a phone set that can then sit on your desk or computer table.

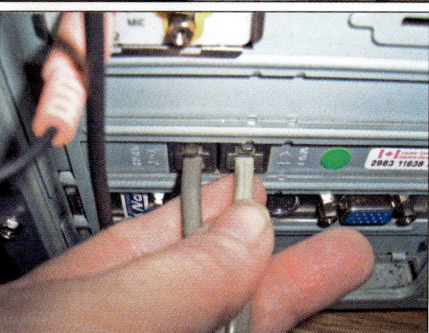

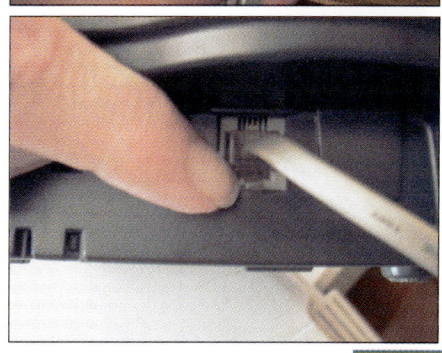

Chapter 16: Installing Your Modem

193

Special Considerations

Do you want to add your Windows Media Center PC to a network that you already have in your home or small office? Do you need to share an Internet connection between multiple PCs? Do you only have access to lower-speed, dial-up Internet access?

Connect to the Network

If you already have a network set up in your home or small office, you may want to bring your new Media Center PC, after it is fully assembled, online with it. After you have the new PC up and running, you can use the Network Setup Wizard in the Windows Control Panel to set up the new system so that it can be seen by and access the rest of the network — that is, of course, after you install the network card in Chapter 17.

If your network already has high-speed Internet access installed to it, you want to add the new Media Center PC to that network so that you can share its Internet connection. Again, run the Network Setup Wizard found in the Control Panel to do so.

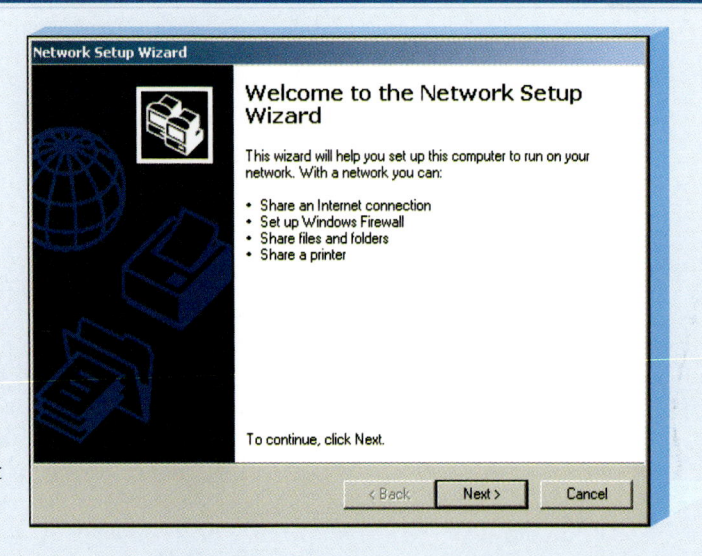

The Hardware Needed to Add a Network

What if you do not have a network currently set up? With two or more PCs in a home or small office, it makes sense to join forces across a network. Each PC needs a network interface card, such as the one that you will install in Chapter 17, and one of the following:

- A network cable for a standard network that plugs into the RJ-45 jack located on the network interface card on each PC

- A wireless setup in which you install a wireless network card on each PC and then use something like a wireless access point (WAP), which sits between the PCs to connect them

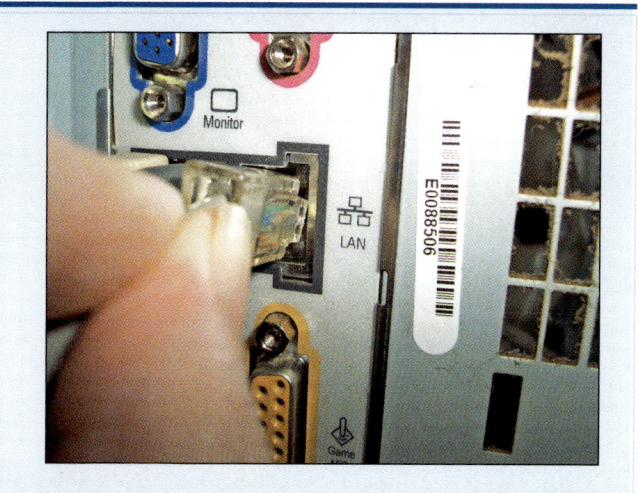

Setting Up and Using a Network

After you install the hardware needed, you then use the Network Setup Wizard in Windows Control Panel and let it step you through the process by which it uses the network cable or wireless point to connect the PCs together. Then you can use the network to do the following:

- Share your Internet connection and modem installed to just one PC.

- Move files around between the computers.

- Otherwise communicate and use the resources of all the computers together, which can include the ability to run an application installed to one PC on another or to share a single printer between multiple PCs.

High-Speed Internet Access

Remember, if you have Internet access only through a standard phone line, you should really investigate broadband access because then you can more readily download movies, share very large sound files, and take advantage of other features that a Windows Media PC can handle.

Chapter 16: Installing Your Modem

195

My Choice for the Network Interface Card

The Biostar K8NHA-G motherboard I chose for the Windows Media Center PC includes integrated components for both sound and for the network interface.

Because of this, I chose to use the integrated network feature so that we would have more money for other hardware. However, if you want to, you could also install a separate network interface card (NIC) that will take over the job from the integrated chipset in the motherboard.

LAN

Add a Network Card

If you chose a different motherboard, however, especially one without an integrated network interface, you will need to add a network card. This may be true even if you do not plan to place your PC on a network because some broadband, high-speed Internet services require a network card to handle broadband access. Check with your service provider to determine what you need.

Alternative NIC Choices

Networks are no longer just for busy commercial offices. Any home or small office with two or more PCs can benefit by tying the systems together on a network.

Different NICs

If your motherboard does not have an integrated network interface, you will need to obtain and install a network card either to connect this system to an existing network and/or to share a high-speed Internet connection.

Consider these alternatives to the integrated network interface:

$

- Realtek Chipset 10/100 PCI network card ($9.99) (shown here)
- StarTech.com 10/100/1000 PCI Gigabit Ethernet card ($15.93)

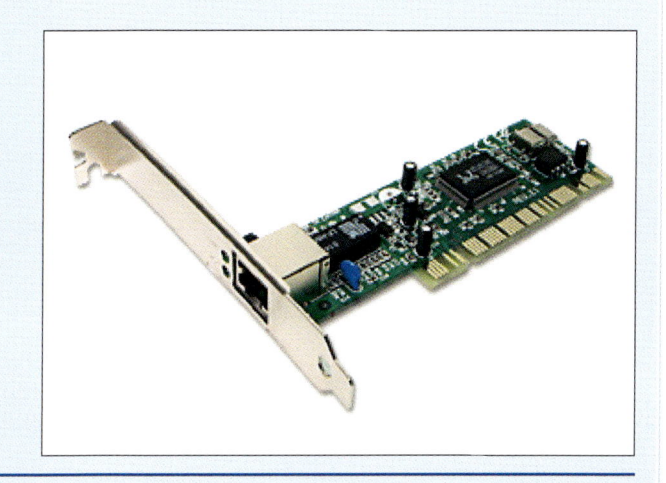

$$$$

- Realtek Gigabit PCI 10/100/1000 network card ($19.52)
- D-Link 10/100/1000 PCI network card ($28.24) (shown here)

Chapter 17: Installing Your Network Interface Card

197

The Wireless Network

A traditional network requires that each computer has a network card and that a network cable, also called an *Ethernet cable,* runs between each PC to carry data. Yet, more and more, people choose to go wireless.

Although a wireless network can cost quite a bit more than a traditional network, there are some benefits. For example, you may not want to run network cables throughout your home or small office. Network cables also can damage easily if you step on them or sit heavy furniture on them or can get pulled as you move about.

Disadvantages of Wireless

Yet there are also some drawbacks beyond cost and configuration. Certain structures, such as massive walls, heavy-duty appliances, and devices that create interference can block a wireless signal as it travels back and forth between different computers in your home or small office. Some cordless phones, such as the 2.4GHz models, also interfere with the wireless signal.

Go Wireless

Although this book and chapter focus on a wired network, you can purchase and install a wireless setup instead. Usually, you will need a wireless network card for each PC you want to include on the network as well as one or more wireless access points that serve to help transmit the signal back and forth. This wireless hardware includes tiny transmitters and receivers that help send and receive the data on each PC.

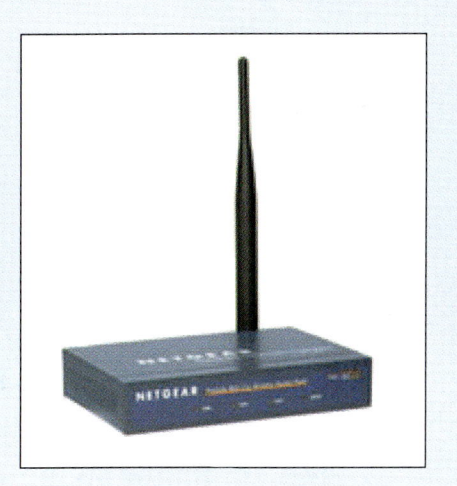

A Wireless Network Setup Kit

Your easiest solution may be to research and obtain a wireless network setup kit, which packs anywhere from two to several different wireless network cards as well as one or more wireless access points, along with the software that you need to configure and manage your wireless network.

The cost of this can vary from less than $200 to several hundreds of dollars, depending on how many PCs and mobile devices such as laptops or notebooks you need to bring together on the network. Check prices and compare features before you buy.

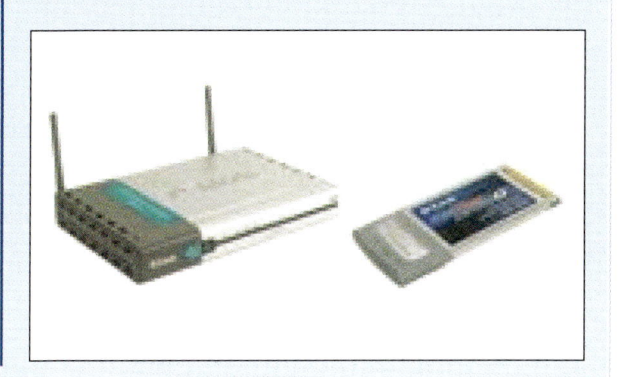

Identify the Connections and Cable

Before you install your network card, you need to be sure that you have a network cable, unless you decide to go the all-wireless route. Normally, the cable will not come with your network card; you need to purchase this separately.

You need a cable for each PC that is part of the network. This cable will be used to connect two PCs together or to connect a PC to an additional network hardware device such as a network router or hub that you may have in place on an existing network.

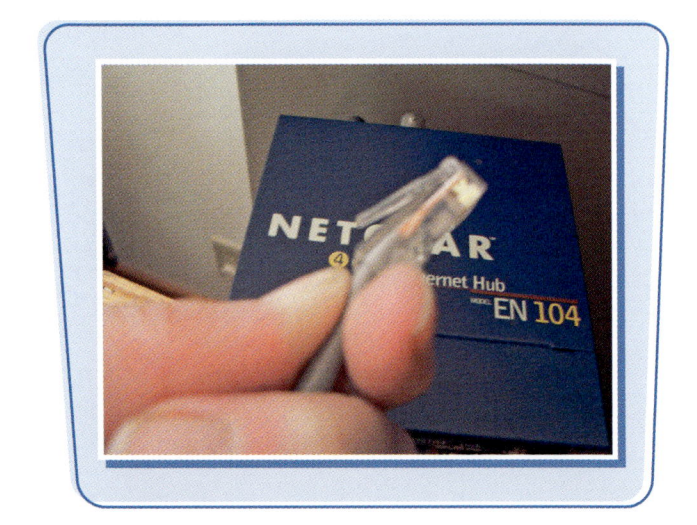

The Network Port

A network cable inserts into the RJ-45 jack — sometimes labeled "LAN" or "Network" — at the back of the network card as it intersects with the rear of the PC. This is the case, too, if you use a motherboard that has the network interface integrated directly into it.

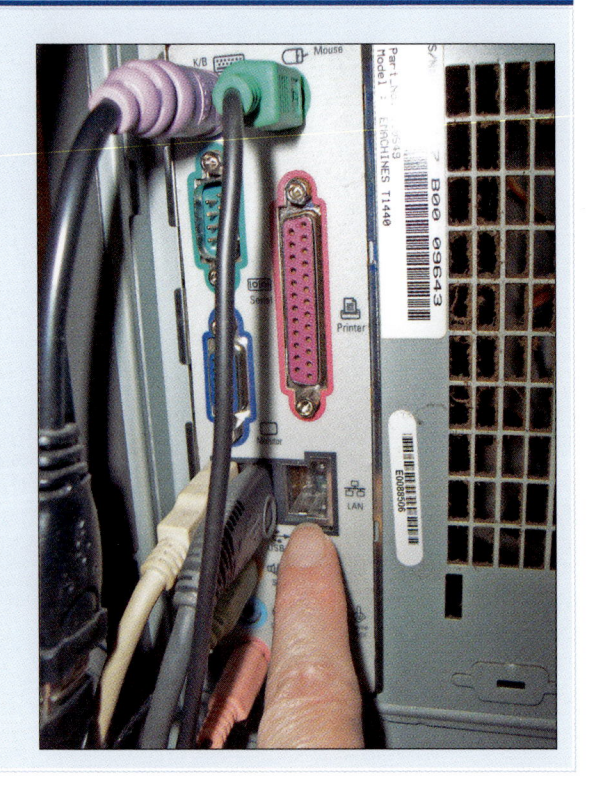

The Network Cable and Connector

Note that each end of the cable ends in a very special connector that looks very much like — although larger — a modular phone connector because these are based on very similar technology. If these connectors suffer damage — such as from the cable getting yanked out of a PC — the connectors and perhaps the cable itself will need to be replaced.

Many computer stores and online vendors sell network cable. You probably want to purchase assembled lengths — meaning that the connectors have been installed to the ends of the cable — because this is much easier than if you purchase a roll of network cable and the connectors and add the connectors yourself.

How Much Cable You Need

Before you purchase one or more cables, you need to know how much distance exists between the different PCs that you plan to connect together on the network. You may want to pull out a tape measure or something similar so that you can measure the distance with some accuracy. You do not want a cable length that is much longer or shorter than the exact measurements. Make sure that you have as many cables as you will need based on the number of PCs that will go on the network.

Install the Adapter

The actual installation of the network card or adapter is usually the easiest part of a network. Unless integrated into the motherboard so that you do not need a separate network card, the card inserts into a PCI slot on the motherboard.

Install the Adapter

1. Locate the PCI slot that you want to use.
2. Remove the screw or retainer at the slot base.
3. If present, remove the faceplate that covers the interface at the rear of the PC. 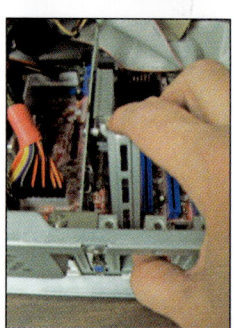
4. Remove the NIC from its package.

Note: If you need to set the NIC down temporarily, place it on its antistatic bag.

5. When ready, orient the connector edge of the network card to the PCI slot.

Note: The connector edge is the side with "teeth" that matches the notches or spaces found in the PCI slot.

6. Firmly and evenly insert the network card into the slot. 
7. Double-check to be sure that the card is evenly and fully seated.
8. Replace the screw or retainer to secure the card at the base of the slot.
9. Check the back of the PC to make certain that the back edge of the network card is fully visible and accessible so that you can install the network cable.

Insert the Cable

With the network card — or integrated motherboard — now in place, you are ready to install the network cable to connect your new system to the network.

These steps assume that you already have a PC set up on the network, with a cable attached to its NIC that you will extend to the Windows Media Center PC. Make sure that the cable will not be stretched because that can cause damage to the cable or to the PCs.

Insert the Cable

Note: *If you are assembling your Media Center PC in a room other than the one where you will use it, wait until the PC is in its final place to connect the cable.*

Note: *If you decide to use a wireless network setup instead, read and follow the instructions that come with your wireless setup. The main difference is that you will not connect cables between your PCs.*

① Extend the network cable from the first PC to the room where the new PC is located.

② Check to be certain that after the cable is run, it is still firmly connected to the network port at the back of the first PC.

③ Plug the free end of the network cable into the RJ-45 LAN port at the back of the Windows Media Center PC.

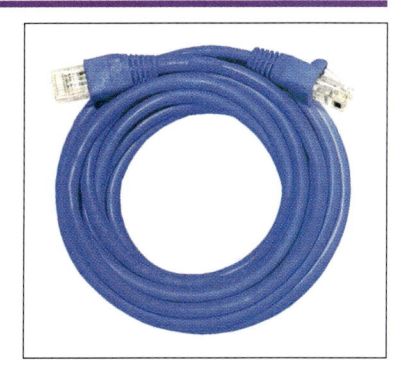

④ Follow the network cable between computers and try to move the cable out of the way of traffic.

You may want to tape or secure the cable along the baseboard or otherwise keep it safe from damage and to be sure that no one steps on it.

Chapter 17: Installing Your Network Interface Card

203

Know Your Options

Can you think of anything else you need to include in your new Windows Media Center PC that you should acquire and install before you finish your assembly? Now is the time to determine this.

A TV Tuner and Video Capture Card

For this system, you will add a TV tuner and video capture card that will enable you to watch television right from your PC as well as capture both still frames and small scenes from movies or programs that you watch for your personal use or enjoyment. This, like the sound card, modem, and network interface card that you have already installed, you will insert into an available PCI slot on your motherboard.

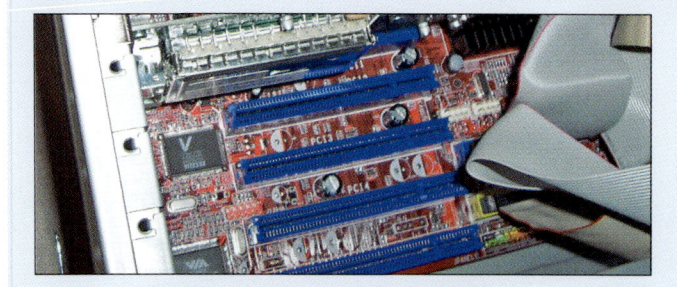

Available PCI Slots

Your only real limitation here is how many PCI slots you have available. If you chose to add a network card and a sound card, for example, and you have the recommended Biostar motherboard, then you should have three PCI slots free for additions. If, instead, you use the integrated sound and network capabilities built into this motherboard, you may have all your PCI slots still open.

The Job of Extra Adapters

After you have the basics such as graphics, sound, network, and Internet capabilities under control with your PC, you may want to look at what your motherboard or some other part of your PC does not offer. For example, if you have not done so already, look at your motherboard and review the motherboard manual to see what it features and what it does not.

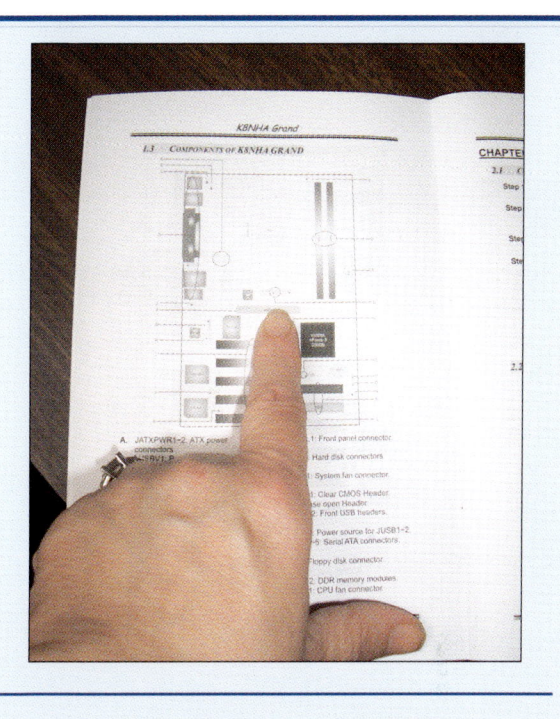

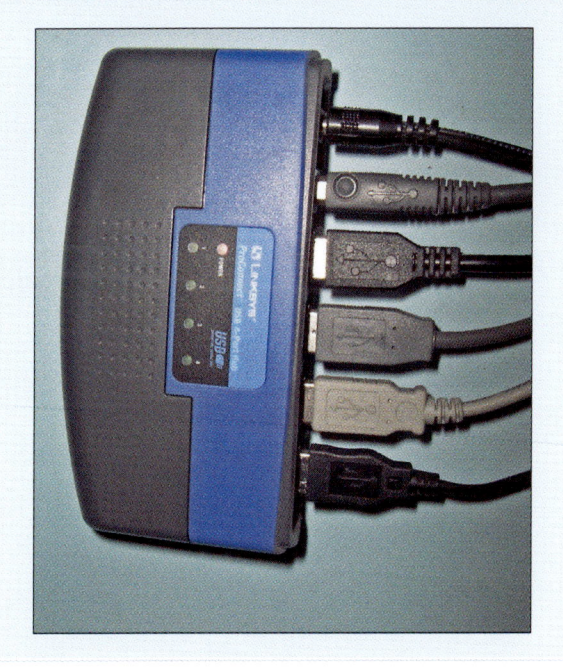

Extra USB Capability?

You may have just two USB ports on the motherboard, yet you know that you may connect several more USB devices. If so, you may want to purchase one of the following:

- A USB hub that connects through a single USB port to offer 4, 8, 12, or 16 additional ports.

- An I/O card that adds extra USB ports; if your motherboard does not have an IEEE 1394 port but you want to install and use a digital video camera, there are I/O cards that enable you to add up to three IEEE 1394 devices to your system through an adapter you add to a PCI slot.

continued

Know Your Options *(continued)*

Some of the additional adapters that you may want to think about for your Media Center PC each adds some special capability or functionality to your system, such as the TV tuner/video capture adapter will.

Consider These

Here are some of the additional adapters that you should consider:

- **I/O cards:** Enable you to connect external devices such as game hardware and USB and IEEE 1394 devices through the addition of extra ports.

- **Special drive controller cards:** Enable you to add high-speed drives such as serial ATA (SATA and SATA II) drives if the motherboard you choose does not happen to support them directly.

- **A SCSI host adapter:** If you decide to change your drives from IDE/ATA to SCSI drives, the host adapter installs to a PCI slot, and then the drives and other devices connect by SCSI cable to the adapter. Software with the adapter helps you control the various drives and devices.

- **Special cooling devices:** Add a fan built into a card that installs to your PCI slot. This is worth your consideration if your office or PC room is especially warm and you think that the PC operation is affected by the heat.

- **A wireless network adapter:** Enables you to turn your regular wired network into one that requires no cables running between different PCs and different rooms; you can buy a wireless setup kit that starts at around $150 to connect two PCs.

Recommended Additions

Now that you have a sense of what you can add through adapters you insert into available PCI slots and you have had the chance to consider your options, think about whether you should include something like one of these recommended options:

- If you chose not to order the ATI TV tuner/video capture card, reconsider it now; for only $100, you turn your desktop into a full-fledged entertainment center where you can grab images from your favorite programs.

- Another good TV tuner card that is less expensive is the ATI E-Home Wonder ($66.70).

- For those without IEEE 1394 ports — which the Biostar motherboard does offer — consider the VIA VT6306 3+1 IEEE 1394 adapter, which gives you three ports for your external Firewire devices ($12.46).

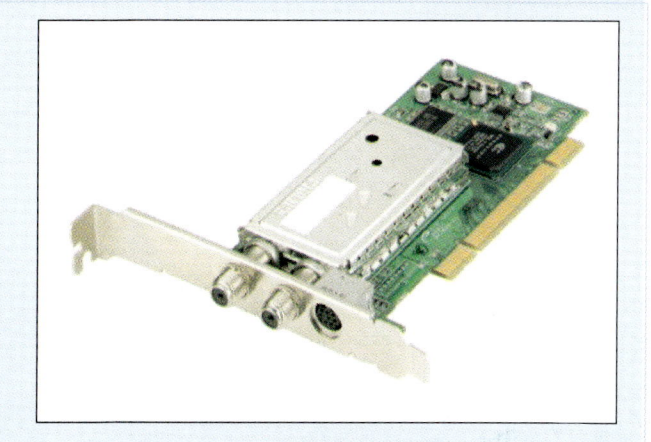

- An ALI 3-port USB 2.0 and IEEE 1394 port addition I/O card ($16.88).

- A SATA controller card for use if your new motherboard choice does not permit the addition of the new high-speed serial ATA drives (starts at $45).

Check Compatibility

Remember to check for PC/Windows compatibility for any additional hardware that you decide to add to your system. You want to be certain that your new hardware will work well with your setup before you pay money to get it.

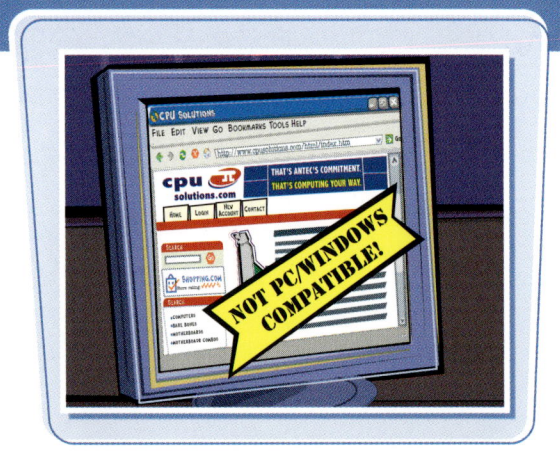

Check Compatibility

CHECK THE PRODUCT INFORMATION

① Review the product information on the vendor site, such as CPU Solutions if you click **Product Details**.

OR

① Check the information available on the product box if you shop at a brick-and-mortar store.

CHECK WINDOWS CATALOG

① Click **Start**.

② Click **All Programs**.

③ Click **Windows Catalog**.

Windows Marketplace appears.

④ Check different product categories for select devices that are compatible with Windows Media Center.

Note: Most products that work with Windows XP usually work with Windows Media Center. However, it is best if compatibility with Media Center is specifically stated.

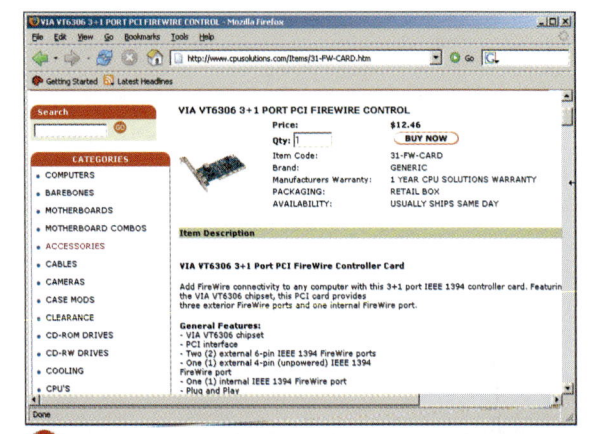

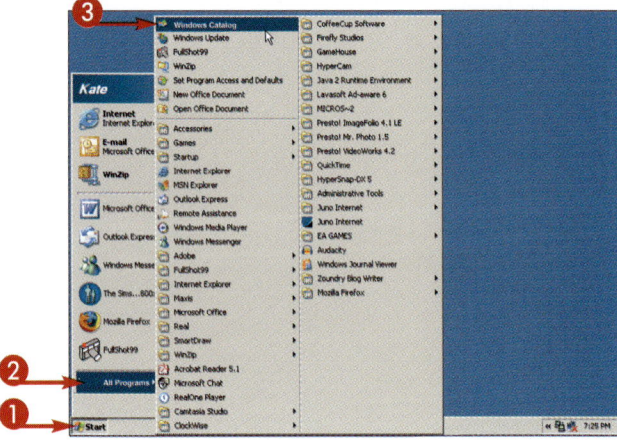

Scope Out Space

Whether you add more adapters before you finish your PC assembly or after the new system is in service, you always need to consider how many PCI slots you have available to be sure that you have room.

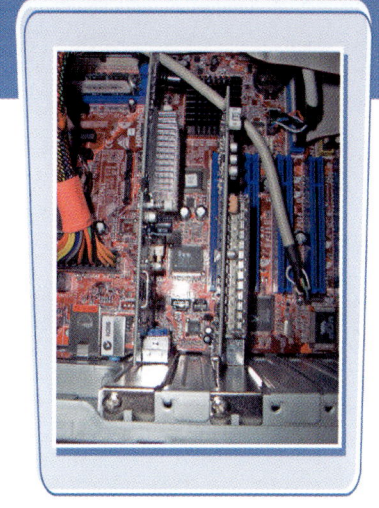

Scope Out Space

PCI SLOTS

If you keep the PC journal recommended earlier in this book, you can keep track of available PCI slots there. This can eliminate your need to open up the case to check for an empty slot before you order new PCI adapters.

REARRANGE ADAPTERS

Normally, it does not matter in what order you install PCI adapters. However, as your PCI slots begin to fill up, you may find it necessary to move adapters around within the slots to accommodate room needed by something such as a drive controller or SCSI host adapter, so you have space for the cables that attach to the adapter.

Move such an adapter to the first or last slot, for example, to give you more room for these cables.

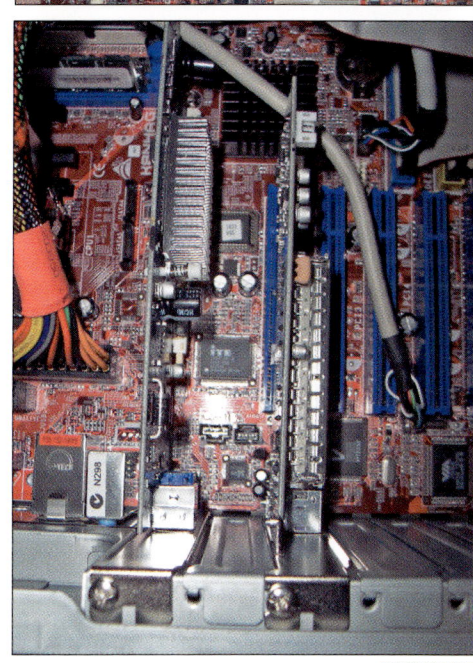

Install the Additional Adapters

First here, you connect your new adapter to the motherboard. You install additional PCI adapters very much like you have already added a sound card, modem, and network card earlier in this book. Then there are steps showing you how to add a new adapter after the PC is already assembled.

Here, you learn to install the TV tuner/video capture card that I chose for the target system — the ATI Wonder Pro TV tuner. Except for specific connections, what you do here will be almost identical to the steps that you perform to add something else.

Install the Additional Adapters

INSTALL THE NEW ADAPTER

① Review the documentation and follow its instructions to set a switch or a jumper, if needed.

② Locate the PCI slot where you want to insert the new adapter.

③ Remove the retainer or screw at the base of the slot and pull away the faceplate at the rear of the PC covering the space the adapter needs.

④ Remove the adapter from its package and inspect it again.

Note: If there appears to be dust or lint or anything on the adapter, use a can of compressed air to blow the debris off.

Note: If you need to set the adapter down, place it on the package or on the antistatic bag.

⑤ Orient your adapter to the PCI slot.

Note: Do not touch any of the components on the board as you work. Handle it by its sides only.

⑥ Insert the adapter firmly and securely into the slot.

7 Check the installation.

8 Replace the screw or retainer at the slot base.

9 Check the back of the PC to be sure that you can easily access the connectors at the edge of the adapter to install any external components.

INSERT A NEW ADAPTER AFTER ASSEMBLY

1 Shut down and turn off the PC.

2 Disconnect the computer's power cord.

3 Remove the PC case cover.

4 Attach your grounding wrist strap and remove any jewelry.

5 Install the adapter into an open PCI slot.

6 Replace the cover and secure it.

7 Connect the power cord and turn the PC on.

Windows should detect that there is new hardware.

8 Have the disc that came with the new adapter in place in your CD/DVD drive so that Windows can load the driver.

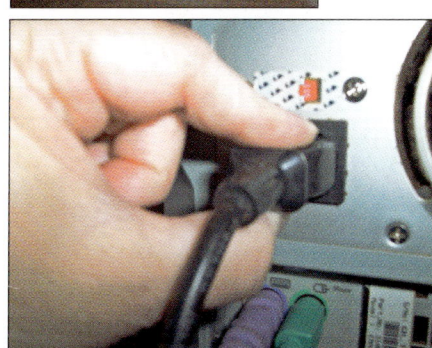

Chapter 18: Adding More Adapters

211

Part VI

Setting Up Peripherals

With the internal components of your new system now in place, your work shifts to the peripherals that you set up around the system and connect to ports and connections at the front or rear of the PC.

You start with the monitor, which you both plug into a wall outlet or surge suppressor/power strip and into the video port located on the connector edge of the graphics card at the back of the PC. Then you connect your speakers and keyboard and mouse and set up your printer and any other external devices that you choose to add to your system. Such components can include external drives and special devices such as digital video cameras, personal media players, and game and drawing tools that install through the USB or IEEE 1394 ports.

A key advantage with USB and IEEE 1394 devices is that you can add them while your PC is on and Windows is up and running; if you did this with some other types of equipment, you could damage the part or the PC itself. You can also unplug them the same way and then store these components, when not in use, out of the way of your busy desktop. Many people have five or more such devices that they can swap in and out as needed.

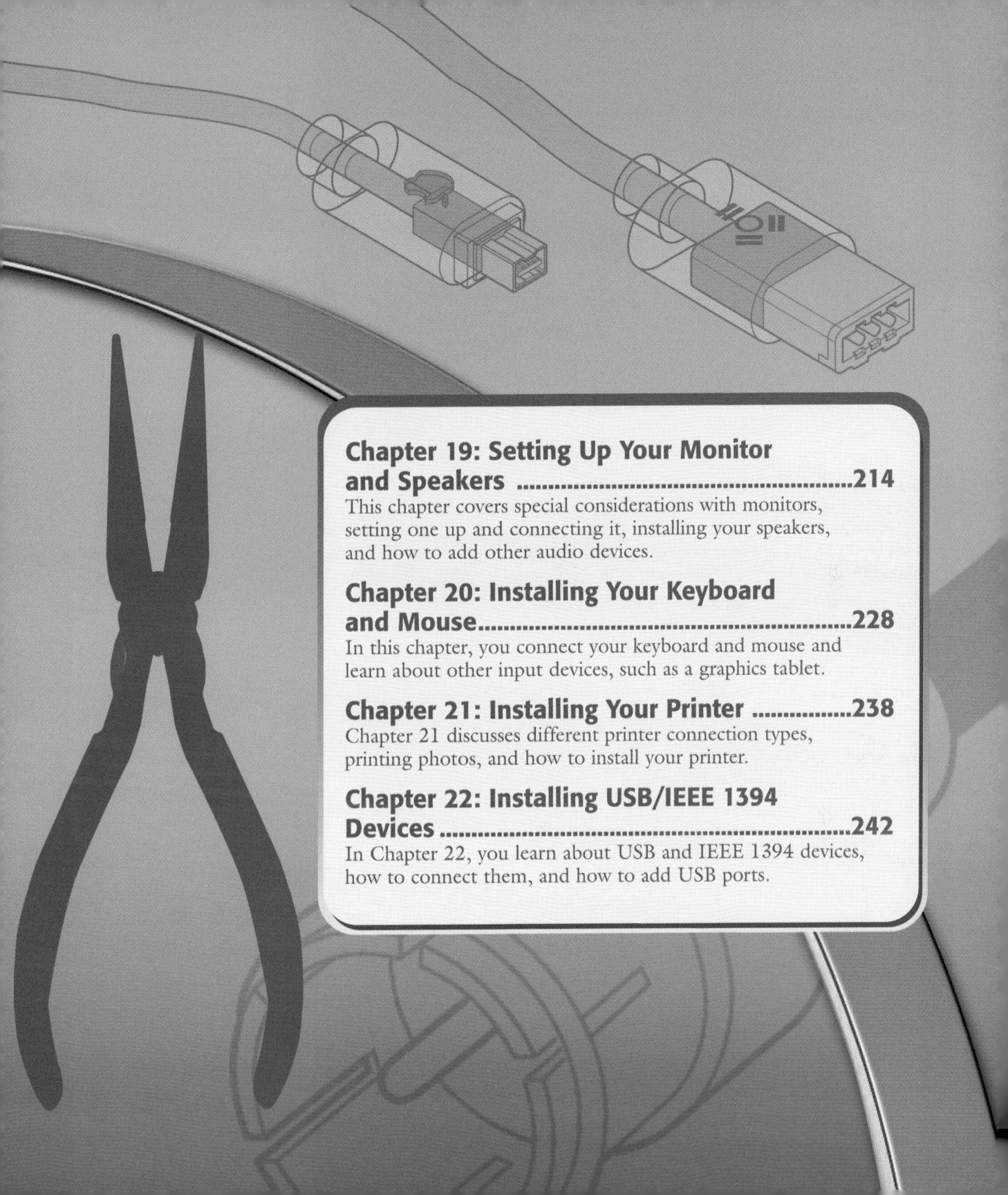

Chapter 19: Setting Up Your Monitor and Speakers 214

This chapter covers special considerations with monitors, setting one up and connecting it, installing your speakers, and how to add other audio devices.

Chapter 20: Installing Your Keyboard and Mouse 228

In this chapter, you connect your keyboard and mouse and learn about other input devices, such as a graphics tablet.

Chapter 21: Installing Your Printer 238

Chapter 21 discusses different printer connection types, printing photos, and how to install your printer.

Chapter 22: Installing USB/IEEE 1394 Devices 242

In Chapter 22, you learn about USB and IEEE 1394 devices, how to connect them, and how to add USB ports.

My Choice for the Monitor

Because I want to save a little money on the monitor, my choice is a standard cathode ray tube (CRT) monitor to supply the display for the Windows Media Center PC. As you can afford it, you can replace this monitor with a 20" or 21" flat-panel liquid crystal display (LCD) unit. LCD monitors are becoming less expensive with time.

A 17" CRT Monitor

My choice, an AOC 720G for $124.99 has a 17" display — the diagonal measurement — and is available in black, which matches the appearance of the PC case chosen in Chapter 5. Although appearance and color matches do not always matter, this is a media system that may be set up in a living room or den where others may see it, so I want it to blend in with other equipment such as the case, my stereo, and home theater components.

If you want to save even more, you could order a 15" display instead. But the 17" is easier on the eyes and provides a higher resolution, which matters when you watch movies or do graphics work. It is also a better choice for a game system than the 15".

Alternative Monitor Choices

Would you prefer an LCD monitor to take advantage of the much narrower depth and the bright display? Even if you are budget conscious, you can go LCD without a big pain in your wallet.

Different Monitors

CPU Solutions offers a number of other makes and models, with both smaller and larger screens, in both LCD and CRT. Consider one of these:

$

- Acer 17" 450-1 black LCD flat-panel monitor with 1280 x 1024 maximum resolution ($249.99) (shown here)
- Acer 19" ALI912B LCD black monitor with 1280 x 1024 maximum resolution ($299.89)

$$$$

- AG Neveo F-17C 17" LCD monitor with built-in speakers ($338.66)
- NEC 20" AccuSync LCD flat-panel monitor, with wall-mount capability and maximum resolution of 1600 x 1200 ($781.96) (shown here)

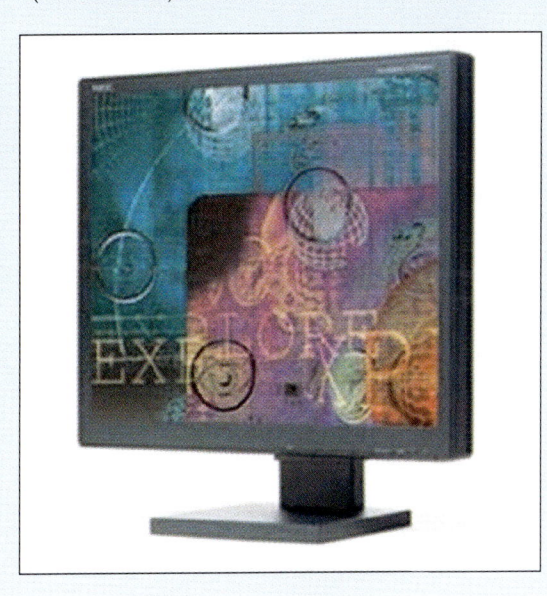

Chapter 19: Setting Up Your Monitor and Speakers

215

My Choice for the Speakers

Speakers — along with your choice of sound card — often have a major impact on how much you are able to appreciate the quality of the music or overall audio experience of your new Windows Media Center PC.

For this system, I selected a three-piece setup, the Altec Lansing VS2121W 2.1 for $38.01. This manufacturer has an extremely good name in speaker technology, and this setup is a good mid-range selection that should make listening to songs and movie soundtracks quite enjoyable.

The Cost of Cheap Speakers

Most preassembled PCs, even those with a very good sound card, come with extremely inexpensive speakers that result in not wonderful sound playback, perhaps with the addition of crackles, poor stereo sound, and a lack of audio balance.

At the other end of the range, you can spend hundreds of dollars on extremely sophisticated speakers designed to give you the ultimate in media playing.

Alternative Speaker Choices

Are you in the market for something a bit more sophisticated than the chosen Altec Lansing model or for something less expensive? You have many choices in a wide range of prices.

Different Speakers

Here are some alternative speaker sets to consider:

$

- Altec Lansing 120W powered speakers ($11.51)

$$$$

- Creative Labs SBS 5.1 70W speaker set ($62.92)
- Altec Lansing VS4121 2.1 speaker set ($77.33) (shown here)
- Altec Lansing VS3151 5.1 speaker subwoofer set ($77.92)

Considerations with Monitors

When you select a monitor, you must consider far more than the overall size of the display or whether it is a standard CRT-style monitor or a flat-panel LCD.

First, you need to match your monitor to your graphics card. You will not benefit from a sophisticated graphics card if you couple it with a bargain-basement monitor that cannot reach the high levels of screen resolution or has a slow refresh rate (or slow response times for LCD monitors) — the speed at which the on-screen image is updated.

VGA or DVI Connectors

Be aware of what type of connection your monitor choice uses because it needs to match the connection available on your graphics card. Most graphics cards today allow for both the standard VGA connection as well as the newer DVI (digital video interface) connector typically found on flat-panel or LCD monitors. Those that do not may allow you to purchase — or pack right in the box — an adapter so that you can install either type of monitor.

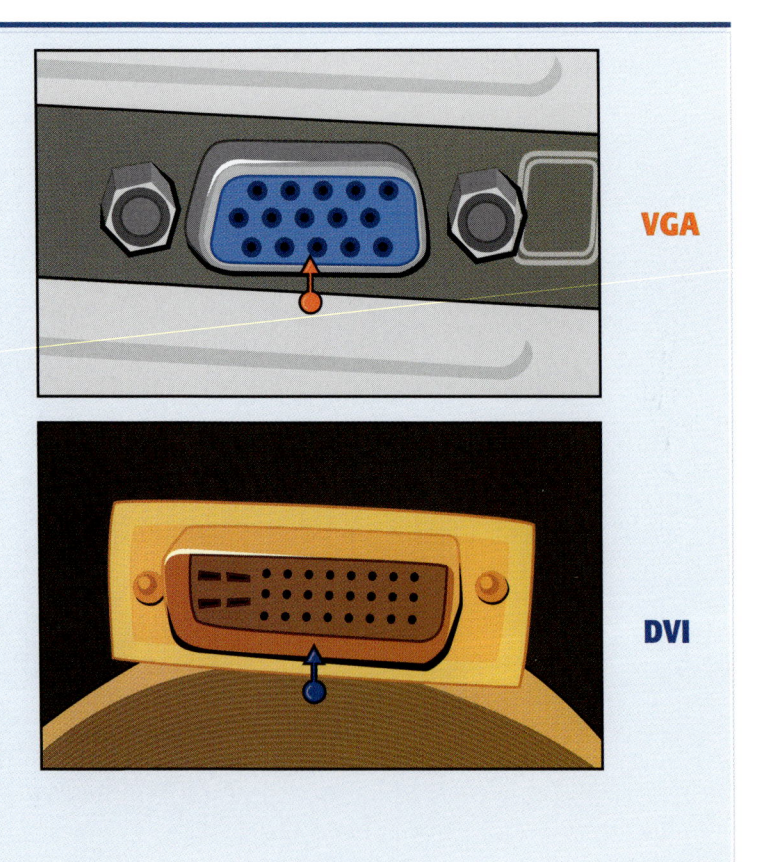

VGA

DVI

Read the Product Information

Read through the product information for each graphics card and monitor that you consider. Compare features, learn what it says about picture control, and see if you can determine which graphics card and monitor seem to make a good match. For use today, you probably do not want a graphics card or monitor with a resolution anything less than 1024 x 768.

```
(ALL-IN-WONDER® 9800 PRO Chipset)

Unleash THE BEAST Within

Banding digital mediums of Gaming, TV and Video together in a virtual
world of multimedia wonderment, THE BEAST RADEON 9800 PRO, with
features such as: TV-ON-DEMAND™, THRUVIEW™, VIDEOSOAP™, support
for DirectX® 9.0 and OpenGL, will liberate your creative BEAST within!

Features:

Powered by the RADEON™ 9800 PRO visual processing unit
Unparalleled TV and DVD features: TV-ON-DEMAND™, Gemstar GUIDE
Plus+™, mulTView™, VIDEOSOAP™, THRUVIEW™ and much more
Easily edit video into your own creations: Video CD and DVD Authoring
*Optional*Radio frequency wireless remote for your PC provides a hand
held 30-foot user interface. Control your mouse and PC applications at
the click of a button.
Stereo TV tuner with 125 channels
Intelligent Teletext on your PC
Zoom & pan - zoom in on the action on-screen and choose your own
close-ups
128MB DDR memory accelerates the latest 3D games
256-bit memory interface removes hardware performance bottleneck and
provides end users with faster 3D graphics
```

A Home Theater

Take into account whether you will truly use your Media Center PC as a place to watch movies. If so, you may want a much larger monitor than the standard 17". Some monitors can even be mounted on a wall instead of sitting on a desk. This may be a nice bonus in a living room or den where you want the appliance to blend in.

The Available Space

Consider the space that you have available. If you have limited desk or table space, this gives you an excellent reason to spend the extra dollars on a flat-panel display, which takes up a fraction of the desktop depth of a standard CRT-style monitor.

Review the Documentation

Read through the documentation for your new monitor as soon as the box arrives. Remove the manual perhaps before you take the monitor out of its package.

The Monitor Manual

The manual usually provides installation instructions, as well as details about adjustments that you can make to the picture, and informs you of any special warnings that you need to know before you press the new monitor into service. The manual should also suggest the placement of the monitor on your desktop.

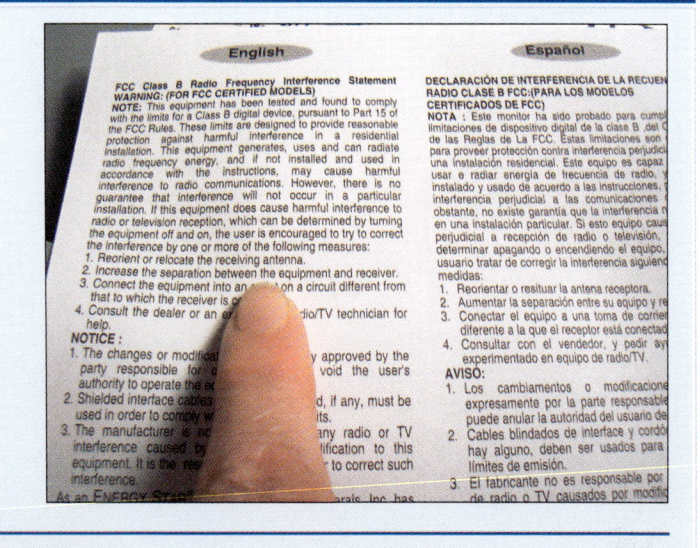

Included Hardware

Consult the monitor manual for information about any hardware that should be included. Normally, you should receive a power cord to connect the monitor to a wall outlet or power strip/surge protector and a video cable to connect the monitor to the graphics card installed in the PC or the video port that terminates the integrated video chipset built into the motherboard.

Check the Cables and Discs

Check the materials that come with the monitor in its shipping box.

Cables, Adapters, and CDs

The included materials should be the following:

- A power cable, one end of which may be permanently attached to the monitor
- A video cable, again, one end of which may be permanently connected to the monitor
- An adapter that can be used to help you connect a monitor to a different style video port on the graphics card
- A CD that contains drivers and special software for the monitor

Check the Cables

Inspect the cord and cable for any sign of damage. Such damage can be a crushed end connector or a rip, tear, or crimp in the length of the insulated housing. Anything like this may hurt the ability to use the monitor to its full capacity, so you need to replace the cord or cable as soon as possible, preferably before you actually connect the monitor to the system.

Chapter 19: Setting Up Your Monitor and Speakers

221

Set Up the Monitor

Finally, you are ready to set the monitor up. Yet, before you pull it out of its shipping box, you need to decide where you want the monitor to reside.

Placement Requirements

Clear the space that you need on your desktop or tabletop, exactly where you want your new monitor to sit. As you do this, try to calculate if the position you choose meets these requirements:

- Close enough to a power outlet to plug the monitor in
- Within reach of the PC case so that you can connect the monitor to the video port on the graphics card at the back of the PC

Consider Where You Will Sit

You also should factor in where you will sit and how far back on the desktop or table the monitor will be. The larger the monitor is, the more distance should lie between you and the screen. Too close and you will develop eye fatigue much more quickly. Too far away and it will be difficult to see.

Unpack the Monitor

With your planning done, now you can remove the monitor from its packing box. Take extreme care that you have a good hold on it because even a short drop or a bang against a desk or table leg can ruin the monitor.

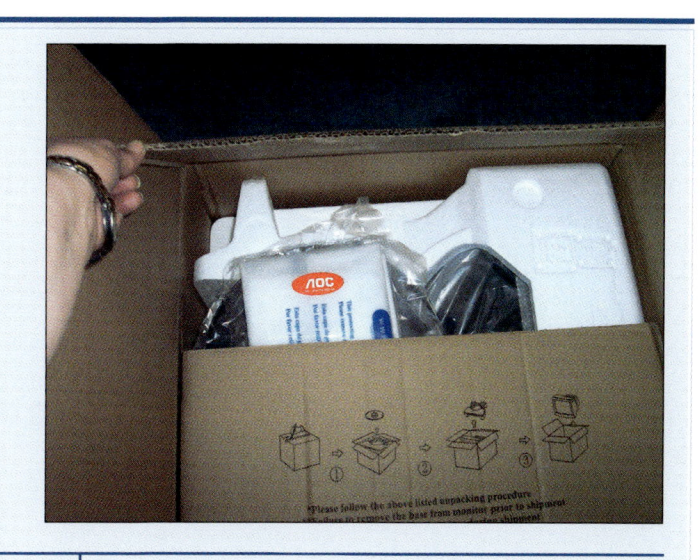

Clean and Inspect the Monitor

Get a clean, preferably antistatic cloth to wipe down the monitor, especially the screen, to remove dust and particles from the styrofoam and shipping materials from the box. As you do this, inspect the monitor to make certain that there is no sign of cracks in the housing and no other obvious damage to the unit.

Locate Monitor Connections and Controls

Now locate the connections on the monitor for the power cord, which may be permanently attached or not, and the video cable that will connect the monitor to the graphics card. Also, open your manual and use it to locate the monitor controls that will enable you to adjust the picture quality after you have the new PC fully assembled. These controls usually sit at the lower front, beneath the screen, much like a television.

Connect the Monitor

Here, you connect the monitor both to a power source and to the graphics card at the back of the PC to prepare it for actual operation.

You may want to wait until you have the entire PC together before you connect the monitor, so you do not have to work around the cables or connectors. If you choose to wait, make a note to yourself to follow these steps later.

Connect the Monitor

CONNECT THE POWER

1. If the power cord is not permanently attached to the monitor, connect the proper end to the cord plug at the back of the monitor.

2. Make sure that the cord is firmly seated.

3. Plug the other end of the cord into a wall outlet or other power source.

4. Press the power button and check to see if the power indicator lights up. You can then turn it off again.

CONNECT THE MONITOR TO THE GRAPHICS CARD

1. Connect the first end of the video cable to the video connector at the rear of the monitor, if it is not permanently installed.

2. If the video cable is wrapped to shorten its length, remove the twist ties or rubber bands and extend the cable to its full length.

3. Locate the video port on the graphics card at the rear of the PC.

4. Insert the other end of the video cable into the video port.

5. Tighten the thumbscrews at either side of the video connector to secure the cable in place.

Install Your Speakers

Good placement of speakers is always an issue, whether you set up a home stereo or a PC. You want the right distance between each speaker component and an unobstructed field around each speaker so that the speakers can deliver your sound.

Avoid the placement of speakers close to a fluorescent light, a telephone, a radio, or any other device or appliance that may create interference and produce crackles or static when you play music.

Install Your Speakers

1. Consult your speaker documentation for recommendations on optimum placement.
2. Remove the speaker components from their package.
3. Wipe them down with a clean, static-free cloth.
4. Place your speakers around your PC areas.

Note: Consider the distance from the back of the PC where you will connect the speakers.

5. Take the first speaker connector and plug it into the appropriate jack at the back of the PC — for the sound card or for integrated sound.
6. Repeat step **5** for the second connector.
7. Make certain that the speaker wires are free and loose, with no crimps.
8. Press the power button on the speakers and make sure that the power indicators light up.

Note: If your speakers are powered (they have a power cord), you also need to plug the cord into a wall socket or other power source.

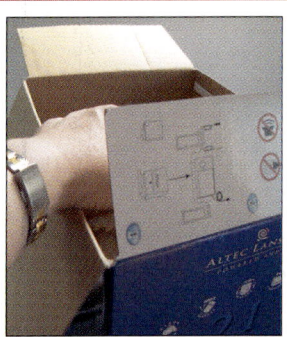

Chapter 19: Setting Up Your Monitor and Speakers

225

Add Other Audio Devices

If you have additional audio devices such as a microphone, headphones, and a digital instrument such as an electric keyboard, drumpad, or sound mixing board, you may want to connect these now to complete your sound system installation.

Add Other Audio Devices

PREPARE TO CONNECT

① Review the connections available at the rear of the sound card at the back of the PC or – where you use sound integrated into the motherboard – the connectors also found at the rear or front of the PC.

② Determine how each audio component connects.

Note: Some may use a USB port — located at the front or rear of the PC — rather than a sound card connection.

③ Bring your audio devices together into your workspace, so you can see them and begin to connect them.

④ Have any documentation that accompanies these devices at hand so that you can refer to it as needed.

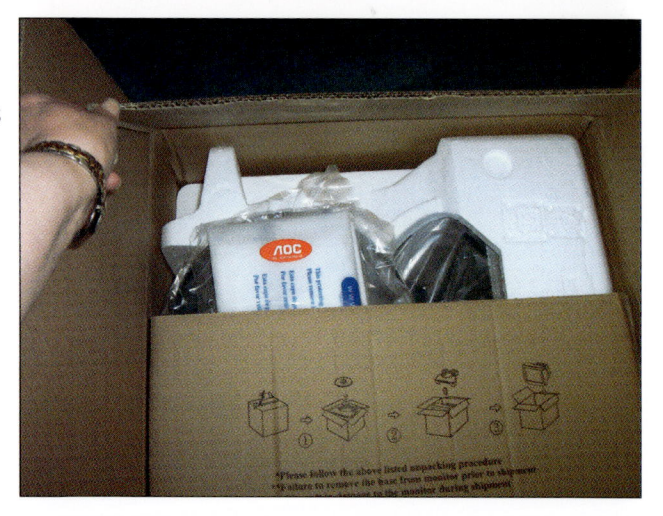

CONNECT YOUR MICROPHONE

1 If your microphone cord is bound, unwrap it so that you can extend the cord to its full length.

2 Take the connector at the end of the cord and plug it into the microphone or "Mic" jack at the rear of the PC.

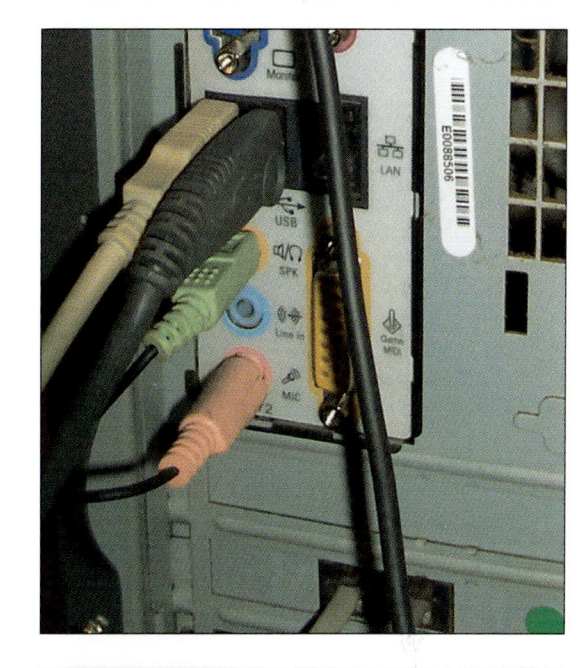

CONNECT HEADPHONES WITH A MICROPHONE

1 Consult the documentation with the headset.

2 Locate the two connectors at the end of the headset.

3 Plug the microphone connector into the "Mic" jack.

4 Determine where you need to connect the headphones connector.

Note: This may require that you temporarily disconnect one or more of the speakers if there is not a separate headphones jack.

Q&A

How do I connect other audio devices, such as an electric keyboard and a sound mixing board?

You connect them similarly to the way that you connect a microphone or headset, but you use the "Line In" jack instead.

Can I wait until later to connect my additional audio devices?

I suggest that you go ahead and connect these devices now to be sure that everything will install correctly. You can then disconnect them if you want to and put them away until your assembly is complete so that you do not have to work around the extra parts.

Chapter 19: Setting Up Your Monitor and Speakers

227

My Choice for the Keyboard and Mouse

To take advantage of the great pricing on a keyboard and mouse combination, the package I chose is a Logitech Internet Pro Desktop pair, in black to match the case. Together, they cost just $16.68.

This combo has some nice features besides the fact that Logitech is a respected name in hardware. It offers a full set of keys, including programmable ones that can be set to automatically perform certain functions. Also, the mouse is optical, which often means less wear and tear.

The Keyboard

Notice that there is a fair amount of room between the final row of keys and the bottom edge of the keyboard; this is a good ergonomic design and will act as a wrist rest to reduce the amount of stress for fast and/or frequent typists.

Alternative Keyboard and Mouse Choices

You want a keyboard and mouse that is a good match for your hands, the way you type, the desktop space you have, the kind of connections you have available on the PC, and usually, the overall appearance of the rest of the PC because a Media Center PC often becomes part of a living room or den.

Different Keyboards and Mice

Among the alternative choices available on CPU Solutions, you can opt to buy a different bundled pair (keyboard and mouse together) or buy each piece separately. The latter can result in a higher total price. Plan on anywhere between $9 and $50 for the keyboard and $10 to $50 for the mouse.

Your choices include the following:

$

- Black Chicony Multimedia keyboard only with a PS/2 connection ($9.99)

$$$$

- Microsoft Natural keyboard with optical IntelliMouse and PS/2 connection ($27.11)
- Logitech 967461 Cordless Desktop Pro in black with multimedia controls ($33.14)
- Saitek's Gamer's Keyboard (keyboard only) with blue LED backlighting, programmable command pad, and a wrist extension ($44.48) (shown here)

Determine Your Connection Type

Review the documentation with your mouse and keyboard to determine how these should be installed to your system. As you check the manual, also look at any additional hardware that may be in the box.

Connection Types

Almost all keyboards and mice connect one of a few different ways:

- To a PS/2 style or mini DIN 6-pin connector usually labeled "keyboard and mouse," respectively, at the back of the PC.
- Through a USB port at the front or back of the PC.
- Without any cord; these operate via radio frequency up to six to ten feet away from the main PC.

An Optical Mouse

If you have a cordless optical or other style of keyboard or mouse, pay particularly close attention to the documentation to make sure that you set it up properly. If you experience problems, be sure that nothing is in the way between the device and the PC itself that could block the signal.

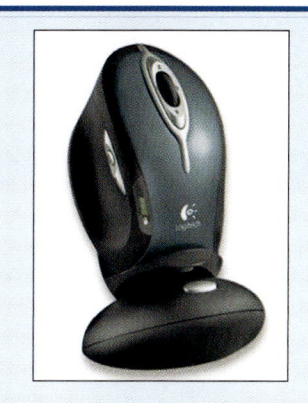

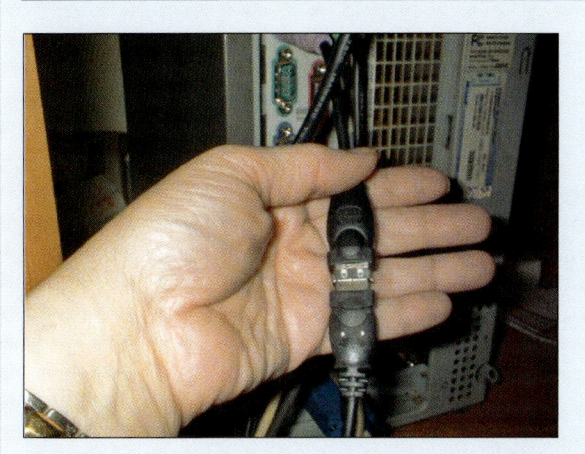

A USB Adapter

Remember the recommendation to check your manual and for additional hardware? There is a reason for that.

Some USB-style keyboards/mice come with an adapter to enable you to connect them either through a PS/2 6-pin connector or a USB port. If you find such an adapter and want a USB-style keyboard and/or mouse to connect via the standard keyboard/mouse ports, follow the manual instructions to install the adapter now. Also, some keyboards and mice come with an adapter that enables you to connect them regardless of whether your PC has a standard PS/2 port or one of the smaller, 6-pin connections.

A USB Keyboard

Also, if your new keyboard connects through a USB port, it may come with additional USB ports located somewhere on the keyboard itself. This means that other USB devices can be attached to the keyboard, which acts as a USB hub or connection point when the keyboard is then connected to a USB port on the PC.

Install the Keyboard

Your first step is to read the documentation accompanying your keyboard or keyboard/mouse combo, if you have not already done so. Then follow the steps here to install your keyboard.

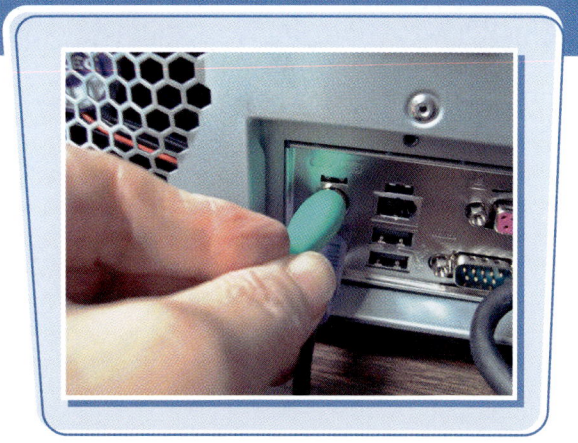

Install the Keyboard

1 Remove the keyboard, along with any accompanying hardware, from the box.

Note: The mouse, if packed with the keyboard, can stay in the box for the time being.

2 A twist tie or rubber band may hold the keyboard cable together, if this is a standard corded keyboard. Remove this holder and set it aside.

3 Fully extend the keyboard cable and note its connection for the end that connects to the PC (again assuming that this is a corded keyboard).

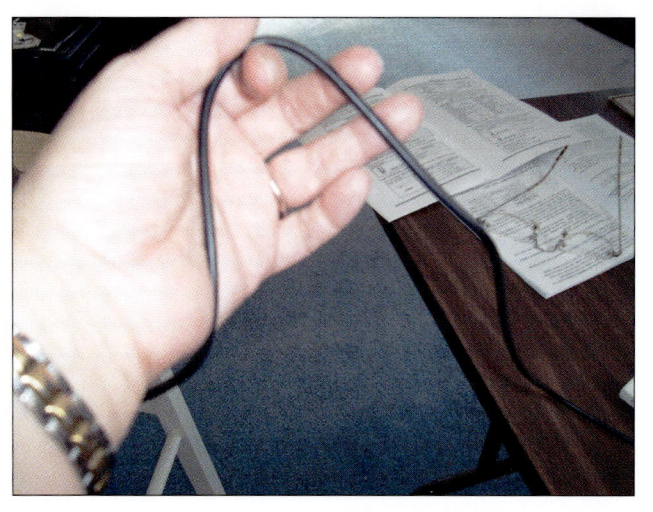

232

④ Locate the keyboard connector, which should be labeled either "keyboard" or "KB" at the back of the PC or the required USB port for a USB keyboard.

⑤ Position the keyboard basically where you want it to sit in relationship to the case and monitor that you have already put together.

⑥ Insert the connector end of the keyboard cable into either the keyboard connection or USB port.

Note: Make sure that it is firmly seated.

⑦ If the keyboard has a power switch — some do — turn it on.

How can I make sure that I am inserting the connector correctly?

A standard keyboard connection has a unique way of inserting the connector. Look at the connection on the PC and the connector at the end of the keyboard cable to match them up before you install it.

I am having trouble getting the keyboard cable to reach the connector at the back of my PC. What should I do?

You need to place a corded keyboard close enough to your PC to have enough cable to reach the rear of the PC. If you want to place your keyboard away from your PC, I suggest that you purchase a cordless one.

Chapter 20: Installing Your Keyboard and Mouse

233

Set Up Your Mouse

With your keyboard now connected, you are ready to connect your mouse, to move you another step closer to having your PC fully assembled and ready to go.

Set Up Your Mouse

① Consult any documentation that packs with your mouse or keyboard and mouse combination.

Note: This should give you the basic steps along with any additional information you need to know about connecting your mouse.

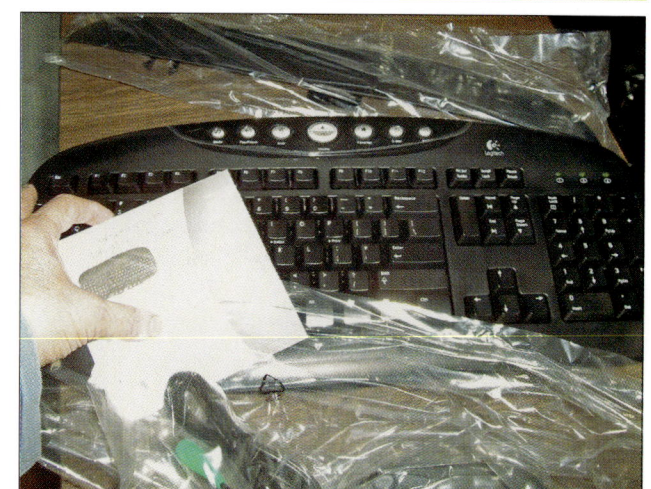

② If the mouse is not already out of the package, remove it.

③ Unwrap the cable that leads between the mouse and the back of the PC.

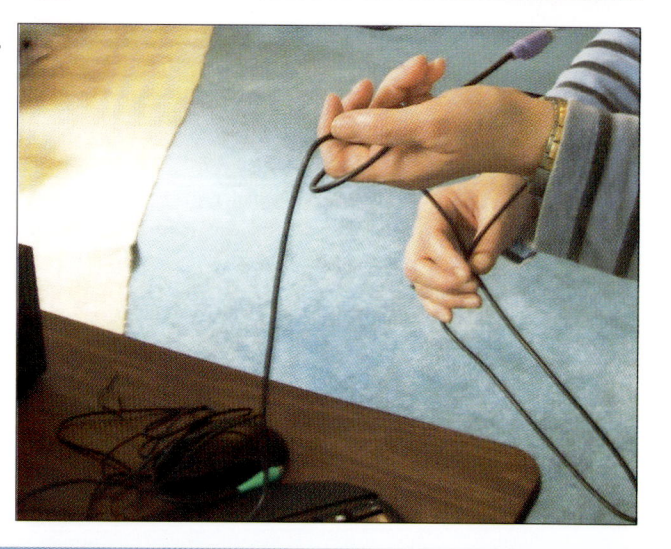

④ Position your mouse where you want it to sit on your desktop.

⑤ If you have a mouse pad, make certain that it is clean and dust free and place it beneath the mouse.

⑥ For a corded mouse, take the other end of the mouse cable and pull the cable out straight.

Note: *You will want a bit of slack.*

⑦ Connect the end of the mouse cable to either the port labeled "mouse" — usually positioned next to the keyboard or PS/2 port — or insert it into the USB port.

I have not purchased a mouse pad for my Media Center PC yet. Can I use something else for now?

For the time being, you may be able to press a fresh manila folder, the glossy side of a magazine or brochure, or some other smooth surface into use until you can purchase a mouse pad.

I have an optical mouse that can be connected either through the USB or the PS/2 port. Is one connection preferred over the other?

Whenever you use an optical mouse that gives you a choice between connecting through the USB or PS/2 port, always connect via the USB port. The reason is that USB allows for somewhat faster and usually much more precise movement. As a bonus, the optical light beneath the mouse allows for better tracking, too.

Install Other Input Devices

If you have any additional input devices, now is the time to connect them. After all, you are just steps away from the finish line in having your Windows Media Center PC all assembled, so you can install the operating system, tweak the system, and then sit back and enjoy.

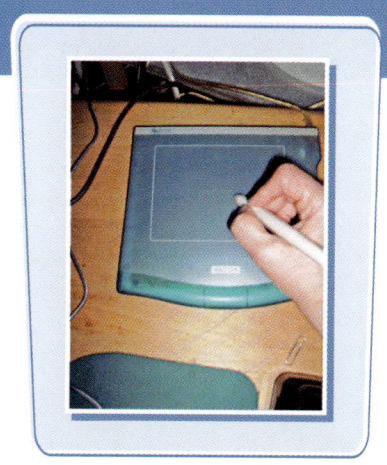

Install Other Input Devices

DIFFERENT TYPES OF INPUT DEVICES

A trackball or an additional keyboard

Gaming hardware such as a joystick, digital game pad, or steering wheel for car racing games

A scanner

A digital camera of any type such as still, Webcam, or video

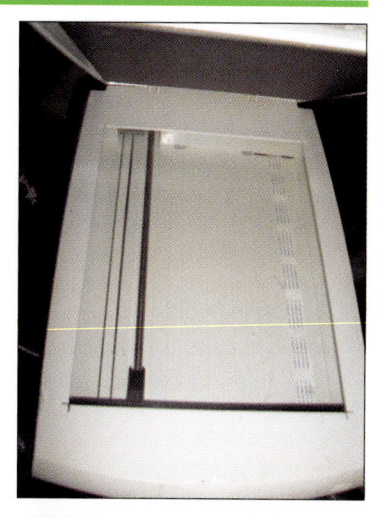

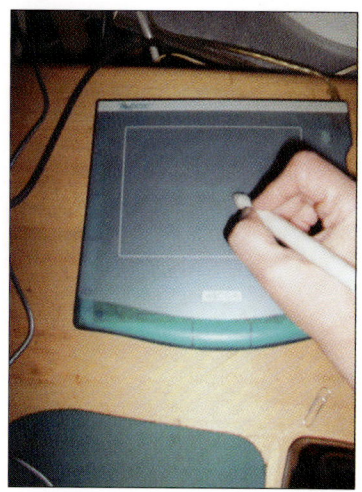

A graphics tablet or digitized pen for drawing

A digital voice recorder to transfer memos that you record into your PC

236

CONNECT THE INPUT DEVICES

① Determine how your input devices connect, which will be through one of the following: a USB or IEEE 1394 port (see Chapter 22), a game port or microphone/headset jack often found on the sound card or added I/O adapter at the back of the PC (see Chapters 15 and 18), a PS/2 or input connection like you used earlier to install the keyboard and mouse, or a serial/COM port or printer port at the rear of the PC.

② Read the accompanying documentation.

③ Connect the device to the PC.

④ If there is a power switch on the device, turn it on before you finish assembly and begin to install the operating system.

⑤ Check the hardware as you learn to do in Chapter 25.

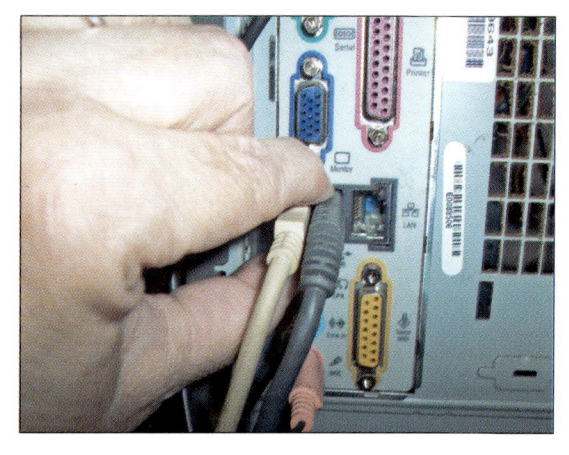

What other types of input devices are there?

Even a headset microphone that you use for dictating into voice-supported applications such as Microsoft Word and other software is often considered an input device. So, too, are special devices that you may use if you have certain physical challenges, such as an assistive reader or alternative input hardware.

You mention being able to work in applications with a microphone as an alternative to just typing. What is required for that?

You need a good, quality microphone and to then train Windows's speech-recognition setup to recognize your speech. Click **Start → Control Panel**, double-click **Speech**, and regularly go through the exercises listed there. Each time you go through the wizard, the system should get better at understanding what you are saying.

My Choice for the Printer

Acquiring a new PC today — by purchasing one or building one yourself as you are doing here — does not always have to mean a new printer as well. I chose for this system, for example, not to add a standalone printer.

Why? There are two reasons: due to cost and the likelihood that you already have a printer. Because the priority here was a robust CPU, more than enough memory, and a graphics card suitable for playing intense games, money went into other hardware.

Your Network Printer

This system will not be deprived. This is because most of you readers already have a printer, which you can share with this Media Center PC through a home network. You may have a good-quality, fast inkjet printer for day-to-day personal-use printing and/or a laser printer for very good output documents. Your new system can share either or both types of printers as needed.

Alternative Printer Choices

If your new Media Center PC will not go on a network, at least not right away, or you do not already have a printer available, then you probably want to add one to your assembly. Even for the most casual purposes, it is good to be available to print copies of digital photographs, documents, and hard copies of orders that you may place online.

Different Printers

Get a printer that is photo print capable, especially if you use a digital camera. If what you print does not have to be fancy or of extremely good quality, an inkjet printer will do. But if you need very good quality and can afford the extra operating cost, consider a laser printer. Also consider the price of replacement ink cartridges and toner cartridges.

Your recommendations from CPU Solutions include the following:

$

- A LexMark Z515 Color Jet printer with a USB 2.0 connection and a print speed of 12 pages per minute (ppm) black and white (also called *monochrome*) and 7 ppm color ($42.37).
- An Epson Stylus C66 inkjet printer with USB and printer port connection and print speed of 17 ppm in monochrome or 9 ppm color ($74.53) (shown here).

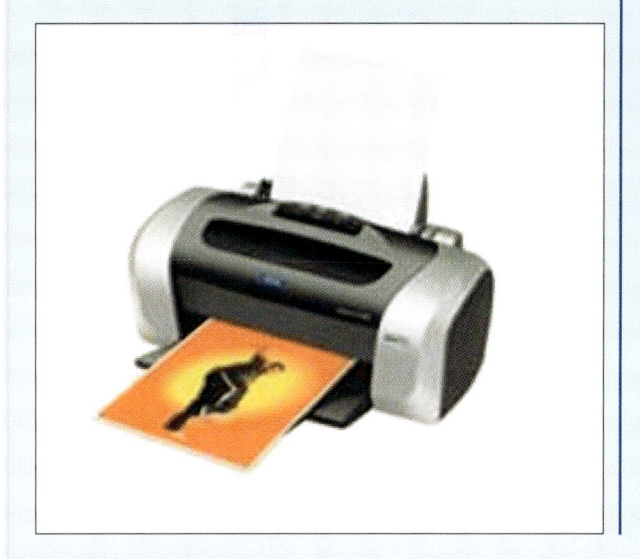

$$$$

- A Samsung ML1740 laser monochrome printer with both USB 2.0 and printer port connections and a TonerSaver feature with a print speed of 17 ppm ($139.99).
- A Samsung ML2150 laser monochrome printer with USB and printer port connections and a print speed of 21 ppm ($424.94) (shown here).

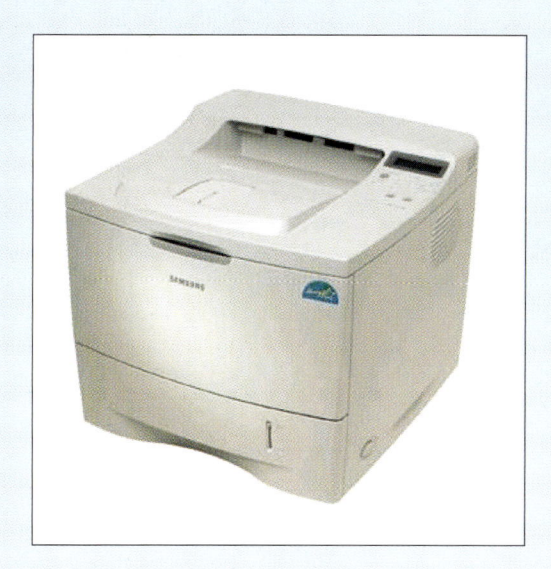

Determine Your Connection Type

Determine which type of connection your printer has so that you will know how to install it. Consumer PC printers connect to the PC through one of two ports: the LPT, or *printer port,* or a USB port.

The box and manual that come with your printer will identify the connection type for you. You will discover that some printers provide both connector types right on the same unit. This gives you the freedom to choose yourself.

Two Connections Can Mean Multiple Printers

There is a special advantage when you get a printer that offers both a USB and printer port connection. Sometimes, you may need more than one printer. Many people today buy both a laser for great quality printouts and an inkjet for standard and cheaper copies.

Printing Photos

Some people have multiple printers so that they can connect both a standard inkjet and a high-quality photo printer and make copies of their favorite images taken with their digital cameras. Although many inkjet printers allow both photo and standard printing, you may learn that you get better results when you buy a photo-specific printer for the images.

Whatever your specific needs, when you have the option of both connections — or even where both printers use just USB ports — it will be easier to connect multiple printers to the same PC or network.

Printer Cables

Each connection type uses a different type of cable. USB printers require a USB cable much like those you have seen with other USB devices in this book. Printer-port–connected printers use a standard printer cable. Do not worry about — or try — plugging the wrong cable into a port because it cannot happen; both ports and their connectors are quite different.

Install the Printer

The process of installing a printer is simple and straightforward. Note, however, that a standard printer-port printer should be connected to the PC when the system is turned off, whereas a USB printer connects when the PC is running.

If you are following the plan here, your PC is not ready to be turned on yet. You can go ahead and install the printer now, though, even if it connects through the USB port. If you have a problem with the printer being recognized later, just unplug it from the USB port and reinsert it after the PC is assembled and running.

Install the Printer

UNPACK AND PREP THE PRINTER

1. Unpack the printer from its box and read the manual.
2. Remove any packing material from the printer.
3. Install the cartridges as directed by the manual.

PLACE AND INSTALL THE PRINTER

1. Place the printer on a flat, sturdy surface within 5 to 10 feet of your PC.
2. Plug the printer's power cord into a wall socket or surge suppressor.
3. Turn the printer on.

   Look for the power light – usually red or green – to indicate that the printer is powered.

4. Connect the printer end of the printer cable to the back of the printer; on some units, the printer cable may be permanently attached to the printer itself.
5. Finally, plug the other end of the cable into the USB port or the printer port at the back of the PC.

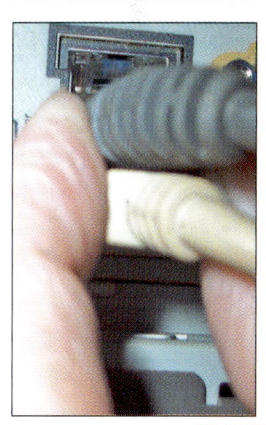

Chapter 21: Installing Your Printer

241

What to Know to Install USB/IEEE 1394 Devices

You are about to discover the reasons why universal serial bus (USB) devices and IEEE 1394 devices, also called *Firewire,* are gaining so much in popularity and usage.

Easy to Install
USB/IEEE 1394 devices are incredibly easy to install and remove because they just plug in and then unplug. Connection and removal are designed to be done while the PC is up and running, unlike most other types of hardware that require the PC to be shut down and turned off.

Very Fast
The latest generation of USB and IEEE 1394 devices are ultra-fast, which means that hardware designers and buyers are no longer limited in the types of hardware that work well externally. With the original USB devices, for example, people were stuck with slow devices such as keyboards, mice, and older-style digital cameras.

Many Different Devices Available

There is an extremely wide range of these externally connected devices available, from digital musical instruments such as electronic keyboards and drumpads to digital sound-mixing devices and personal media players such as MP3 units, to high-speed and high-capacity drives of all types, to great cameras, recorders, and beyond. When not in use, you can store these devices in a cabinet or drawer off the desktop to save space, too.

Installation/Removal Considerations

There are three primary things that you need to remember when installing and working with USB devices after you have your new system fully assembled and ready to use:

- The first time that you connect such a device, special software will install to support the hardware. You can then remove the device, but the system will remember that the device is installed so that you can connect it again later without reinstalling it.

- For best results, the PC must be up and running Windows when you connect or disconnect the device.

- Before you physically detach a USB or IEEE 1394 device, click the Remove Hardware icon in the system tray at the bottom-right corner of your desktop. If you fail to do so, you could experience problems the next time that you reconnect the device.

Connect the Devices

Before you start, understand that you may want to wait until after your PC is completely assembled and your Microsoft Windows Media Center operating system is set up to actually connect your USB and IEEE 1394 devices. Remember that they are designed to install and connect with the PC on and running.

Connect the Devices

CONNECT THE DEVICES

1. Review the documentation that comes with each of the devices to determine what additional steps you may need to take in the installation of them.

2. Locate your USB and IEEE 1394 port at the rear — or front — of your new PC.

    There should be at least two USB ports, but, depending on your choice of motherboard, you may have one or no IEEE 1394 ports.

3. Unpack your devices from their packages and make sure that each has a cable, which may or may not be permanently attached to the device itself.

4. If required, attach the USB/IEEE 1394 cable to the device.

Note: Again, this may be permanently attached to the device.

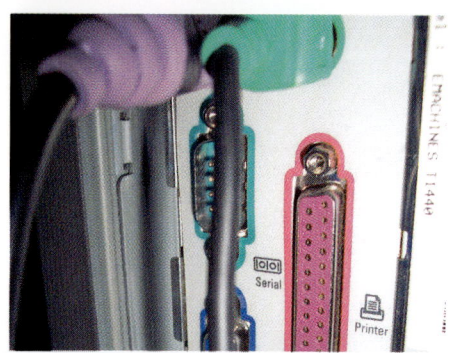

5 If there is a separate power cord for the device, install it as directed in the documentation and plug it into a wall socket or surge suppressor.

6 Turn the device on; many of these devices have a power switch or toggle button.

7 Connect the other end of the USB or IEEE 1394 cable to the port on the front or back of the PC.

8 With the PC already on, you may be prompted to insert the install CD into your CD/DVD drive to finish configuration of the new hardware. Do so.

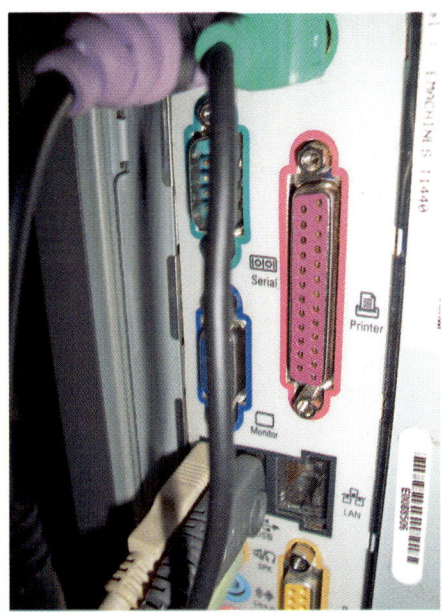

Q&A

I have an IEEE 1394 device but no IEEE 1394 ports. What should I do?

You can buy and install an IEEE 1394 adapter to an available PCI slot in your motherboard. Chapter 18 covers the installation of additional adapters.

Can I share a USB or IEEE 1394 device with the Macintoshes I use at work?

Yes, you can. Almost any device that connects through these ports, which are used by both PCs and Macs, can be used by both. There are exceptions, however, and these are usually noted in the product description. Some keyboards, for example, are strictly designed to be used with one or the other, not both.

continued

Connect the Devices *(continued)*

Your desktop system usually has just two USB ports, and a laptop or notebook computer often has just one. This can be a big problem if you begin to buy more and more PC hardware that uses USB because, if you need to connect more than two devices at a time, you will run out of ports to do so.

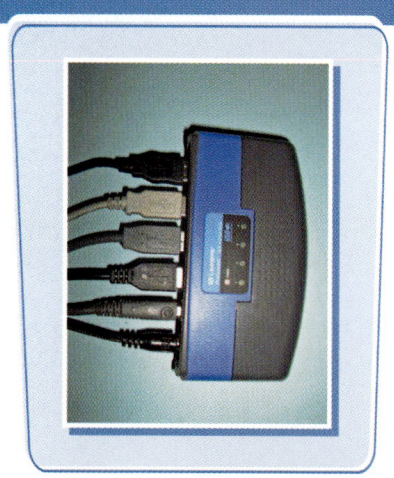

Connect the Devices *(continued)*

OPTIONS FOR FIXES

You could do a few different things to handle this: One option is to replace your motherboard with one that offers more USB ports, but this is not very cost effective. Another option is to install an add-on adapter into your motherboard that can give you several additional USB — or IEEE 1394 or both — ports.

THE BEST OPTION: ADD A USB HUB

Yet the best solution is to purchase and install a USB hub. This is a device that acts something like a smart power strip. Just as you can turn a single electrical wall outlet into one that accepts four or more plugs, a USB hub gives you 4, 8, 12, 16 or more USB ports.

A USB hub installs to just a single USB port, just like other USB devices.

THE DIFFERENT USB AND IEEE 1394 VERSIONS

- Check the information on most USB and IEEE 1394 devices, and you will see that version numbers are listed, such as USB v1.1 and 2.0 and IEEE 1394 v1.0 and 2.0.

The earlier versions of USB and IEEE 1394 are substantially slower than v2.0. For some devices such as keyboards, many digital cameras, printers, and scanners, that much lower speed is fine because this type of hardware does not need an ultra-fast connection.

But with external drives such as hard disks, you always want to buy products that are rated as USB 2.0 compatible, or the speed will be far too slow for data to move back and forth from the PC to the drive.

New PCs — or specifically, their motherboards — support v2.0 of both USB and IEEE 1394 devices, so take advantage of them.

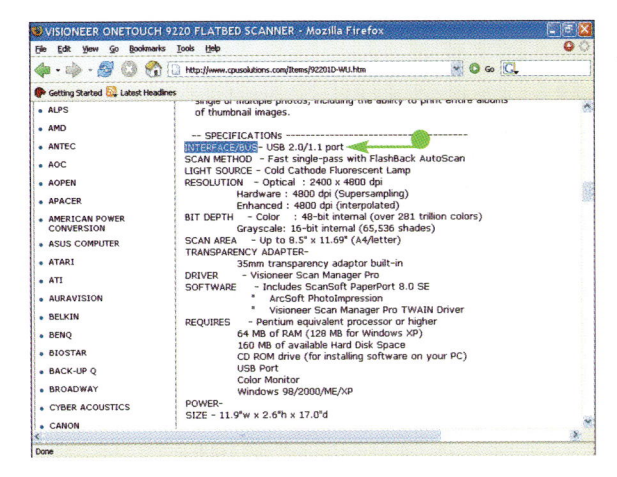

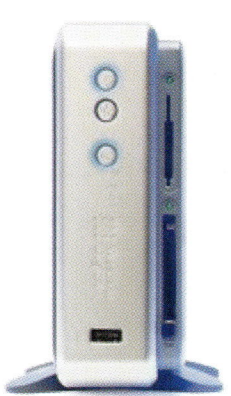

Q&A

Are there other ways for me to add USB ports?

Many USB keyboards and a few other USB devices have extra USB ports built in to enable you to connect additional devices.

What will happen if I use an older version device with a newer version port?

USB and IEEE 1394 are both backward and forward compatible. This means that you can insert a USB or IEEE 1394 v1.1 device into a USB 2.0 slot and have it work; you can also insert a USB 2.0 device into a v1.1 port. Bear in mind, however, that the device or the port will always drop to the lower v1.1 speed when you mix and match v1.1 and v2.0 hardware/ports.

Chapter 22: Installing USB/IEEE 1394 Devices

247

Part VII

Turning Your Components into the Ultimate Media Center PC

The final part of this book brings together everything you have done so far into the first real test of your new system — plugging it in and turning it on. But your work is not quite done yet.

First, you need to get the new system to boot; this is when you learn whether you were successful with all your detailed installations. If not, you will go through the steps for troubleshooting as you try to search out the source of a problem and resolve it so that you can proceed.

Then, after the system boots, you need to prepare the hard disk to install your Microsoft Windows Media Center operating system. After Windows is loaded on your PC, the operating system detects your new hardware and installs drivers to manage the components.

After that, you get the opportunity to test your newly constructed PC to determine how well it works. You will tweak and tune settings until you get the results that you want. Finally, you learn how to use Windows Device Manager to check your hardware, troubleshoot issues, and update drivers. After you complete Part VII, all that is left is to sit back and enjoy your custom-built Media Center PC.

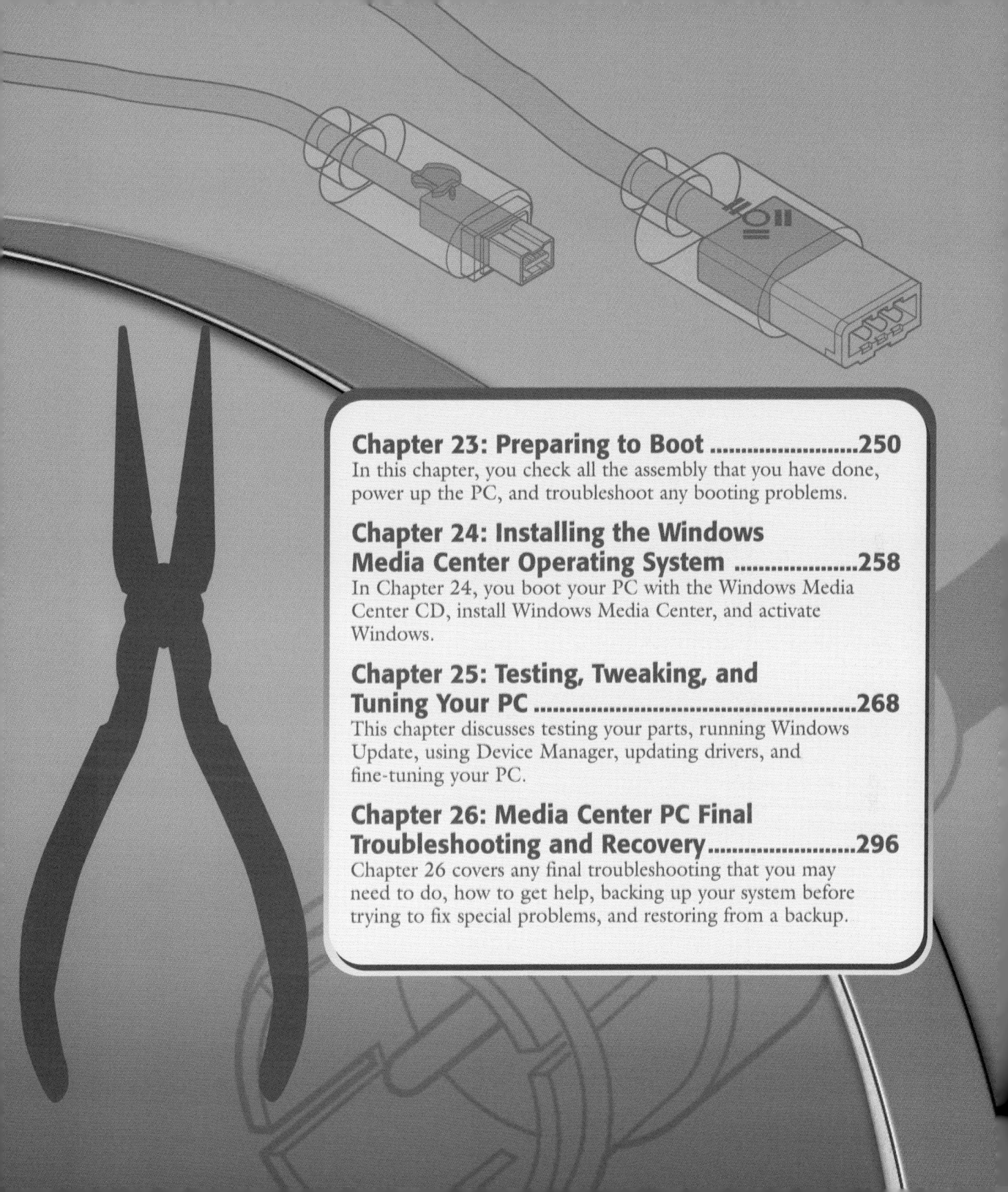

Chapter 23: Preparing to Boot 250
In this chapter, you check all the assembly that you have done, power up the PC, and troubleshoot any booting problems.

Chapter 24: Installing the Windows Media Center Operating System 258
In Chapter 24, you boot your PC with the Windows Media Center CD, install Windows Media Center, and activate Windows.

Chapter 25: Testing, Tweaking, and Tuning Your PC 268
This chapter discusses testing your parts, running Windows Update, using Device Manager, updating drivers, and fine-tuning your PC.

Chapter 26: Media Center PC Final Troubleshooting and Recovery 296
Chapter 26 covers any final troubleshooting that you may need to do, how to get help, backing up your system before trying to fix special problems, and restoring from a backup.

Check All Your Work

You are finally at the moment you have been working up to and waiting for: watching your new PC start up, called the *boot process*.

Now is your final opportunity to review all the assembly you have done so far, double-check that everything is connected properly and remains securely attached, and verify that you have not forgotten anything special you may have meant to add to your new system.

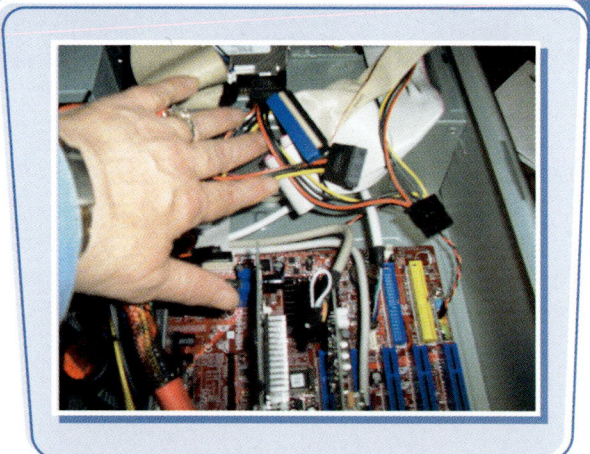

Check All Your Work

① If you have replaced the cover on the PC, remove it and set it aside.

② Consult Chapter 5 through Chapter 22 for each part, checking that you have installed all your components and that they remain firmly attached in the correct place.

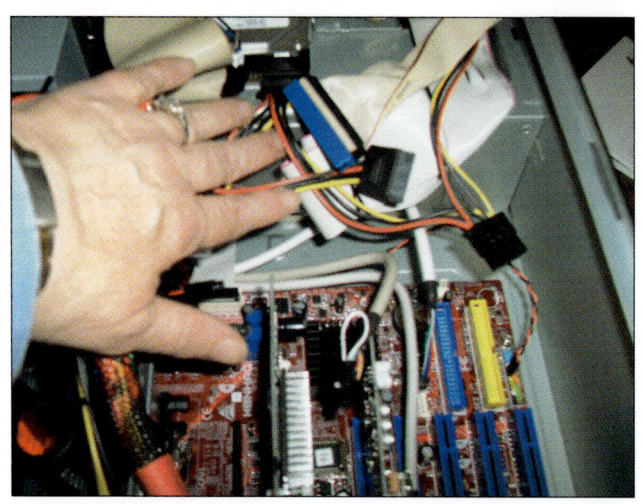

③ Replace the cover and screw it into place.

④ Check the front and rear of the PC to be sure that all the hardware is connected and seated firmly.

⑤ Look around your workspace and in any boxes remaining from your assembly. Make sure that you have not forgotten anything.

⑥ Collect the manuals, other documentation, and the warranties together from the devices and insert them into a folder or notebook that you have labeled to easily find them again later.

⑦ Set the install CDs – including your Microsoft Windows Media Center disc – near the system, so you have them available when you set up the PC.

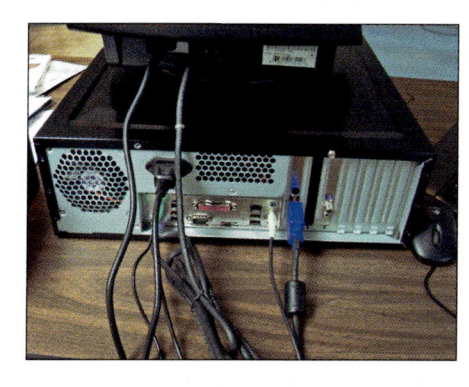

My PC is still in my work area. At what point should I move it to where I will use it?

Now is the time to move your new system from the work area to its final resting place. If you have a small but strong cart, that may be ideal to move everything at once. If not, you may need to disconnect the keyboard, mouse, monitor, and speakers temporarily and then reconnect them again after all the components have been moved.

After I moved my PC, my printer stopped working, and it was fine before. Do you know what may be the problem?

Check your cable and connections. It sounds like one is loose. If all else fails — and you are sure that the power indicator on the printer is lit, so it has power — remove the device. Click **Start → Printers and Faxes**, right-click the printer name, and click **Delete**. Click **Yes** in the dialog box. Then restart Windows and let it install support for the printer all over again.

Install the Power Cord and Start the PC

Now you will connect your PC to power and boot it to see how it starts. However, the PC will not be fully ready to start and boot until you install the operating system, which you cannot do until your hard disk is prepared for use.

Right now, you just need a sense of whether everything is connected properly so that you can get to the step of preparing your drives and installing the operating system.

Install the Power Cord and Start the PC

1. If it is not already installed, locate and connect the power cable to the back of the PC.

2. Plug the other end of the power cable to a wall outlet or a surge suppressor.

3. Press the power button to turn the PC on.

Cover a Few Basics

Now that you have started the PC, what happens? If you are very fortunate and followed every single direction to the letter, you will see an error message telling you that the drive is not ready or the operating system is not found. Believe it or not, this is normal because the hard disk is not ready and the operating system is not installed yet.

If Problems Come Up

If instead, you see — or hear because of a series of beeps — something different, you need to investigate why. Here are some detective tips:

- Do you see or here anything? If not, go to the next section.
- Check the monitor screen for any messages displayed there. If present, jot the message down to see if you can find some reference to it in your motherboard manual or other resources that you learn about in the next section.
- If the system beeps repeatedly, count the beeps. The number means something. If necessary, restart the PC and count them.

Troubleshooting Boot Issues

If you are fortunate to see what you should see — an error message telling you that the drive is not ready or the operating system is not found — you can go ahead to Chapter 24. If not, you need to troubleshoot to determine what is wrong and resolve the problem before you can proceed.

Read through this section to see what problem and response best matches your situation and then try the suggestions provided to overcome them.

No Activity

Problem: Nothing at all happens.

What to try: If you see or hear absolutely no activity, one of the following is likely the culprit; check these and try again:

- You do not have the PC plugged into a working electrical socket.
- The surge suppressor or uninterruptible power supply you use is not set up, either not plugged in or turned on.
- The PC is not turned on.

Still No Activity

Problem: After checking the power and trying a different wall outlet, you still have no activity.

What to try: There is the possibility that your power supply is bad and is not supplying power to the system. Obtain a replacement power supply, install the new one in place of the existing one, and try again.

An Unexpected Error Message

Problem: There is an error message on the screen.

What to try: First, make sure that the error message is not one of the two you should see — telling you that the drive is not ready or the operating system is not found; if it is, just proceed to Chapter 24. If the error message differs, what you do depends on what the onscreen message reports, such as these:

- A message about missing or problem hardware: If so, turn off the PC, disconnect it from power, remove the cover, put on your antistatic wrist strap, and check the connections and installation for the device noted in the error message before you replace the power and try to start it again.

- A message about CMOS Setup: Follow the onscreen directions to go into CMOS Setup to check your hardware there. Have your motherboard manual handy, open it to the troubleshooting or CMOS Setup section, and try to find information about your problem. If you make changes there based on manual instructions, save your changes before you leave CMOS Setup and then try to start the PC again.

Troubleshooting Boot Issues *(continued)*

The Monitor Is Blank

Problem: You can hear the PC operating, but nothing shows on the monitor.

What to try: Turn off the PC and check the connection between the monitor and the graphics adapter or video port at the back of the PC; make sure that it is properly and firmly seated before you turn the PC on again.

If all appears well with the external connections, disconnect the PC from power, remove the cover, don your antistatic grounding wrist strap, and check the installation of your graphics and other adapters before you reconnect power and try again to start the PC.

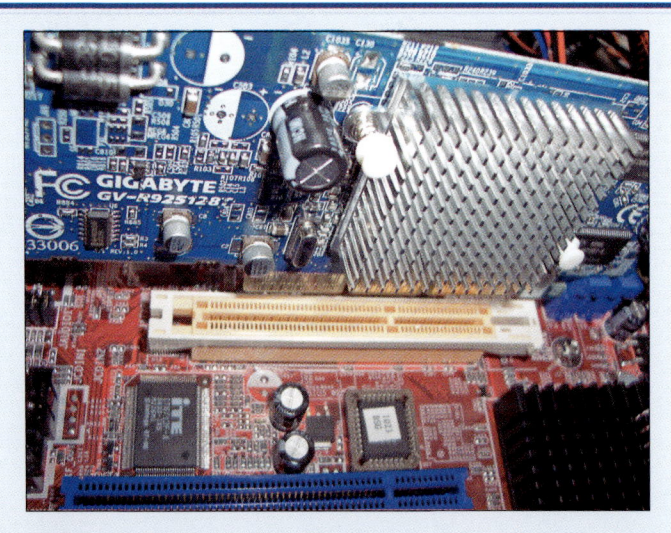

Only the Power Supply Is Working

Problem: You hear the power supply whirr, but nothing else appears to work.

What to try: Turn off the PC and disconnect it from power, remove the case cover, and put on your grounding wrist strap. Exercising extreme care, reconnect power and turn on the PC again, making sure that you *see* as well as hear the power supply working. When verified, disconnect the power again with the PC off and then check all the connections running from the power supply to other components such as the motherboard and drives. A problem with the power supply is possible; you may need to remove the existing one and replace it to proceed.

256

A Series of Beeps

Problem: Instead of the PC trying to start, you hear a series of beeps but see no onscreen message.

What to try: The very first thing to do after you count the number of beeps is to consult your motherboard manual. The manual should specify what the set number of beeps indicates. Follow the recommendations noted to try to resolve the situation. If you cannot locate this troubleshooting information in the manual, try the online support site for the motherboard manufacturer.

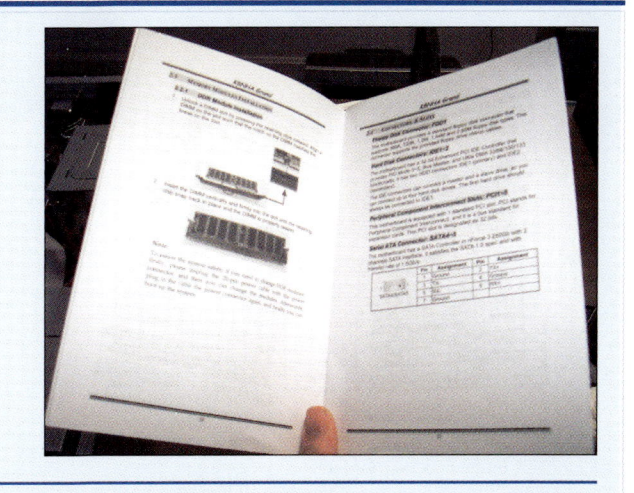

The PC Still Will Not Start

Problem: You tried what the manual recommends but still cannot start the PC or cannot figure out what is wrong.

What to try: First, do you have a sense of exactly what component is not working? If you purchased all your components through CPU Solutions, your first call should be to them. Have a phone near the PC because the CPU Solutions representative may ask you questions or to check something for which you need access to the system. He or she also may recommend that you contact the manufacturer of a specific part directly before CPU Solutions replaces it.

When All Else Fails . . .

Problem: You have now tried everything, including calling the technical and manufacturer's support, but you still cannot find what is wrong.

What to try: Although you may want to consider asking CPU Solutions to allow you to ship the system back except for those components that you can verify do work, your best bet at this point may be to disassemble the PC and build it again from scratch, paying careful attention to detail. This will eliminate — for the most part — the chance that you may have simply installed a core component incorrectly, which is preventing the rest of the system from working properly. You can also just remove one component at a time and reinstall it.

Boot Your PC with the Windows Media Center CD

Now you will perform your last two major tasks before you troubleshoot, tune, and tweak your new system, which you do over the course of the last two chapters of this book.

The Last Two Steps

The two major steps left to the assembly and setup process for your personally customized, built-all-by-yourself system are preparing your hard drive(s) and installing Microsoft Windows XP Media Center Edition.

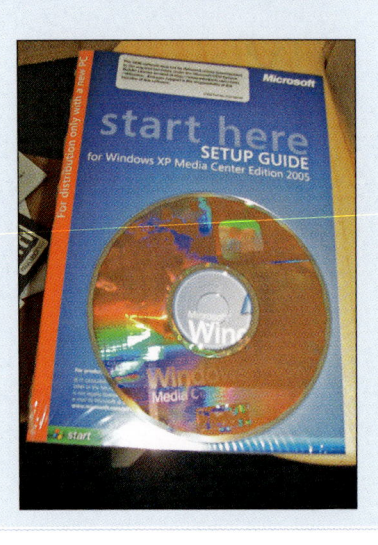

Check That You Are Ready

Before you start, you need to be sure that you can answer yes to the following questions, based on instructions and recommendations from Chapter 23:

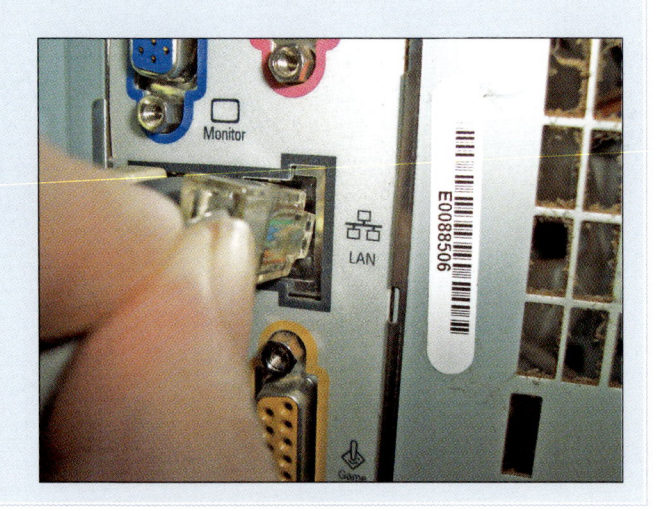

Check That You Are Ready *(continued)*

- Did you do a thorough review of your system and setup to verify connections and installations?
- Were you able to get as far in the boot process as outlined in Chapter 23?

If You Are Not Ready

If you respond "no" to either question, you need to stop and either perform your checks or troubleshoot why you cannot start to boot before you try to set up your operating system. It is very likely that if you do not, you will not be able to get very far as you run the Windows install; if you somehow manage to do so, the results are apt to be problematic. You could have the system report a failure of one or more devices, or the operating system may run in a very unstable condition.

If your answer to both of those questions is yes, you are good to go. You can insert your Microsoft Windows XP Media CenterEdition CD into your CD/DVD drive and run setup.

Set Up Your Operating System

You want to have up to an hour available to get the installation of Windows Media Center started. After that, you will want to monitor the setup every few minutes or so to make sure that it is proceeding as it should and does not require your attention or input.

For the first several minutes, you will have to step through selections to configure the operating system and prepare the hard drive to accept Windows and a file system.

Set Up Your Operating System

START WINDOWS SETUP

① Insert your installation disc into your CD/DVD drive.

② Press the power button to turn the system on.

③ If the Setup screen appears, skip the next subsection and go on to the subsection following that, "Continue the Basic Setup."

If you receive an error message instead of the Setup screen, you need to change the boot sequence. See the following subsection, "Change the Boot Sequence."

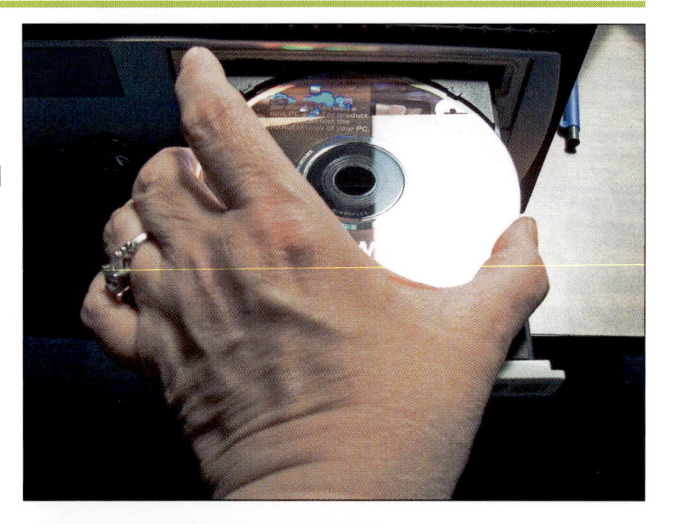

CHANGE THE BOOT SEQUENCE

① Press the power button again to restart the PC.

② Check the monitor.

At some point, you will be instructed to press a key or key combination to enter Setup or CMOS Setup, the programmable part of BIOS on the motherboard.

③ Press this key or key combination.

④ From the CMOS Setup menu, locate the section that indicates that it deals with startup configuration.

⑤ Locate the entry to specify boot drive(s). Follow the onscreen instructions to modify this entry to add the CD/DVD drive to the sequence.

⑥ Save your changes and exit CMOS Setup.

The PC restarts, and the Windows Setup screen appears.

CONTINUE THE BASIC SETUP

① When you see the Welcome to Setup message, press Enter.

② Read the end user license agreement.

③ Press your F8 key to agree and continue.

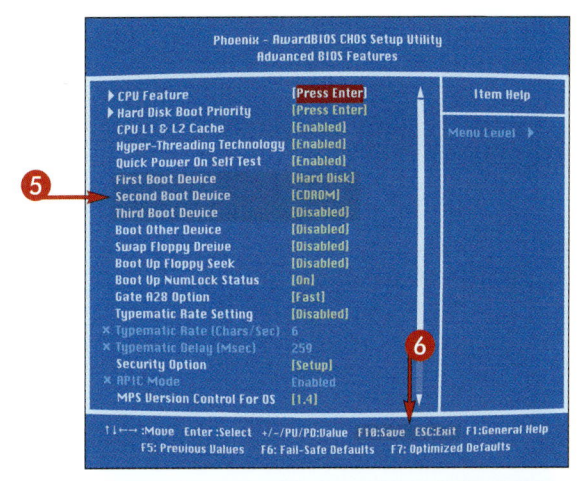

Why would I need to change the boot sequence?

If your system behaves as if it does not see the Windows install disc, you may need to adjust your drive booting sequence to tell the BIOS to try to boot from the CD or DVD drive where the installation disc has been inserted.

If there are some changes I want to try in CMOS Setup, can I make them at this time?

The safe answer is no. You probably first want to get the PC up, with Windows installed, and operational, and then make a complete backup of your system before you make custom changes. Even then, you should be very careful that you know what you change in CMOS Setup, or you could stop the PC from working properly or at all.

Chapter 24: Installing the Windows Media Center Operating System

continued

261

Set Up Your Operating System *(continued)*

With Setup now running, watch carefully for what the screen tells you as well as what you read here. Have your CD envelope handy, as well as both installation CDs, for the steps here.

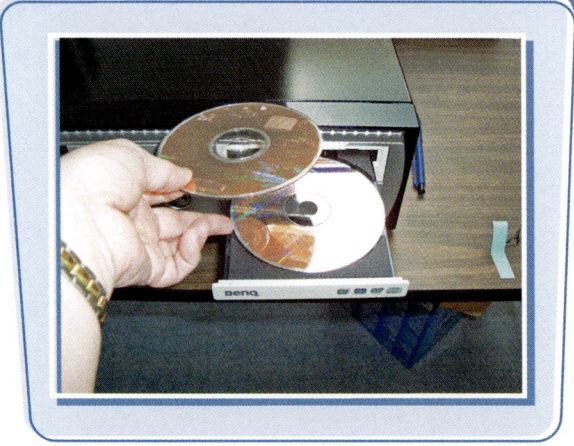

Set Up Your Operating System *(continued)*

④ When you reach the Partition Management section, select the unpartitioned disk space on disk 0 — which is your first installed hard disk if you have more than one — at ID 0 on bus 0.

⑤ Press Enter.

⑥ On the Partition File System screen, select **Format the Partition Using the NTFS File System**.

Note: NTFS is the most secure type.

⑦ Press Enter.

An onscreen message reports that Windows is now formatting the partition. This may take several minutes or more.

⑧ After formatting is complete, a message informs you that setup files are being copied to the drive. Just let it continue.

⑨ At some point, the system will report that it needs to reboot; let it do so.

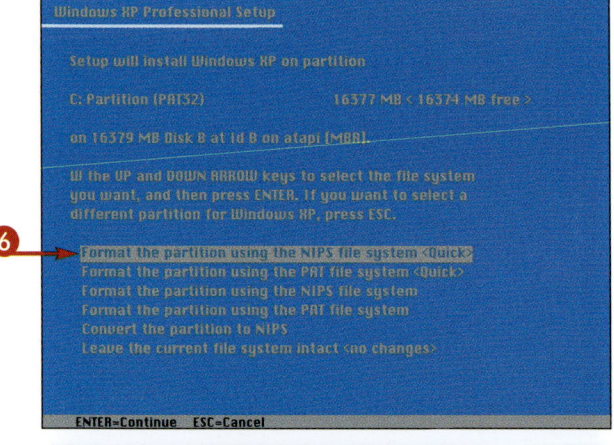

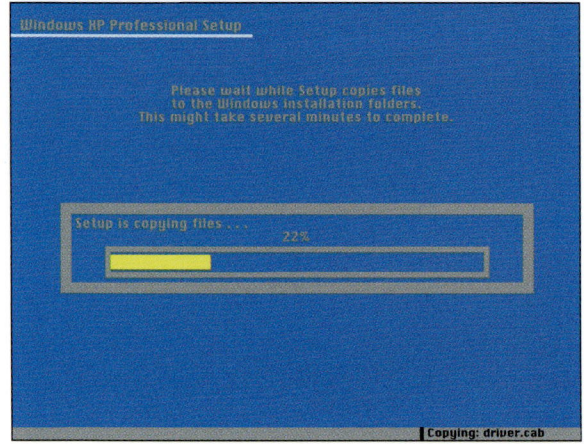

After a reboot, the system will begin to ask you to make selections.

⑩ First, choose your Regional and Language options.

⑪ Click **Next**.

⑫ Type your name and, optionally, the title of your organization.

⑬ Click **Next**.

⑭ Enter your 25-character product key, which should be located on the envelope in which your Windows disc came.

Note: Take care to enter it correctly.

⑮ Click **Next**.

⑯ Provide a name by which this system will be identified – especially useful if the system will become part of a network with other PCs.

⑰ Type your password and retype it to protect the Administrator account on the PC.

⑱ Click **Next**.

⑲ Set the time and date for your time zone and the current time and date.

⑳ Click **Next**.

㉑ When you see the Network Settings screen, accept the default selection and click **Next**.

㉒ On the domain page, accept the default and click **Next**.

㉓ When prompted, remove the first disc of Windows Media Center and replace it with disc two.

Note: Close the drive if it does not do so automatically.

The PC will eventually prompt you again for CD1.

㉔ When it does, remove disc two and insert disc one again.

Note: Again, close the CD/DVD tray if needed.

㉕ Click **OK**.

The PC then reboots again.

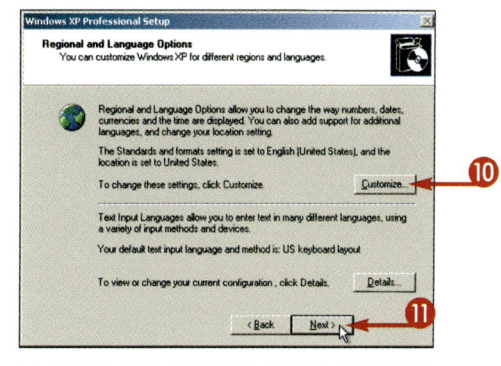

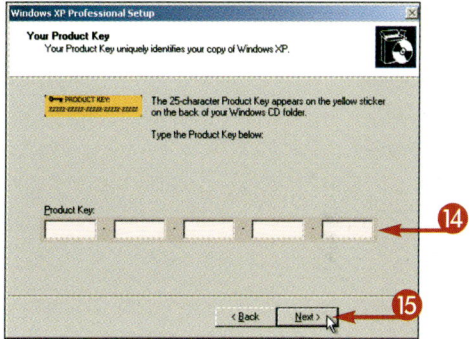

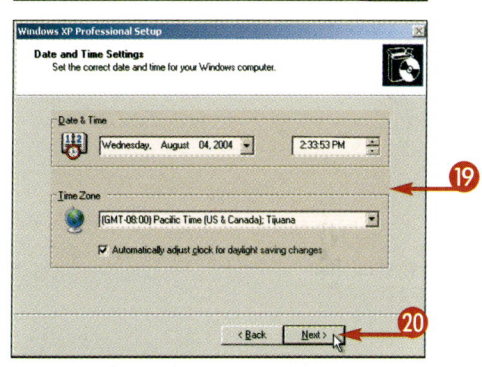

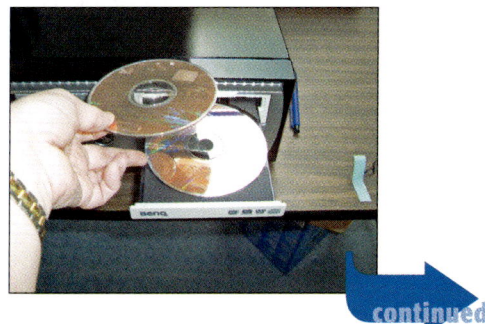

continued

Set Up Your Operating System *(continued)*

Here you will complete your installation steps.

Set Up Your Operating System *(continued)*

The Windows Setup Out of the Box Experience starts.

㉖ At the bottom of the Welcome screen, click **Next**.

㉗ Click **Help Protect My PC**.

㉘ Click **Next**.

㉙ Click **Yes** on the Internet Connection screen.

㉚ Click **Next**.

The Activate Windows message appears.

㉛ Click **No** for the time being because you may need to set up your Internet account first.

㉜ Click **Next**.

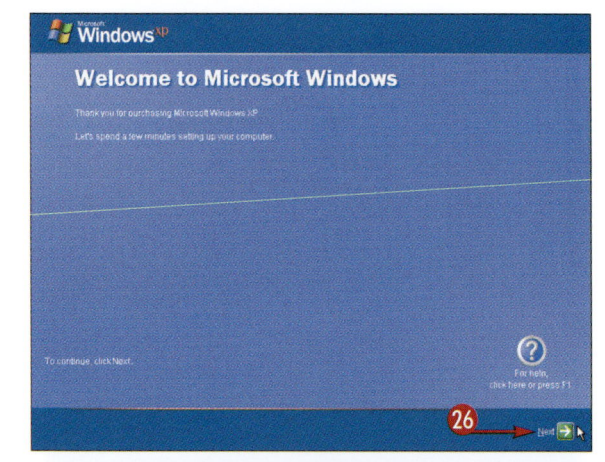

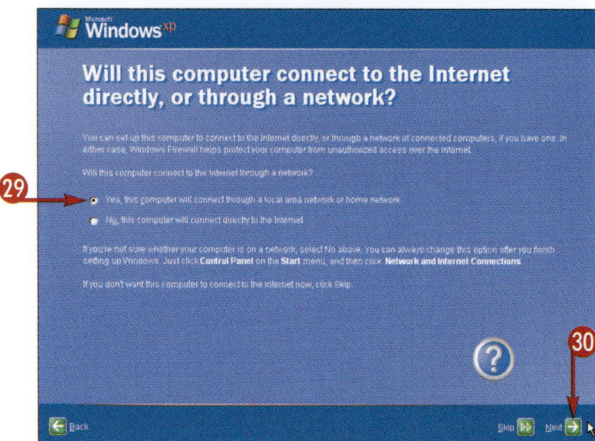

264

㉝ Type your name and then the usernames of anyone else who will share your PC.

㉞ Click **Next**.

Setup finishes.

㉟ Follow any onscreen instructions.

㊱ Remove the final Windows CD, replacing all discs in their installation case.

㊲ Store the disc set somewhere safe and where you can easily locate it again.

㊳ Have all the separate hardware CDs from the devices you installed available so that you are ready if you are prompted to install them.

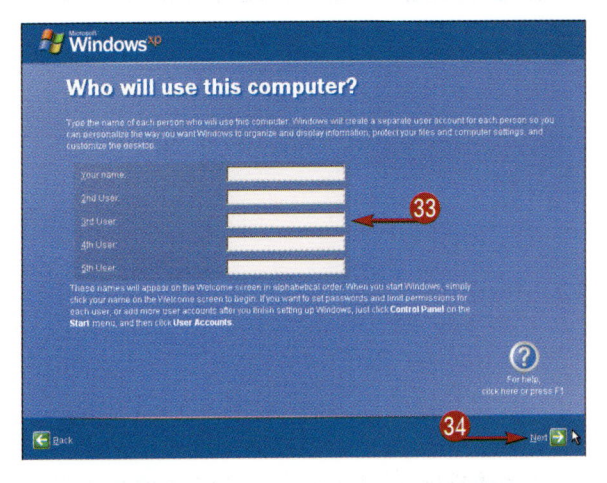

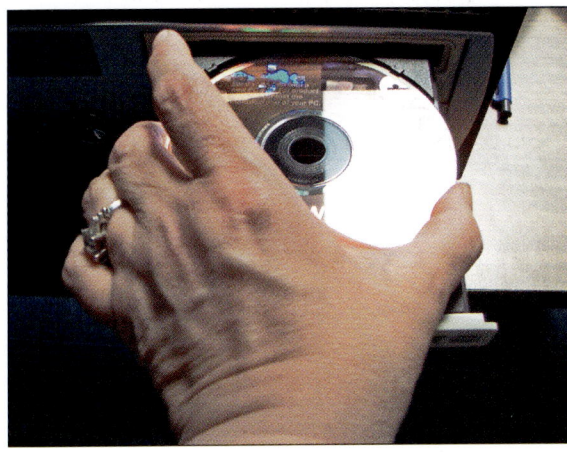

Q&A

Should I install the hardware setup CDs in any special order?

You should start with the biggest items — meaning most important — first. For example, your motherboard will likely be packed with a CD to finalize your setup of it. Then move down through other choices until you work to the peripheral or external devices such as your speakers, printer, keyboard, mouse, and digital camera.

Does the hardware setup CD always contain the latest and greatest drivers for my devices?

Actually, by the time you buy and install a hardware device, its driver and any extra software required may have been updated one or more times. However, some of these device drivers may be installed when you run Windows Update, which is discussed in Chapter 25. With others, you can follow instructions in your documentation to visit the Web site of the manufacturer and update the drivers.

Chapter 24: Installing the Windows Media Center Operating System

265

Activate Windows

You must activate your copy of Windows Media Center within 30 days of the date that you first install it, or the operating system will cease to function. This means that you would not be able to load Windows.

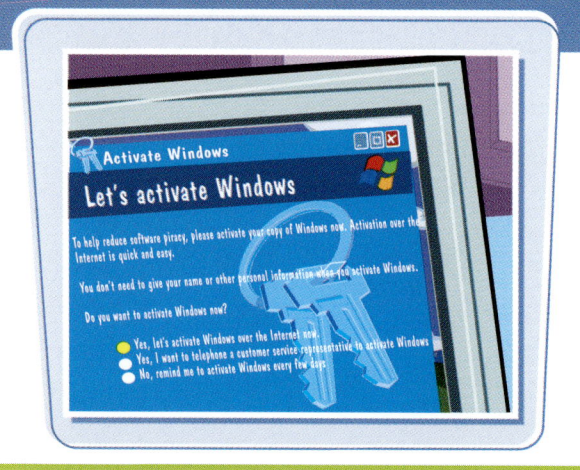

Activate Windows

CONNECT TO THE INTERNET

1. Make sure that your Internet connection is running.

INSTALL HARDWARE AND SOFTWARE PER YOUR ISP'S INSTRUCTIONS

Note: If you have hardware or software that came with your broadband Internet service, such as cable, a DSL, or a satellite modem, and an install disc to help you configure your service, follow these steps.

1. Check with your service provider to make certain this hardware and software is compatible with Windows Media Center.

2. Install the hardware and configure the software as directed by your ISP.

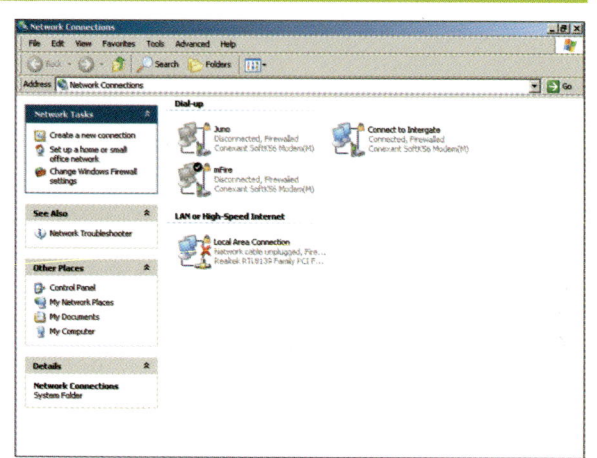

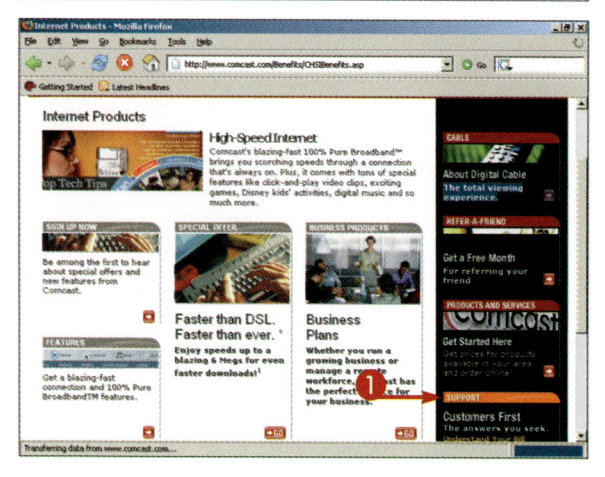

266

IF USING DIAL-UP

① Use another PC to check your ISP's Web site to get configuration information.

② Use the Internet Connection Wizard to set up your Internet service account.

ACTIVATE WINDOWS MEDIA CENTER

The next time you restart your system, the activation reminder pops up.

① Click **Yes, Let's Activate Windows over the Internet Now**.

② Click **Next**.

Alternatively, you can click the key icon in the system tray to launch the Activation Wizard.

③ Connect to the Internet if needed.

④ Follow the Activation Wizard's steps to check and verify the activation.

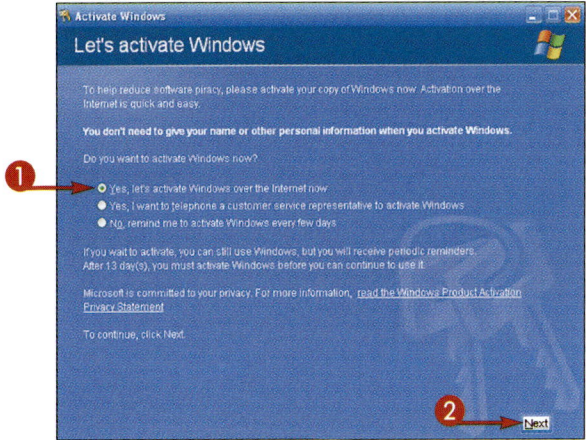

Remember!

If you are using a dial-up Internet service, remember that earlier chapters recommend that you upgrade to a high-speed service to take advantage of some of the Media Center operating system's features.

What happens if I go past 30 days before I install an Internet connection to my Windows Media Center PC?

First, you will be locked out of Windows after the 30-day limit is reached. Because you probably do not want that to happen, use the manual activation option where you choose to call the Microsoft number to activate Windows.

About Testing Your Parts

With your PC fully assembled and your operating system completely installed, you now need to determine how well suited your hardware and configuration is for both work and play.

A Checklist

Essential elements to check your results include the following:

- Clicking **Start** ➔ **Media Center** to run the Media Center Setup Wizard, which takes about 15 minutes
- Running the Windows Update tool to check for any updates to the operating system, software, and drivers
- Determining how well your devices operate when called upon to do so
- Using options in the Control Panel to configure and tune devices such as the audio and video components of your Windows Media Center PC
- Using the feature in Windows called Device Manager to detect problems such as nonfunctioning or missing or conflicting hardware
- Checking and, if necessary, updating drivers used to support your hardware
- Obtaining manufacturer information, as needed, to resolve various issues

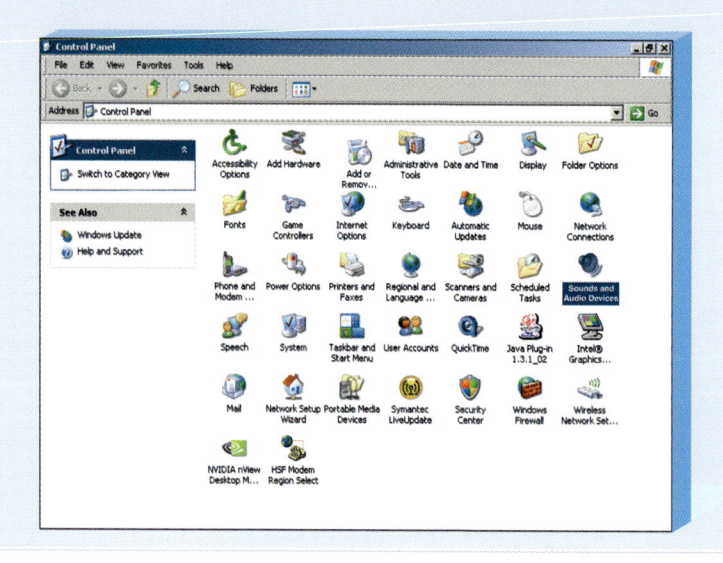

Think about What You Need to Test

Think about the hardware you have installed on your system. When you do, you may be able to think of some of the files you may like to use to test your hardware.

For example, you may want to have the following available:

- A CD of music to try out your sound card
- A DVD movie disc to play to test your movie-watching capabilities
- A graphics-intensive game that you can install to see how well the system performs while playing it

Test the Sound Playback

If you have a microphone set up, you also may want to load Sound Recorder and record a short voice file. When you play it back, you can see if the quality, the volume, and other issues are handled well by the system. To do so, follow these steps:

① Click **Start** ➔ **All Programs** ➔ **Accessories** ➔ **Sound Recorder**.

② When ready, click the red circle to begin recording; click the black square to stop.

③ Click the Play button to play back your recording.

You may want to jot down notes regarding the quality of playback and operation as you try running various files.

Run Windows Update

You should run Windows Update on a regular basis — say, once a week — to automatically update key files on your system, which include Windows patches and driver upgrades for your devices/hardware. Right after you first install a new version of Windows is also an excellent time to run this.

Run Windows Update

RUN WINDOWS UPDATE

1. Click **Start**.
2. Click **All Programs**.
3. Click **Windows Update**.

Your Web browser opens automatically and connects you to the Windows Update site.

The site scans your system over your Internet connection and determines what file and driver updates, if any, you need.

4. Follow the onscreen directions to download files and install them.

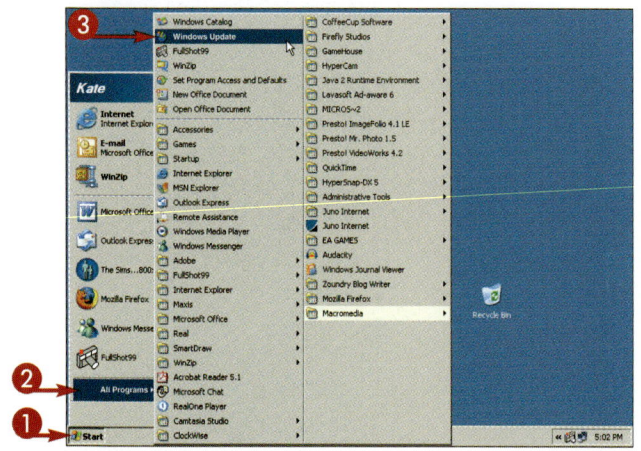

270

SET UP AUTOMATIC UPDATING

1 Click **Start**.

2 Click **Control Panel**.

The Control Panel appears.

3 Double-click **Automatic Updates**.

The Automatic Updates dialog box appears.

4 Click the selection that works best for you (○ changes to ●).

Note: The Automatic option is recommended.

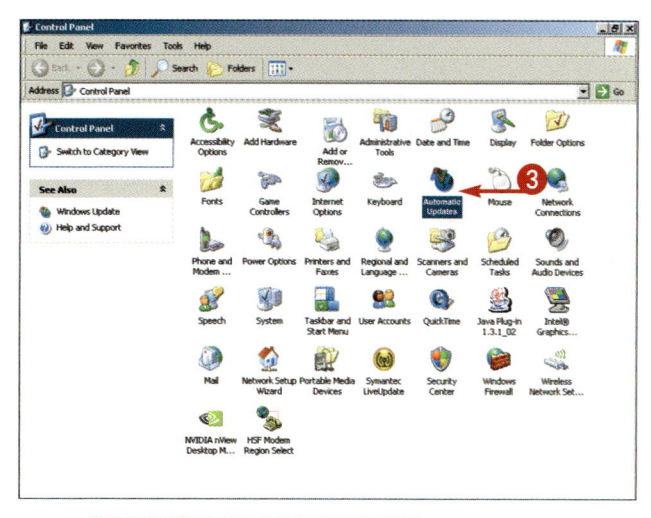

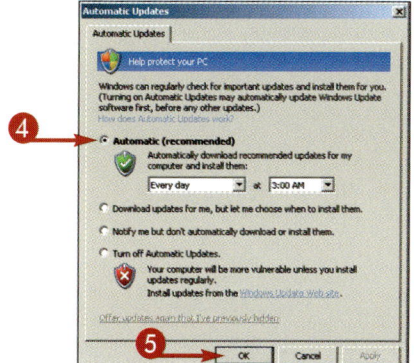

5 Click **OK**.

Can I set up Windows Update to be partially automatic and partially manual?

You can set up Windows Update to be as automatic and invisible or as manual and requiring your assistance as you want it to operate. You will see how you can modify Windows Update to run as you prefer.

Why should I not choose the Turn Off Automatic Updates option in the Automatic Updates dialog box?

This is not a wise choice because it could mean that you never get important updates, such as security fixes. If you go too long between updates, you could end up with a nonfunctioning operating system.

Try Out Your Components

Although you learned why you need to test devices and what you can use to do so, the only component you have tested so far is your ability to record sound files from your microphone; now you will do a test run for other capabilities.

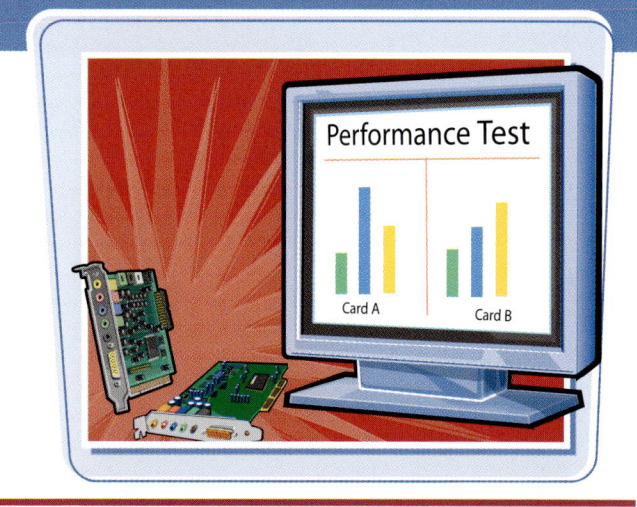

Try Out Your Components

TEST YOUR MUSIC-PLAYING CAPABILITY

① Insert a prerecorded music CD into your CD/DVD drive.

Note: Close the tray if it does not shut automatically.

Windows Media Player loads automatically and begins to play the CD.

② If Media Player does not load, click **Start → All Programs → Entertainment → Windows Media Player** and follow the onscreen tips to play a first song.

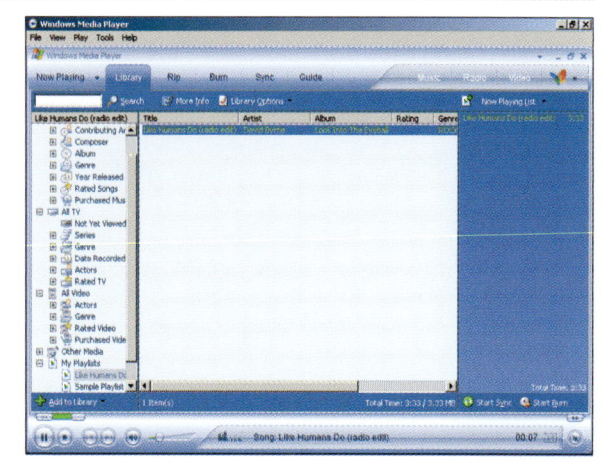

TEST YOUR MOVIE-PLAYING CAPABILITY

① Open the DVD-playing software that comes with your DVD drive.

② Insert a prerecorded DVD video into your DVD drive.

The movie player begins to play the movie.

TRY OUT OTHER COMPONENTS

① Record a CD or DVD by following the onscreen prompts in My Computer.

② Install a game from CD.

③ Play the game as you normally would.

Open Device Manager

After you put together a new PC and whenever you sense a problem with a device installed to your system, you should check Device Manager. This tool provides a roster of the major hardware components or support installed to your PC and allows you to enable or disable devices, as well as check and update device drivers.

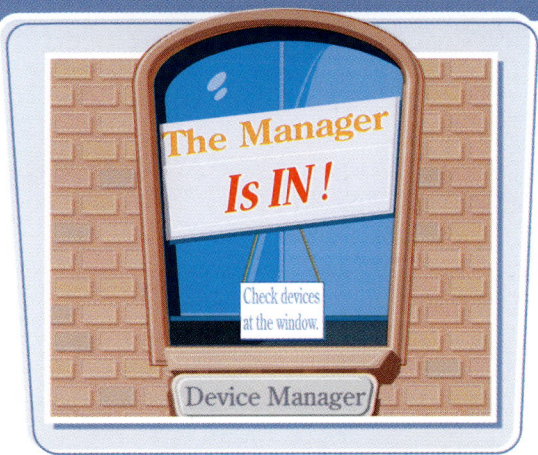

Open Device Manager

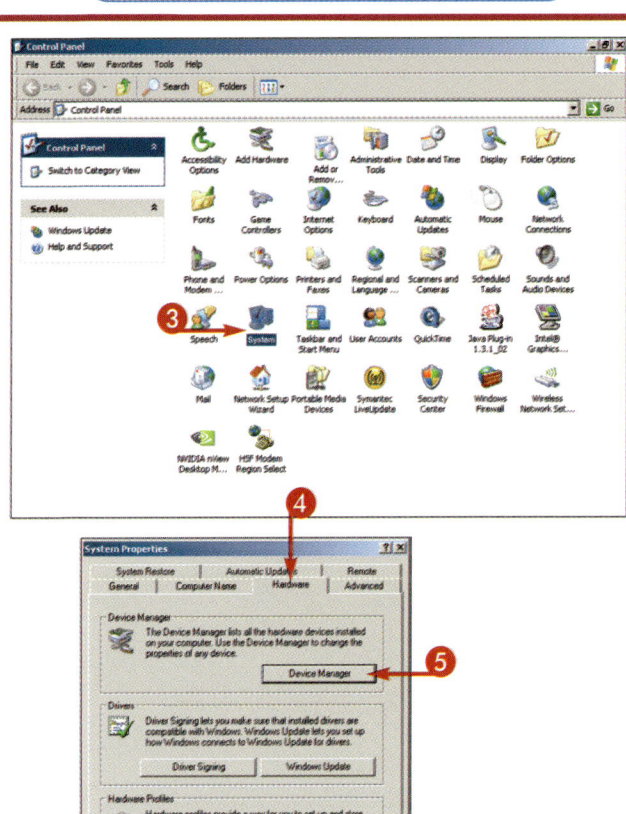

① Click **Start**.

② Click **Control Panel**.

The Control Panel appears.

③ Double-click **System**.

The System Properties dialog box appears.

④ Click the **Hardware** tab.

⑤ Click **Device Manager**.

Device Manager opens.

Chapter 25: Testing, Tweaking, and Tuning Your PC

273

Consult and Use Device Manager

To understand better what Device Manager reports to you, you first need to identify what kind of information it offers. So you will start by exploring Device Manager and its many listings and details.

Consult and Use Device Manager

CHECK THE DEVICE LIST

① Open Device Manager.

Note: See the previous section, "Open Device Manager."

② Note that each major component or component category for your PC hardware is listed.

③ Click **+** next to a category to expand it; to collapse it again later, click **−**.

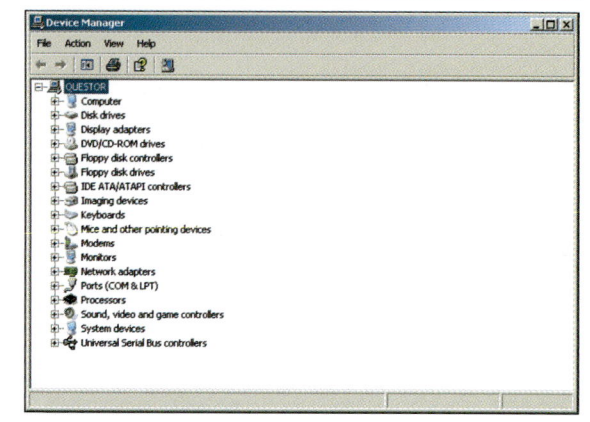

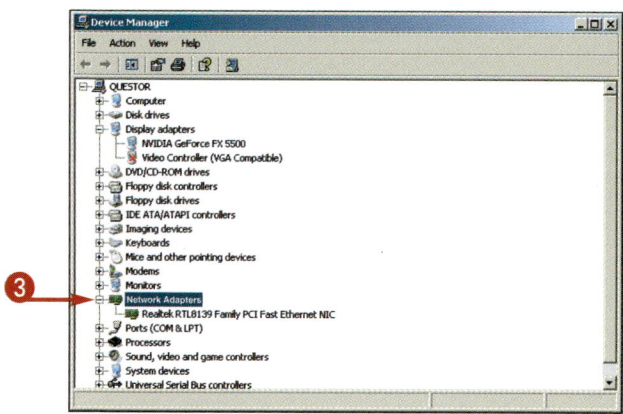

REVIEW PROPERTIES FOR AN INDIVIDUAL DEVICE

① Right-click the chosen device from the expanded category list.

② Click **Properties**.

The Properties dialog box for the chosen device appears.

③ Check out the information on the General tab.

④ Click the other tabs to display specifics about other properties, such as Resources for the PC hardware resources used for this device and Driver to identify your driver version and the date of the last update.

Note: *Be smart and check out the Properties listing for all the devices listed under every category in Device Manager.*

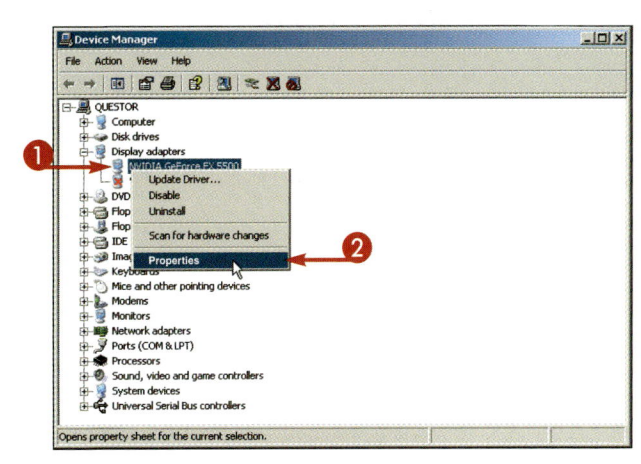

I changed a few settings in Device Manager, and now my system is having a few problems. What should I do?

Making changes you are not certain about in Device Manager may cause problems. To be able to revert back to a cleaner system if you experience a problem *after* making changes, see "Before and After You Resolve Special Problems" in Chapter 26. This is smart advice to follow before you make any of the tweaks and modifications throughout this chapter and the next, and then make a fresh copy after you succeed in fixing the problem.

Chapter 25: Testing, Tweaking, and Tuning Your PC

continued

275

Consult and Use Device Manager *(continued)*

Whenever you encounter a problem with the operation of a piece of hardware or do not know exactly what is wrong with the system, come back to Device Manager and review the information you have already seen.

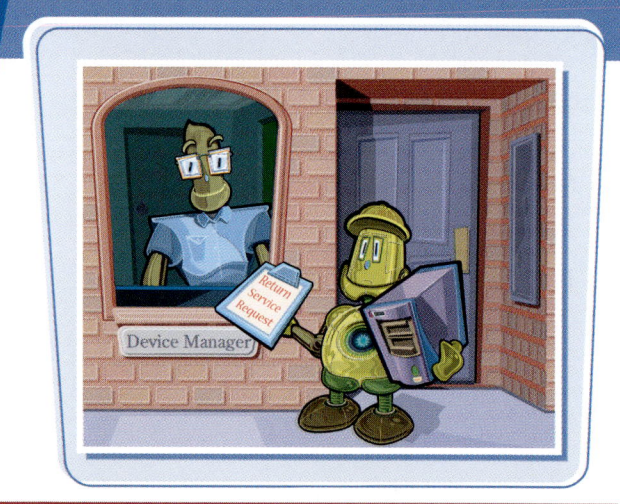

Consult and Use Device Manager *(continued)*

IDENTIFY PROBLEMS IN DEVICE MANAGER

Three features in Device Manager, besides the driver update wizard, help you identify and potentially resolve trouble that you have with devices:

- Trouble indicators on device entries such as a red X for a disabled device and a yellow exclamation point for a device that may not have the correct driver or shares some hardware resource such as memory or a connection with another device that is causing difficulty.

  The **Troubleshoot** button on the General tab in Device Manager properties, which lets you run a special problem-solving help session to see if it can resolve the issue.

  The **Device Status** area of the General tab of the Device Manager properties for a device.

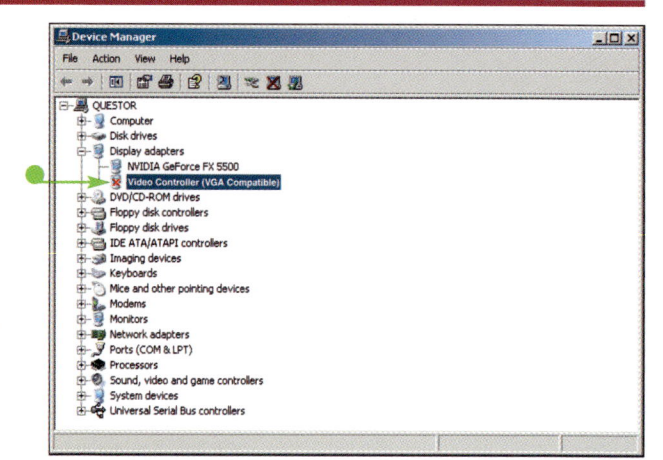

USE THE TROUBLESHOOTER

1. Open Device Manager and locate the entry for the device that you want to test.

2. Right-click the device and select **Properties**.

   The Properties dialog box appears.

3. On the General tab, click **Troubleshoot**.

   The Help and Support Center opens, showing the appropriate troubleshooter for the selected device.

4. Click the closest match to your issue (○ changes to ●).

5. Click **Next**.

6. Follow the onscreen directions and recommendations.

7. When done, close the Help and Support Center.

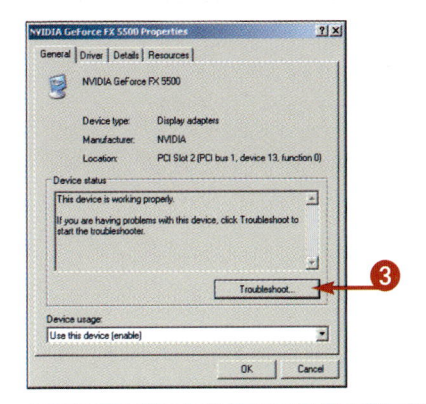

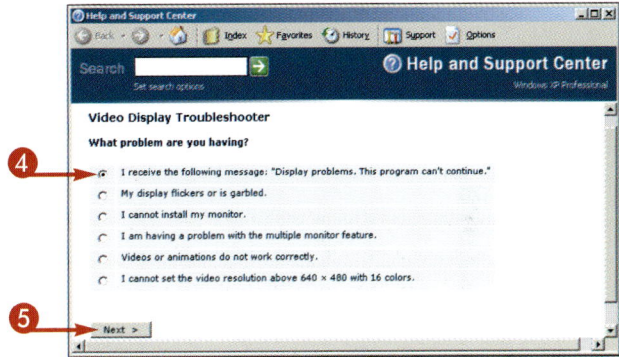

Q&A

What are some ways to resolve device issues?

It could be that a driver update will take care of the identified bit of trouble; you learn how to update drivers on your own — independent of Windows Update — later in this chapter, in the section "Update Drivers in the Device Manager." You may need to remove the device driver as part of a workaround.

What does the Troubleshoot button do?

The Troubleshooting Wizard steps you through questions and concepts that may help you identify your problem or lead you in the direction of assistance. You do not have to wait until a problem is reported through Device Manager to use it.

continued

277

Consult and Use Device Manager *(continued)*

You have the ability to try to enable a disabled device — one showing a red X — and temporarily disable a device that is showing a yellow exclamation point conflict or is otherwise behaving badly.

Consult and Use Device Manager *(continued)*

ENABLE A DEVICE

1. Open Device Manager and locate the entry for the device.

2. Right-click the device and select **Properties**.

   The Properties dialog box appears.

   - If the device is disabled, the Troubleshoot button usually found here is replaced with an Enable Device button.

3. Click **Enable Device**.

   The Enabling a Device page of the Troubleshooting Wizard appears.

4. Click **Next**.

5. When prompted to restart the system, click **Restart**.

6. Check Device Manager again after the restart to see if the problem appears resolved and the device is working.

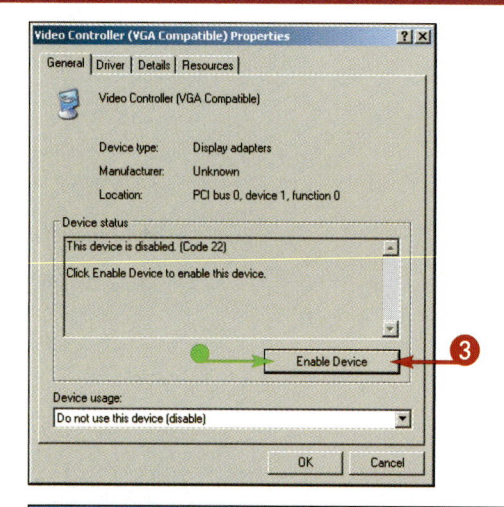

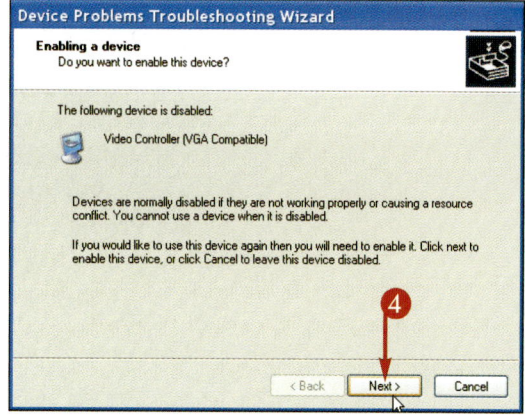

278

DISABLE A DEVICE

1. Open Device Manager and locate the entry for the device that you want to disable.

2. Right-click the device and select **Properties**.

   The Properties dialog box appears.

3. Click ⌄ and select **Do Not Use This Device (Disable)**.

4. Click **OK**.

   The System Settings Change dialog box opens.

5. Click **Yes** to restart the system.

● You can click **No** to restart later.

6. After the system restarts, reopen Device Manager.

   The device will now have a red *X* next to its entry, indicating that it is disabled.

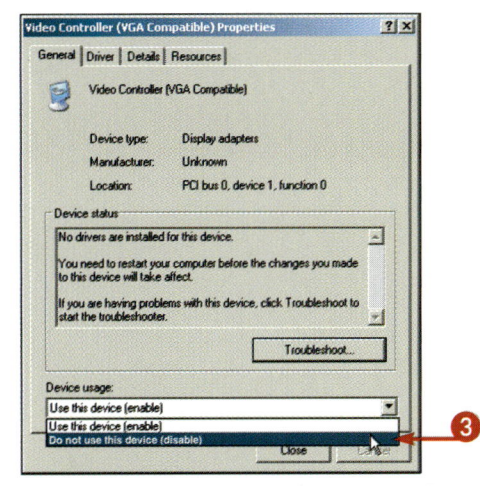

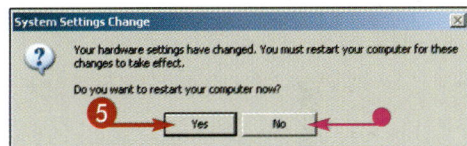

Q&A

Is my new DVD drive dead? I see it in Control Panel, but if I insert a blank DVD-R or DVD-RW disc and try to record files to it, I get an error message such as "inaccessible function."

Do not worry; your drive is not dead. Instead, try first clicking **Start → My Computer**. Locate your DVD drive, right-click it, and click **Properties**. Click to check **Enable Recording**. This enables you to write to your drive. Some setups come with this already enabled; others do not.

If I decide to install a separate network card to the Biostar motherboard and use that instead for networking, how do I stop the network function on the motherboard itself?

Disable the onboard network feature in Device Manager. Now, you will continue to see this option listed in Device Manager, but with a red *X*. That is normal, and no cause for concern. Anytime you disable an onboard chipset such as for the network or video or sound, you need to disable it in Device Manager and live with the red *X* on the device listing.

continued

279

Consult and Use Device Manager *(continued)*

A fairly simple way to see if you can get past a problem in Device Manager is to remove its entry. This does not, of course, physically remove the device, just its driver, at least until you restart the system.

After Windows restarts, it redetects and then reinstalls support for the device fresh; this can cure corrupted files related to the device and/or revert you back to the original, working configuration of the device before you tweaked something.

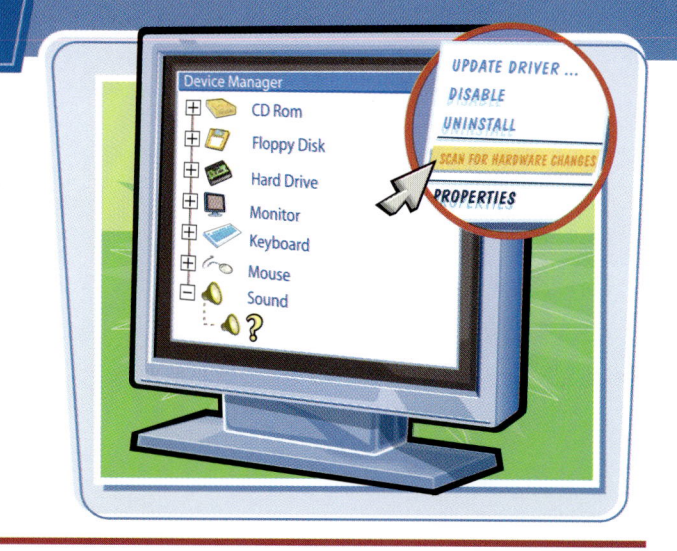

Consult and Use Device Manager *(continued)*

REMOVE AN ENTRY IN DEVICE MANAGER

1 Right-click the entry for the hardware or its support that you want to remove from Device Manager.

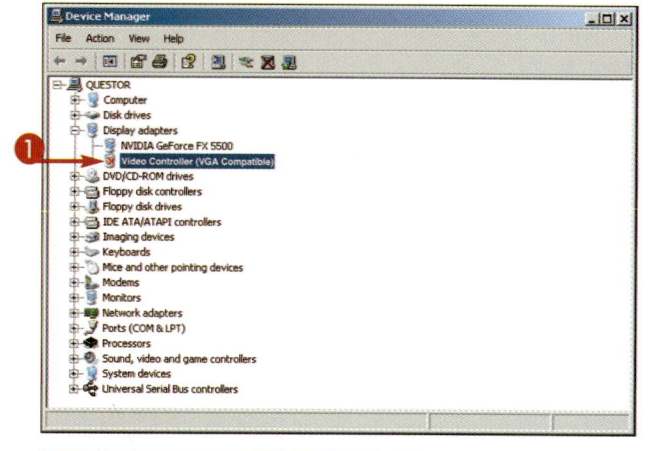

2 Click **Uninstall**.

After Windows removes the device entry, it may prompt you to restart the PC.

3 Click **Yes** or **OK**.

After Windows restarts, if you have not physically removed the device, Windows runs the hardware wizard to reload support for the device.

4 Recheck Device Manager to see that it shows the proper results.

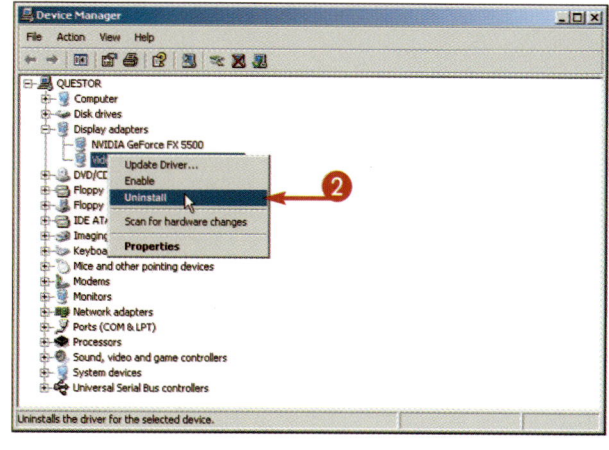

280

SCAN FOR HARDWARE CHANGES

① In Device Manager, right-click the device that you tweaked.

② Click **Scan for Hardware Changes**.

The scan runs, and the Device Manager list is refreshed.

③ Check for changes in the listings.

Note: If you have trouble getting a new device detected and installed to the system, you can run the Add Hardware Wizard from the Control Panel. See the section "Force Windows to Check for New Hardware."

SCAN FOR HARDWARE CHANGES IF YOU ARE NOT CERTAIN WHICH DEVICE TO CHOOSE

① Right-click **Computer** (or the computer name), listed at the top of the Device Manager entries.

② Click **Scan for Hardware Changes**.

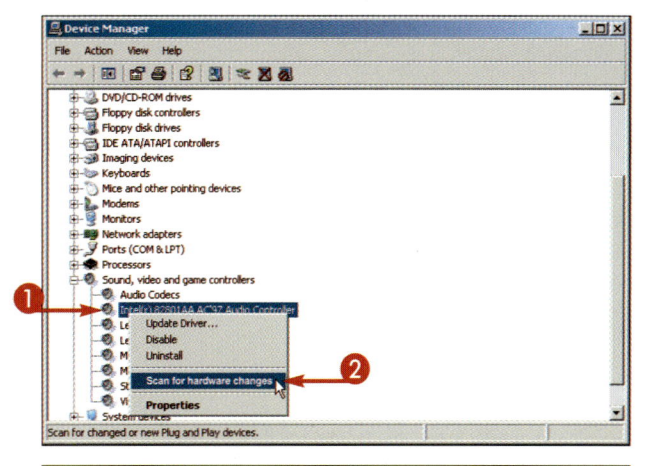

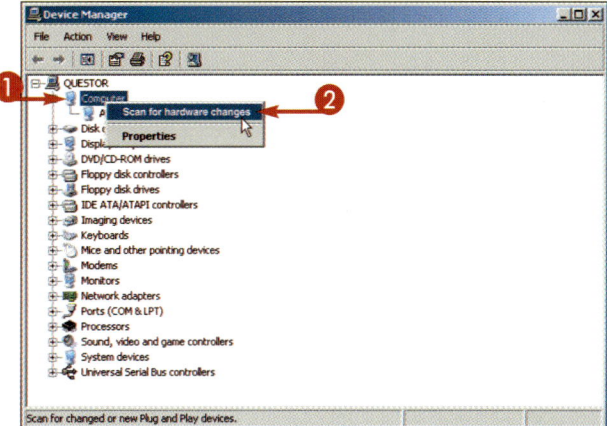

When else would I want to remove an entry in Device Manager?

If you want to physically remove a hardware component or just the support for it, such as a motherboard-integrated sound or network card, you should remove its entry in Device Manager as shown here first. After the hardware — such as an installed adapter because you cannot remove an integrated component — is actually removed, Windows will not redetect it and reload a driver for it.

When should I scan for hardware changes?

Tell Device Manager to scan for hardware changes to your system whenever you have modified your hardware settings through special configuration software, reset switches or jumpers on the device itself, or otherwise changed the physical setup.

Update Drivers in Device Manager

Why do you need to check for and update the drivers for your various hardware devices such as your network card and your sound card support? Just look at this list of some of the most pressing reasons.

Reasons to Update Your Drivers

You should update your drivers whenever you do the following:

- Upgrade a major application such as your Microsoft Office version, your Web browser, or comprehensive graphic and video-editing software. For example, your graphics card may begin to produce strange onscreen results without a driver update after other type of upgrade is performed.

- Notice that a device that formerly worked fine and shows no obvious damage suddenly begins to misbehave. This could be a sign of a corrupted existing driver that may be resolved through a driver update.

Reasons to Update Your Drivers (continued)

- Install the latest and greatest video game; drivers are often updated to support a new game better than the existing driver.
- Add new software that seems to cause some system instability.
- See that the PC is crashing, hanging frequently, or produces more error messages than usual, yet you cannot see anything obvious that is wrong.
- Perform routine maintenance on your system or go awhile since your last Windows Update session.

If You Are Concerned about a New Driver

If you are concerned about the effects a new driver may have, know that you can use the rollback feature, discussed later in this section, to revert back to your previous driver. You can also create a backup or copy of your system that you can fall back on as needed, as outlined in Chapter 26.

Update Drivers in Device Manager *(continued)*

You can check for driver updates several different ways: through the Windows Update tool discussed earlier, by visiting the Web sites of individual manufacturers and downloading and installing the drivers (see "Fine-Tune Your PC"), or through Device Manager, as detailed here.

Unfortunately, you may occasionally discover that a driver update can create more problems than it resolves. If you experience this after an update, you can roll back to the previous driver, which will restore your system to its previous state.

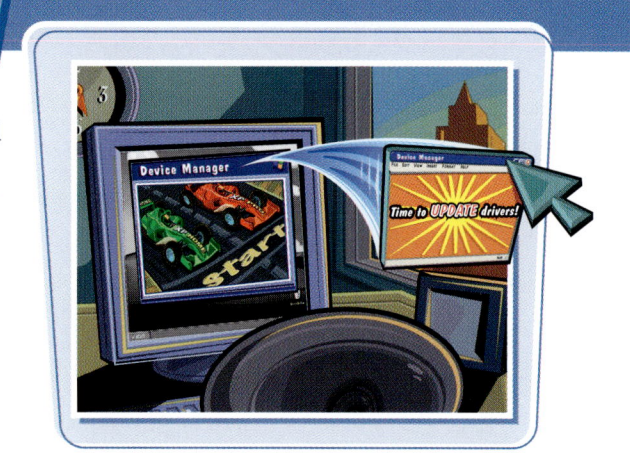

Update Drivers in Device Manager *(continued)*

CHECK FOR AND UPDATE DRIVERS

1. If your Internet connection is currently offline, connect again.

2. In Device Manager, right-click the device that you want to check and update.

3. Click **Update Driver**.

   The Hardware Update Wizard appears.

4. Click the option that best fits (○ changes to ⦿).

5. Click **Next**.

6. On the next page, leave the default choice, Install the Software Automatically, selected.

7. Click **Next**.

8. If a new driver is located, follow the onscreen instructions to download and install it.

Note: The Driver tab, available from the Properties window on many Device Manager entries, also usually contains a button or option for searching for a driver update.

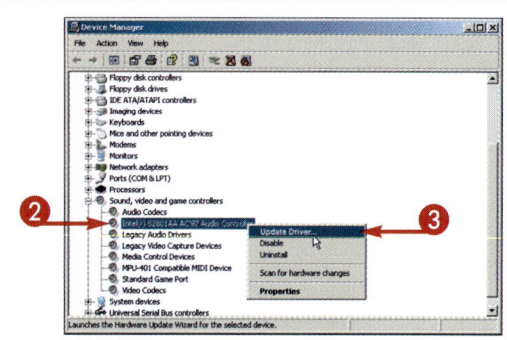

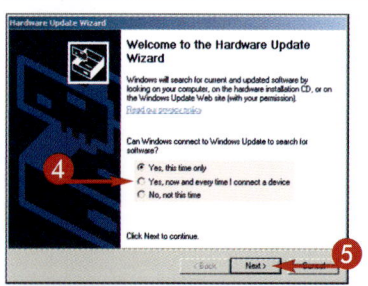

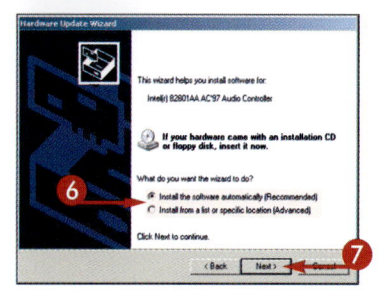

284

ROLL BACK TO A PREVIOUS DRIVER VERSION

① In Device Manager, right-click the device whose driver you previously updated.

② Click **Properties**.

③ In the Properties dialog box, click the **Driver** tab.

④ Click the **Driver Details** button.

The Driver File Details dialog box appears.

⑤ Review information about the driver update.

⑥ Click **OK**.

⑦ Back in the Properties dialog box, click **Roll Back Driver**.

If Windows recognizes a previous driver version, it reports this.

⑧ Follow the onscreen directions to complete the rollback.

If a rollback is performed, Windows will tell you when the operation is successfully completed.

If Windows finds no previous driver, it will ask if you want to load the appropriate Troubleshooting Wizard.

● Click **Yes** or **No** as you prefer.

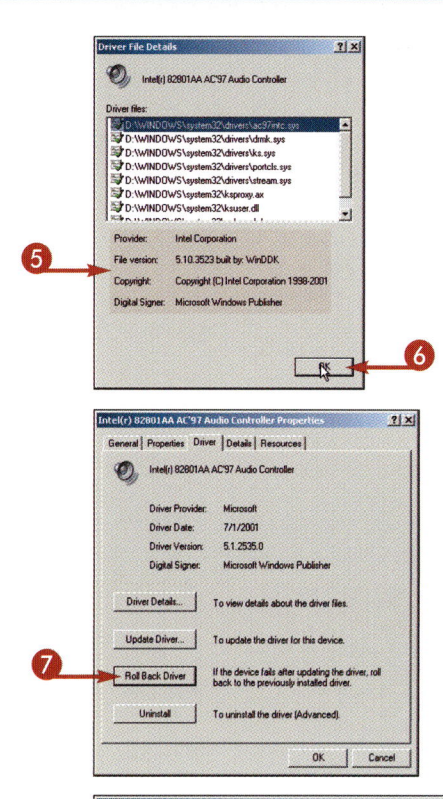

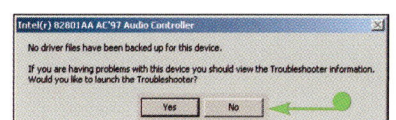

Force Windows to Check for New Hardware

If you install new hardware — or a replacement for existing equipment — you should see Windows detect this on the first restart after the installation. However, if Windows fails to detect the hardware or run the install wizard, you can force Windows to check this manually using an option in Control Panel.

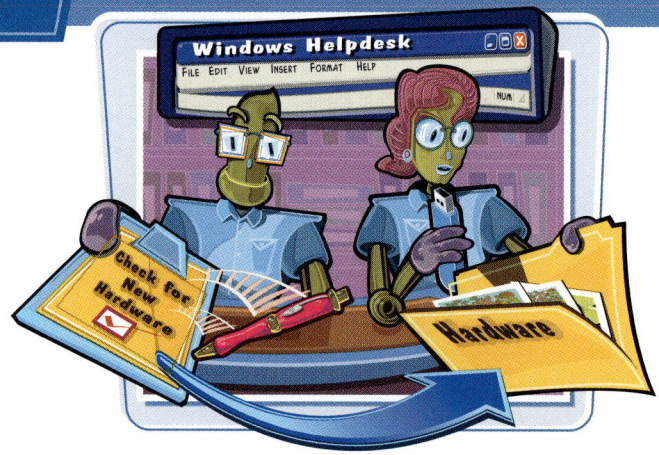

Force Windows to Check for New Hardware

① Click **Start**.

② Click **Control Panel**.

The Control Panel appears.

③ Double-click **Add Hardware**.

④ If you have an installation disc that came with your new device, place it in your CD/DVD drive.

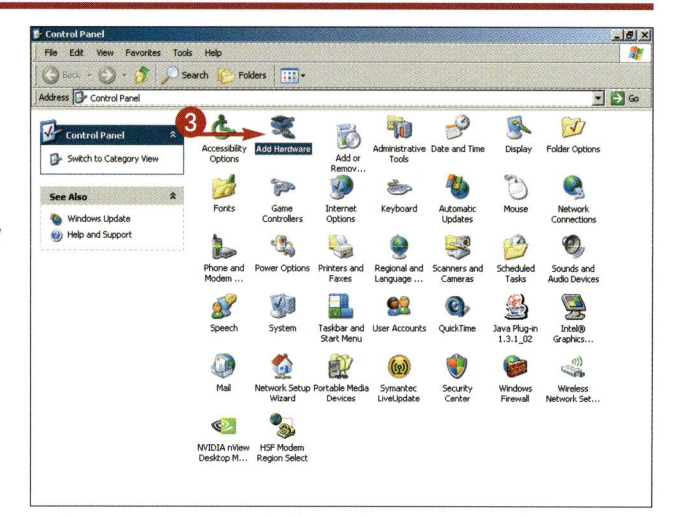

The Add New Hardware Wizard appears.

⑤ Click **Next**.

Windows performs a scan looking for any hardware that it has not previously seen and installed.

Windows tells you that it has found new hardware.

⑥ If Windows displays the device, select it from the list.

⑦ Click **Next**.

⑧ Follow the onscreen prompts to install the driver for the new device.

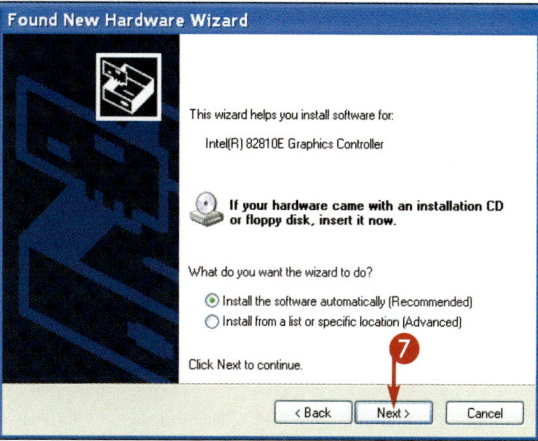

Q&A

The Add New Hardware Wizard did not find my new piece of hardware. What should I do?

If Windows finds nothing, you may want to shut down the PC, remove power, and, for internal devices, ground yourself, open the cover, and check the installation. Also verify that any cables or connections are seated and that, if the device has a power switch, it is turned on.

Every time I restart my PC, the Hardware Wizard tells me that it has just found the same device — my monitor — and goes through the installation again. What can I do to stop this?

Run Windows Update or visit the Web site of the manufacturer to see if there is a device driver update that you can download and install. If this does not correct the problem, contact the technical support line or Web site for the manufacturer to ask for help.

Fine-Tune Your PC

Are you now generally pleased with your Windows Media Center PC and wonder what else you can do to optimize your experience? Here are some tips and tricks to boost speed, tweak the overall operation of your system, customize your configuration, and fine-tune for the best results.

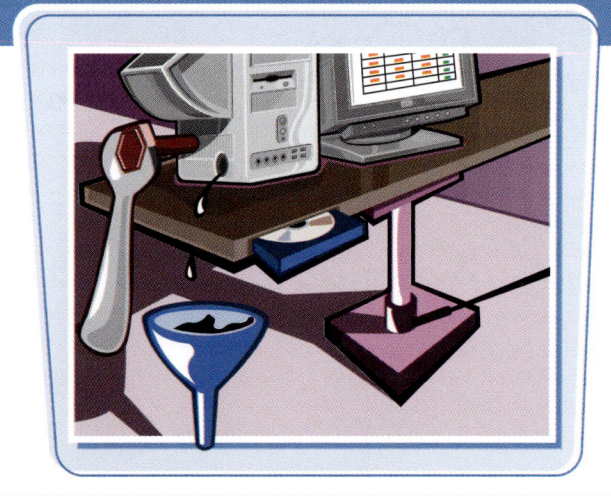

Fine-Tune Your PC

In this section, the emphasis will be on tweaking settings to achieve specific results, such as how to make your display the best it can be and what you can do to customize your speaker setup and sound playback. These are finer points of the detail work to tune the PC the way that you want it to run.

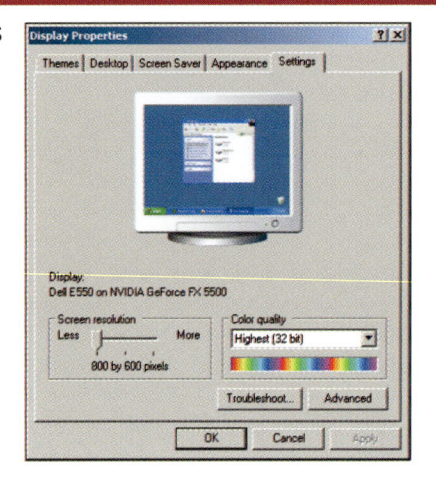

Yet you can find and try other suggestions for getting every bit of performance that you can out of your system. For example, you may be able to locate optimal settings for your graphics card and sound card that you want to test on your setup.

REFER TO MANUFACTURER WEB SITES

To find recommendations for optimized settings, troubleshooting information for minor to major performance issues, and other helpful information, visit the official Web sites of the manufacturers of your various PC components.

These sites often include message boards to post and answer questions or provide specific details; downloads of updated drivers, special help software, and testing utilities; and technical papers that cover all aspects of a particular product.

You can also find installation and removal instructions, frequently asked questions (FAQs) and their answers, and live or regularly scheduled help chats or online discussions.

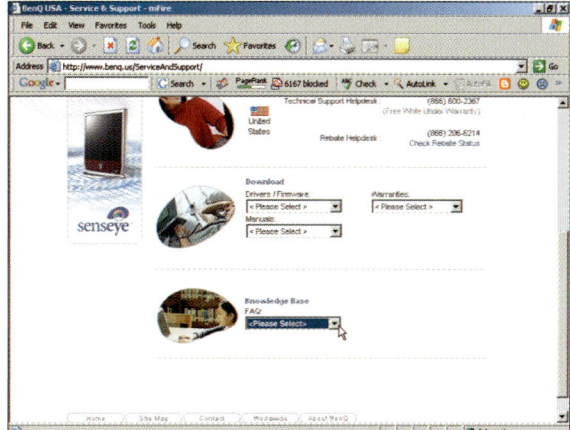

Q&A

What should I do with the tweaks I find at the manufacturer's Web site?

Jot down notes of the tips and tricks that you read at the site and then look through them again later before you rush into tweaking. Acting too quickly can lead to mistakes.

I have several customized parts and tweaks to my setup that I want to perform. How should I go about this?

First, do a full system backup or create a restore point using System Restore in Windows. Then do just one upgrade or tweak at a time and wait for a bit to assess your system behavior after you make this change. If all seems well, you can move onto the second tweak, follow the same cautionary procedure, and so on.

continued

Fine-Tune Your PC *(continued)*

Do you want to change your screen resolution, to make it larger or smaller? or increase the number of colors that are supported? or turn on or off or modify your screen saver? All of these fit under the category of adjusting your display.

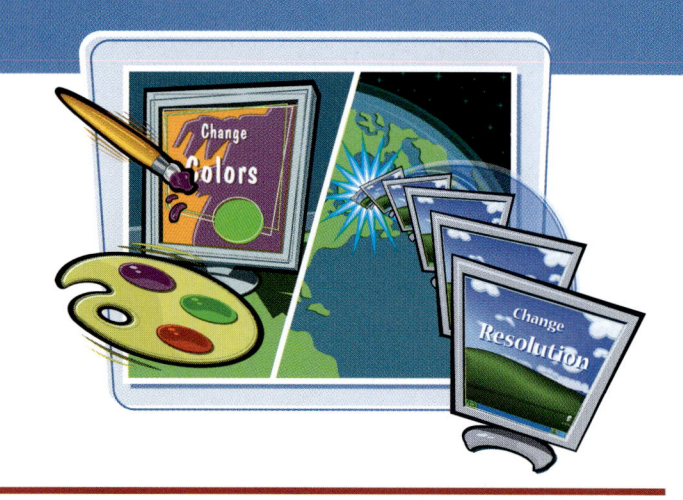

Fine-Tune Your PC *(continued)*

VIEW DISPLAY OPTIONS

1. In the Control Panel, double-click **Display**.

   The Display Properties dialog box appears.

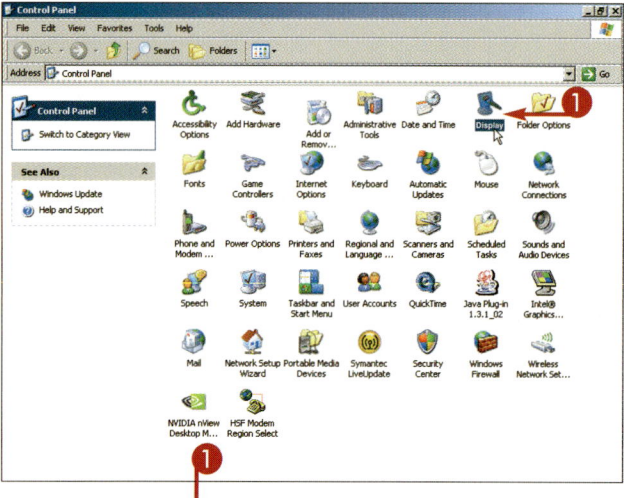

TURN ON THE SCREEN SAVER

1. In the Display Properties dialog box, click the **Screen Saver** tab.

2. Click and choose the screen saver that you want.

3. Click the Wait to specify how many minutes to delay before the screen saver pops up.

TURN OFF THE SCREEN SAVER

4. Click and select **None**.

CHANGE THE SCREEN SAVER

5. Perform step **2**, choosing a different screen saver.

6. Click **OK**.

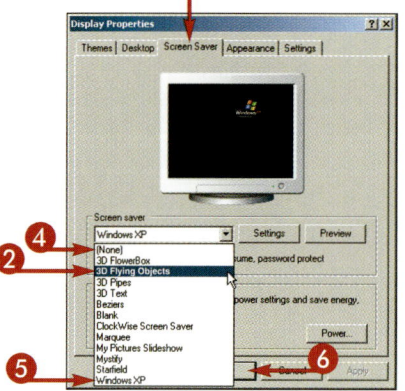

CHANGE THE SCREEN RESOLUTION

1. In the Display Properties dialog box, click the **Settings** tab.
2. Click and drag the slider to the left to decrease the resolution or to the right to increase the resolution.
3. Click **OK**.

   The resolution changes, and an onscreen warning appears, giving you the option to reverse this change as needed.
4. Click **No** to keep the change as is.

ADJUST THE COLOR SETTINGS

1. In the Display Properties dialog box, click the **Settings** tab.
2. Click the Color Quality ⌄ and select **Highest** for best results or **Medium**.
3. Click **OK**.

   Your color settings are changed as you have specified.

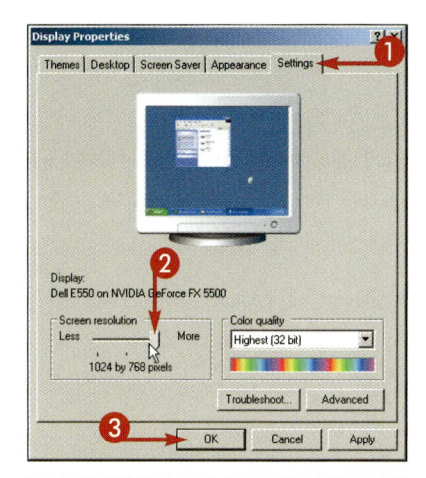

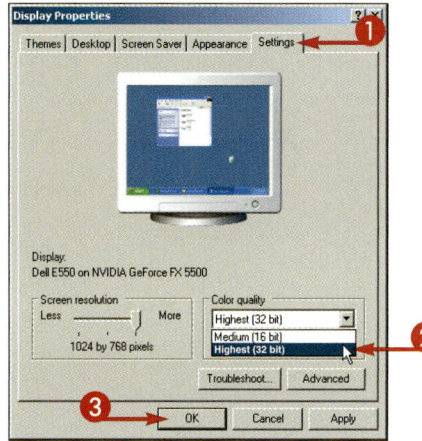

Q&A

Are there any other display tools that I can use?

Depending on the graphics card you selected, you may have an additional set of tools for adjusting the video setup. Check your system tray for a button that has the same name as your graphics card. Double-click that button to open the utility.

What is the difference between 32-bit, or highest, and 16-bit, or medium, color quality? Which should I set?

On some systems, you may see three settings: Highest, High, and Medium. These different color qualities refer specifically to how many colors your display can show. The highest setting, 32-bit, can theoretically show up to four billion shades; 24-bit, or high, color quality shows up to 16 million different hues; and the 16-bit or medium setting shows far fewer, just over 65,000, colors. For a Media Center system, you want this set as high as possible. To view your settings, right-click your desktop, click **Properties**, click the **Settings** tab, and look under Color Quality.

Chapter 25: Testing, Tweaking, and Tuning Your PC

continued

291

Fine-Tune Your PC *(continued)*

If you are not thrilled with the video output on your monitor after your Windows Media Center PC is fully assembled, one property that you can try to tweak is the refresh rate of the monitor.

The refresh rate specifies at what speed — measured in Hertz (Hz) — the monitor will check and redraw information provided by the graphics card to the screen. If you set the refresh rate too high, you can actually make overall performance worse.

Fine-Tune Your PC *(continued)*

ADJUST THE MONITOR REFRESH RATE

1. In the Control Panel, double-click **Display**.

    The Display Properties dialog box appears.

2. Click the **Settings** tab.

3. Click **Advanced**.

    The Properties dialog box for your monitor and graphics card appears.

4. Click the **Monitor** tab.

5. If checked, click to uncheck **Hide Modes That This Computer Cannot Display**.

    Note This is a temporary measure.

6. Click ⌄ and select a refresh rate that is no more than 10% faster or slower than the current rate.

    Note: If you are using an LCD monitor, you adjust the response rate.

7. Click **OK**.

8. Monitor the display and overall system performance since the change in refresh rate.

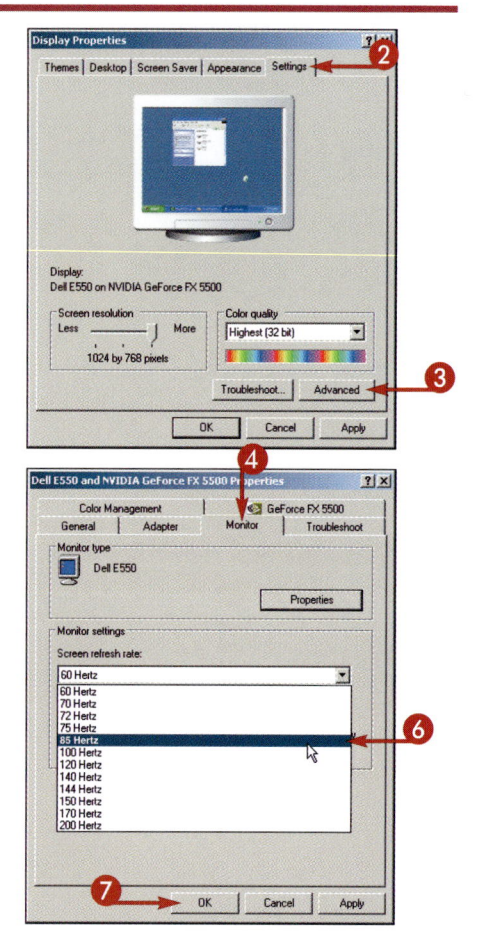

TWEAK YOUR AUDIO PLAYBACK

You can adjust the quality, balance, or the total volume of the audio output of a PC a few different ways.

- You can double-click the Volume icon in the system tray to open the volume controls, with which you can adjust the volume levels for speakers and the CD/DVD drive.

Note: Just as the graphics board adds a control to adjust video in the system tray, your sound card may add one to tweak audio quality, volume, and balance.

Your speakers, headphones, microphone, and other sound-related devices may also have volume and balance controls.

Note: You can also adjust audio settings using the Sounds and Audio Devices Properties dialog box, which is accessible from the Control Panel.

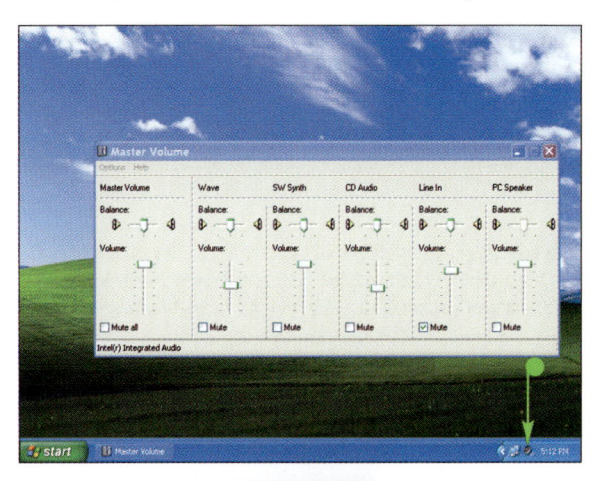

Q&A

Is there another way that I can check problems with my monitor?

You can use the Troubleshooting Wizard to check the monitor, much as you did earlier using Device Manager, by clicking **Troubleshoot** on the Settings tab of the Display Properties dialog box.

I opened the volume controls, but it did not help with my volume problem. What do you suggest I try?

When you are working through an issue with audio volume, you may want to check all of the control tools that I discuss here, including the normal volume controls, the sound card's volume controls, any controls on the hardware itself, and the Sounds and Audio Devices Properties dialog box.

continued

293

Fine-Tune Your PC *(continued)*

Virtually all of your audio hardware can be custom set using the Sounds and Audio Devices Properties dialog box, accessible from the Control Panel. This includes the setup of your speakers.

Fine-Tune Your PC *(continued)*

SET UP SPEAKERS USING THE CONTROL PANEL

1 In the Control Panel, double-click **Sounds and Audio Devices**.

The Sounds and Audio Devices Properties dialog box appears, with the Volume tab showing.

2 Under Speaker Settings, click **Advanced**.

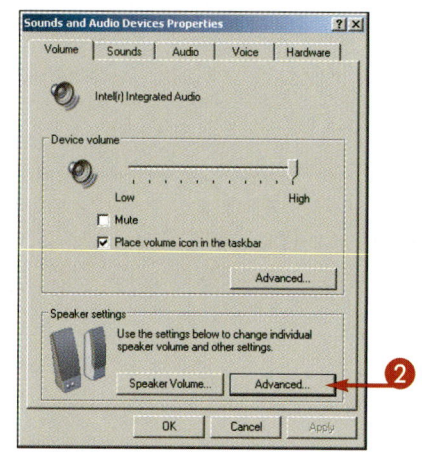

The Advanced Audio Properties dialog box appears, with the Speakers tab showing.

3 Click and select the closest match to your speaker setup, such as **5.1 Surround Sound Speakers**.

4 Click **OK**.

5 Click **OK** back in the Sounds and Audio Devices Properties dialog box.

Note: Play a sound file to check your new speaker volume and balance settings.

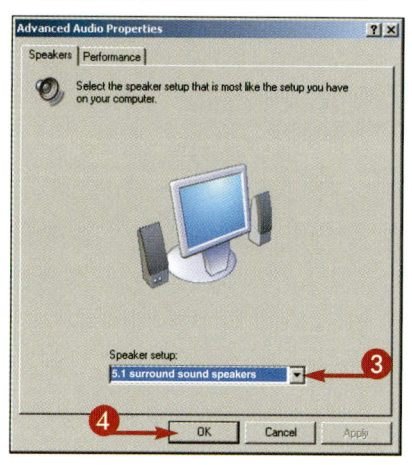

294

Chapter 25: Testing, Tweaking, and Tuning Your PC

VERIFY YOUR PRINTER USING THE CONTROL PANEL

1. In the Control Panel, double-click **Printers and Faxes**.

   The Printers and Faxes window appears.

2. Make sure that the printer is properly listed.

3. Right-click the printer icon.

4. Click **Properties**.

5. Verify that the correct device is in place.

OPTIMIZE POWER SETTINGS USING THE CONTROL PANEL

1. In the Control Panel, double-click **Power Options**.

   The Power Options Properties dialog box appears.

   To save power, you can have your monitor, hard disk, and other devices shut off or go into very low power mode during prolonged times of inactivity.

2. Click ⌄s and select the choices that you want.

3. Click **OK**.

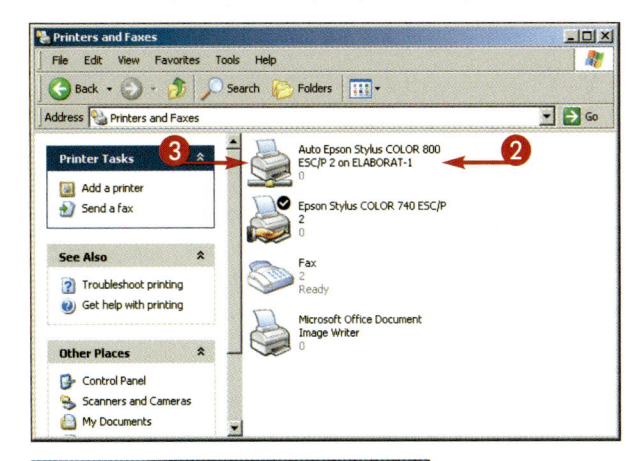

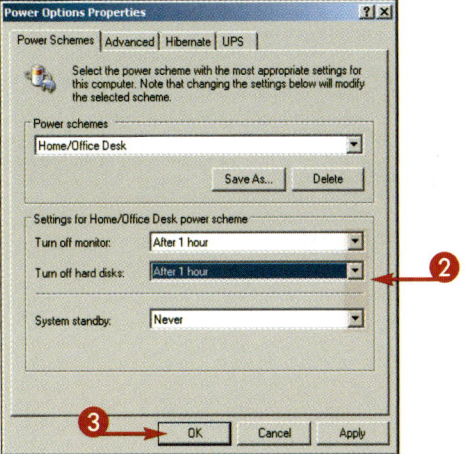

Are there power options for an uninterruptible power supply?

Yes, if you add a UPS to your Media Center PC, you can select the **UPS** tab in the Power Options Properties dialog box to view and modify the UPS's usage settings.

I do not want to turn my PC off and on all the time, but I hate wasting a lot of electricity by letting it run for hours with no one using it. What can I do to conserve power?

Explore the options available in Control Panel when you double-click **Power Options**. If the Always On setting is selected on the Power Schemes tab, you are consuming more power than you need to use. Choose **Home/Office Desk** instead and then set options for how many minutes or hours to wait before Windows begins putting devices such as your monitor and hard disk into low power mode.

Final Troubleshooting

If you have anything on your system that continues to behave badly, you want to try to resolve it at this time, so you can finish up your assembly and enjoy your new PC.

Write Down the Problems

If you have not done so already, write down the problems that you are experiencing — such as error messages, improper behavior, and any onscreen warnings that appear when you restart the system. Documenting this comes in handy so that you forget nothing if you need to contact someone for assistance or go searching through an online help resource for technical support.

A Systematic Approach

With your troubleshooting, try to be as systematic and logical as possible. This approach can help almost as much as technical acumen because you are less likely to panic and break something or make changes thoughtlessly without being able to remember what you have done.

Troubleshooting Tips

As you work through the issues and try suggestions you read or get imparted to you, keep these troubleshooting tips in mind:

- Assume nothing. When you assume, you are much less apt to check on the facts of a detail and depend on your memory, which may be faulty.
- Try just one thing at a time; if that change does not resolve the situation, set it back as it was before you started and then try something else.
- When you find several different suggestions for things to change or try, organize them into a list from the easiest and least invasive to the hardest and most invasive. Then perform these suggestions in that order, from easiest to hardest.
- If you become frustrated or panicky, step away and relax before you tackle the work again.
- Make a backup, restore point, or drive image before you get too deeply into the work. See the section "Before and After You Resolve Special Problems" for details.
- Be careful that you do not proceed too far along a point where you do not know what you are doing; this could result in creating new problems rather than fixing the current one.
- When you find assistance online, make a print copy of the suggestion to refer back to later.
- Also when you find assistance online, read all the information; do not jump, skim, and ignore big chunks of the text because all the steps or details may be important.

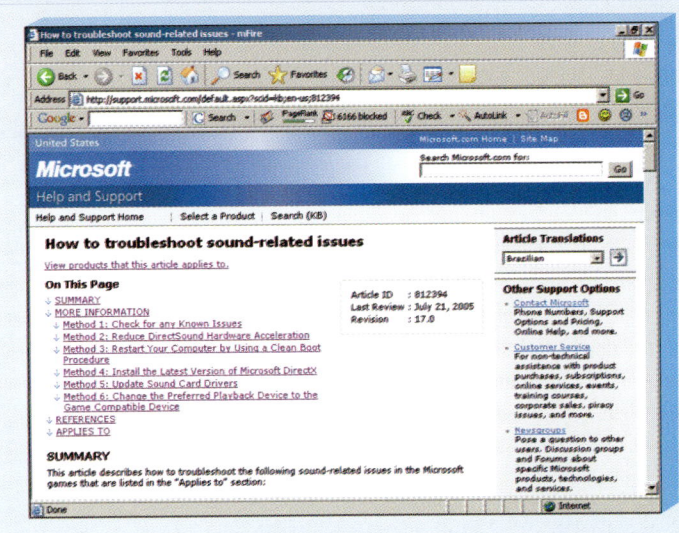

297

Getting Help

When you need help in troubleshooting remaining pesky issues with your newly built Media Center PC, it helps to know where you can find assistance and information.

You also should know exactly who would be the best to contact for help: whether it is your vendor CPU Solutions, the individual hardware manufacturers, or Microsoft as the creator of Windows Media Center. This section tries to explain where to go for what type of assistance.

Check Your Documentation

One place to start is to review all the information that came packaged with your hardware, such as documentation and manuals. These often provide a troubleshooting section that helps with common problems in installing and getting a product to work; warranties, which spell out what coverage you have as the consumer and exactly what parts or services are offered, and any material from CPU Solutions that details whom to contact if you have a problem with the components you purchased from them.

Call CPU Solutions

Call your vendor — CPU Solutions or another hardware retailer where you bought the components — when there is any question of damage or the device seems dead through no fault of your own. The vendor should replace the part as soon as possible but will likely ask you to return the problem product first.

Contact Your Hardware Vendor

The actual manufacturer of a piece of hardware is the best resource when, after following the directions to the letter, you cannot get the device to respond or operate as it should. A customer service or technical support number should be available in the documentation that came with your component. First, however, you should go to the company Web site to see if you can locate assistance online in its technical support area.

Check the Microsoft Resources

When you believe the problem lies with the operating system itself or how Windows relates to a hardware item that is working but not quite the way it should, Microsoft is your best contact for assistance. However, Microsoft does not support Media Center directly; instead, it has online help sites that may help you find answers and tips for resolving or working around your issue.

Find Assistance with Microsoft Windows XP Media Center Edition

Although Microsoft develops and produces Windows Media Center, if you call Microsoft for issues that arise with your operating system, you may be referred back to your PC hardware manufacturer instead.

This is because, unlike other versions of Windows that are available in wide general release, Windows Media Center is made available only with new, preassembled PCs or the hardware used to assembly your own PC, as you did here. You cannot simply call the manufacturer who set up the system because you did it yourself.

What may be far more useful for you is the Microsoft Windows Media Center information page available at www.microsoft.com/windowsxp/mediacenter/. You also may want to search for specific issues with Media Center through the Microsoft Knowledge Base found at http://search.support.microsoft.com. Specify Media Center when you search by your operating system version.

Getting Help *(continued)*

Here you will go to the Windows Media Center support page and search the Microsoft Knowledge Base for help.

Getting Help *(continued)*

USE THE WINDOWS MEDIA CENTER SUPPORT PAGE

1. Connect to the Internet, load your Web browser, and go to www.microsoft.com/windowsxp/mediacenter/.

2. Check through the options available there and click links to those that interest you.

*Note: These areas include the **Expert Zone**, which includes message boards where you can post questions and get assistance from other users as well as experts, attend chats, and read columns that provide helpful advice, and **Downloads**, where you can find patches and software that may be able to help you resolve problems or get a feature or function working.*

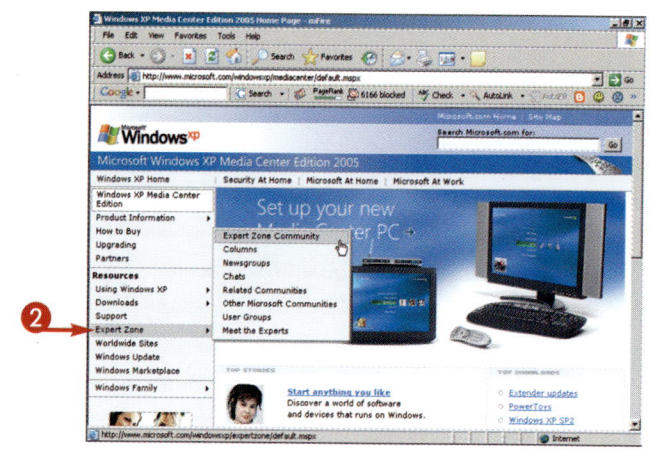

SEARCH THROUGH THE MICROSOFT KNOWLEDGE BASE

1 Connect to the Internet, start your Web browser, and visit http://search.support.microsoft.com.

2 Type in your operating system version and any keywords that relate to the problem you are having, such as **Windows Media Center PC sound card**.

3 Click **Go**.

The Knowledge Base returns a list of links that match the topic for which you searched.

4 Click to open the links to any articles that appear to best match your issue and read the instructions provided.

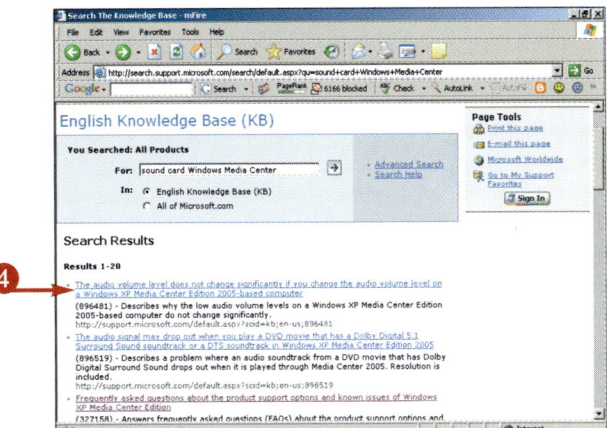

Is there any cost for using the Microsoft Media Center support Web page or the Knowledge Base?

No, these Microsoft Web-based resources are free to use. They can supply incredible levels of help on a whole variety of different topics and problems.

Do help articles that reference Windows XP apply to the Windows Media Center operating system?

Because Windows Media Center is a special version of Windows XP, the answer is usually yes. However, if you find two articles on the same subject, and one references Windows XP generally whereas the second targets Windows Media Center, go with the latter. Just remember to read the articles thoroughly and follow any cautionary tips.

Chapter 26: Media Center PC Final Troubleshooting and Recovery

301

Before and After You Resolve Special Problems

You should make a copy of your system — one that includes its Windows files, drivers, any applications, and configuration software for your devices you have installed — so that you have something to fall back to if your operating system becomes corrupted, a driver makes an awful change to your setup, or your primary hard drive fails.

A Copy of Your System

You may have Norton Ghost or Drive Image, both programs that will create a snapshot or copy of your drive that can be reapplied later to return to a fresh setup. You also may have another program or utility suite that regularly backs up your files. If so, you can install and use one of those.

System Tools

There are two tools packed directly into Windows that enable you to make copies and restore after a disaster of some type. These tools are Backup and System Restore, both found in System Tools (click **Start ➔ All Programs ➔ Accessories ➔ System Tools**). In this section, you will see how to use these tools to create copies and apply them as needed.

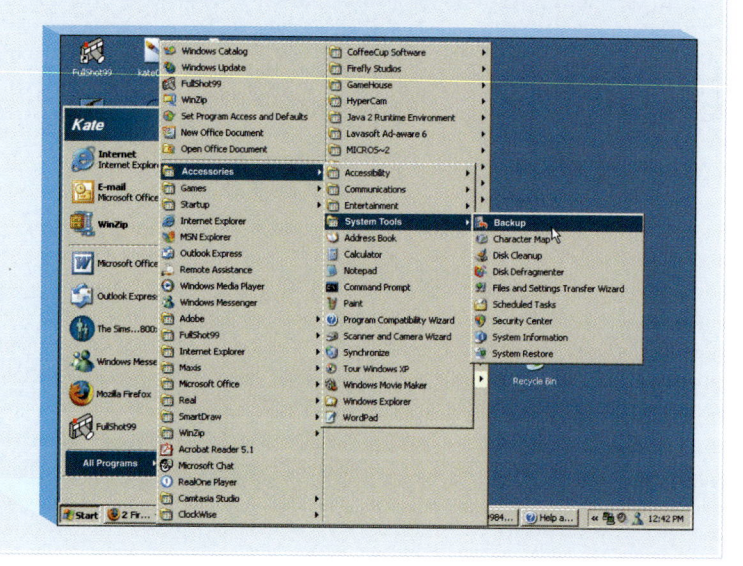

Make a Backup

You should create a backup of your system — or core files stored on your system — whenever you do any of the following:

- You have your system up and running and in very good shape.
- Before you make serious changes to your system that could affect its ability to run or perform properly.
- You fear that some instability with the system may leave you unable to access your files.
- You are about to replace the hard drive or format the existing hard drive.

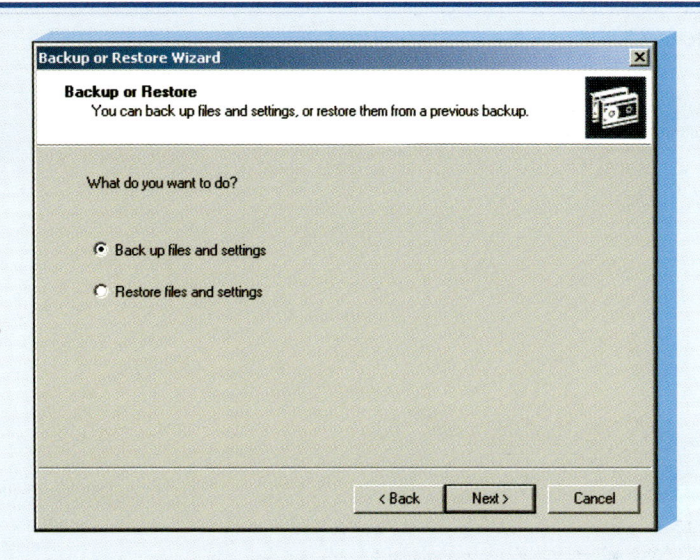

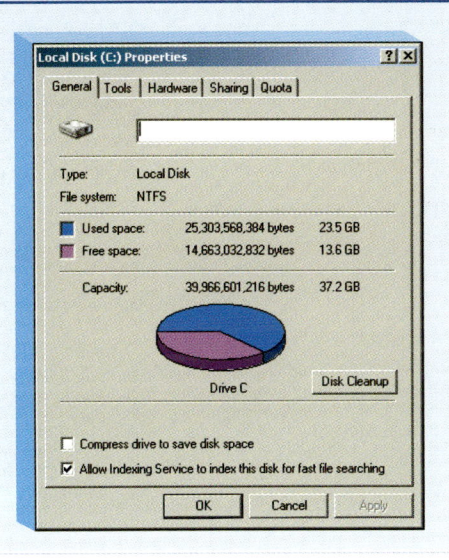

Where to Store the Backup

The file created by the backup process in Microsoft Windows can be stored on a different logical or physical hard disk where it can stay, or you may copy the file to a CD or DVD drive using My Computer in Windows.

Wherever you store this file must have enough room. For example, a backup of a 20GB hard drive with many applications installed and with several files on disk may take as much as 10GB to 12GB on a second hard drive to store; this is too large to fit on single recordable CD with about 650MB free or a single recordable DVD disc with about 4.5GB of free space. To check available disk space, click **Start** ➔ **My Computer**, right-click the drive that you want to check, and then click **Properties**.

Before and After You Resolve Special Problems (continued)

Here, you create a backup of your main hard disk and restore from that backup.

Before and After You Resolve Special Problems (continued)

CREATE A BACKUP

1. Click **Start**.
2. Click **All Programs**.
3. Click **Accessories**.
4. Click **System Tools**.
5. Click **Backup**.

   The Backup or Restore Wizard appears.

6. Click **Next**.
7. Click **Back Up Files and Settings** (◯ changes to ⦿).
8. Click **All Information on This Computer**.
9. Click **Next**.
10. Specify the drive where the backup will be stored and a backup filename.
11. Click **Next**.
12. Click **Finish**.

    Windows creates the backup, showing you a progress bar.

    At the end of the process, you are asked to insert a blank floppy disk.

13. Insert the floppy disk into the floppy disk drive.

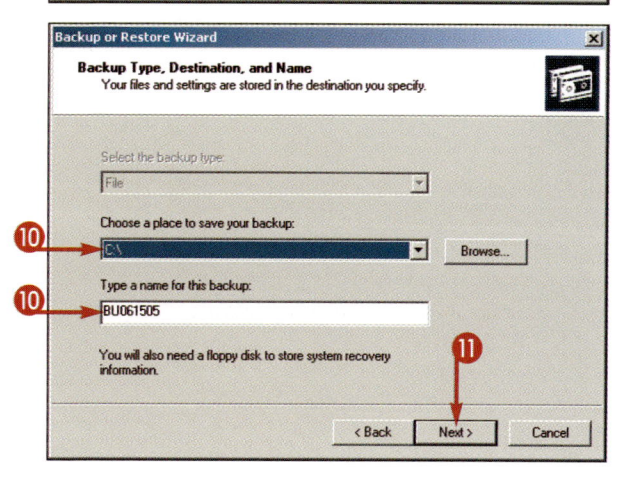

304

RESTORE FROM A BACKUP

① Perform the preceding steps **1** to **6**.

② On the Backup or Restore page of the wizard, click **Restore Files and Settings** (○ changes to ●).

③ Click **Next**.

④ On the What to Restore page of the wizard, click your backup file, usually found on the C: drive.

⑤ Click **Next**.

⑥ Click **Finish**.

The backup restore process begins to apply itself over your existing system.

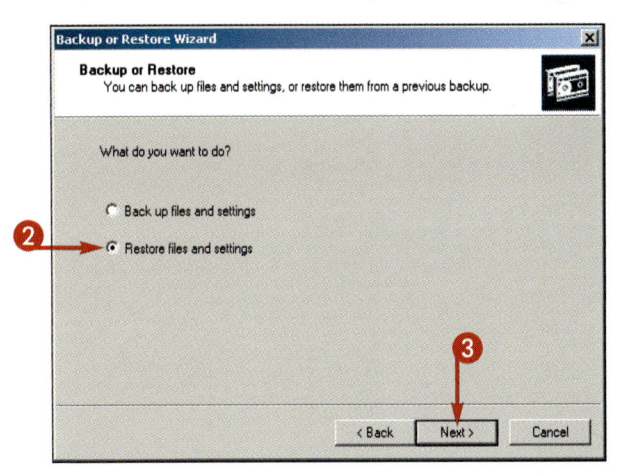

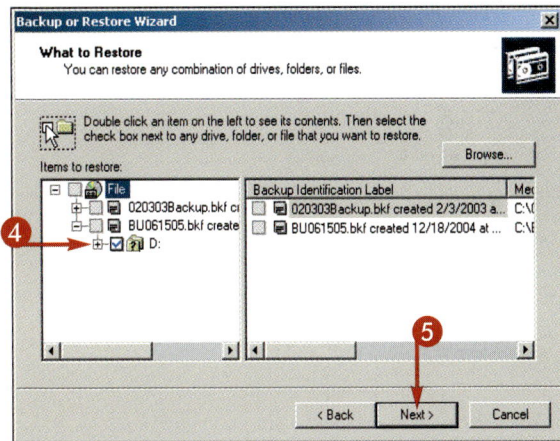

Q&A

What should I name my backup file?

Choose a name that will be easy for you to identify, such as **backup101505**, for a system backed up on October 15, 2005. Note that backup files created with the Windows Backup tool are stored with the .bkf file extension, so this example would be named backup101505.bkf.

I back up only once a month, but my friend insists that I should do it at least once a week, if not every day. Who is right?

The more you use your system and the more you depend on it and store important files on the hard disk, the more frequently you should back up. If you only use your Media Center PC casually, once a month may be enough. But if you use the system daily and create important files, increase your backup frequency.

continued

Before and After You Resolve Special Problems (continued)

System Restore is a tool that enables you to record copies of your basic setup and then restore these copies — called *restore points* — later if you have difficulty starting your system or an unfortunate change has left your PC unstable. To use this tool, you must have System Restore turned on and a restore point made before you need to restore your system.

Before and After You Resolve Special Problems (continued)

ENABLE SYSTEM RESTORE

① Click **Start** → **Control Panel**.

The Control Panel appears.

② Double-click **System**.

The System Properties dialog box appears.

③ Click the **System Restore** tab.

④ Click to uncheck **Turn Off System Restore on All Drives** (☑ changes to ☐).

⑤ Click **Apply**.

⑥ Click **OK**.

RECORD A RESTORE POINT

① Click **Start** → **All Programs** → **Accessories** → **System Tools** → **System Restore**.

② Click **Create a Restore Point** (○ changes to ⦿).

③ Click **Next**.

④ Type a unique name for this recording.

⑤ Click **Create**.

System Restore creates the restore point.

⑥ When it is finished, click **Close** to shut the window.

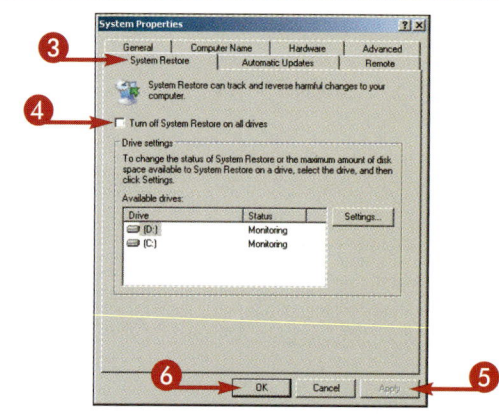

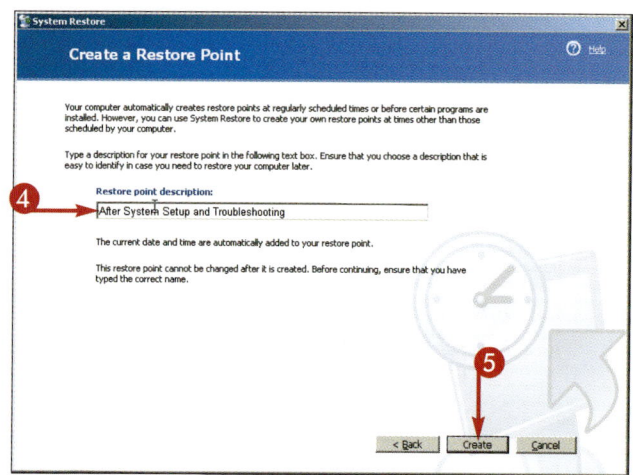

RESTORE USING SYSTEM RESTORE

1. Click **Start** → **All Programs** → **Accessories** → **System Tools** → **System Restore**.

   System Restore opens.

2. Click **Restore My Computer to an Earlier Time** (○ changes to ⦿).

3. Click **Next**.

4. Click the restore point from which you want to restore.

5. Click **Next**.

6. Follow the onscreen instructions to apply the restore point.

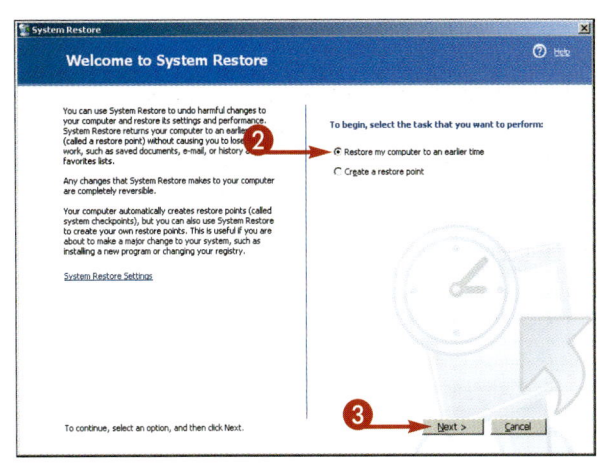

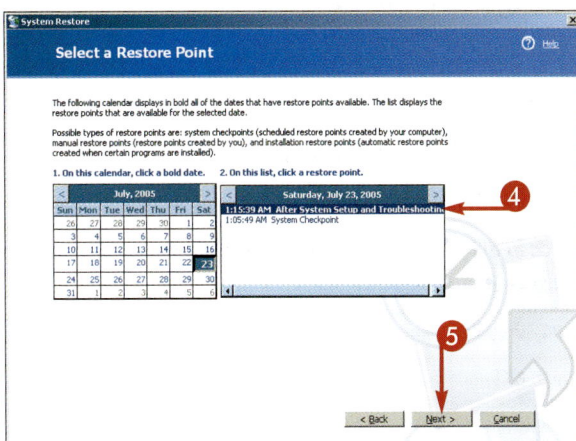

I have multiple drives. Can I turn System Restore on for just one of my drives?

No, you can turn System Restore on for all drives or off for all drives, but you cannot turn it on for just one drive unless you just have a single hard disk/drive partition.

What happens if I start having worse system problems after I restore from a restore point?

After you restore your system using a restore point, Windows will give you the option to undo the restoration, usually after you restart your system right after the restoration. So you can change back then, if needed; when you click to revert back to the previous setup, Windows steps you through the reversion. However, if you do not realize until later that the restore point you chose creates more of a problem, you can use System Restore to recover to a different saved restore point.

Chapter 26: Media Center PC Final Troubleshooting and Recovery

307

accelerated graphics port (AGP): A special expansion slot found on the motherboard that is exclusively available to install an AGP graphics card. On some budget motherboards, there is no AGP port, so you cannot install a separate AGP graphics card; instead, the graphics chipset is integrated directly into the motherboard.

add-on adapter: A printed circuit board providing some function, such as a modem, network capabilities, or special graphics options, that is installed to one of the expansion slots found on the motherboard. Most add-on adapters today are of one of two types: AGP, which handles video exclusively, and PCI.

applications: The programs installed to your hard drive that run under Windows, such as Microsoft Word and America Online software.

ATA drive: See **IDE drive.**

audio adapter: See **sound card.**

basic input output system (BIOS): The programmable part of your PC's motherboard that stores information about the connected hardware, performs a check as the PC starts up, and passes hardware information along to Windows.

bootup: The process of starting up a PC before the operating system such as Windows loads, when the BIOS checks to see what hardware is connected and available.

case: The housing for your internal PC components such as the motherboard, CPU, memory, internal drives, and installed add-on adapters.

case fan: One or more fans installed within the PC case to draw hot air away from sensitive components, send cooler air to the components, and/or push hot air outside the case through the vents to prevent overheating.

CD drive: A generic name for any type of drive that at least plays CD discs. A CD drive alone can only play back CDs.

CD-R drive: A type of CD drive capable of not only playing CDs but also recording music or data files using CD-R disc media.

CD-RW drive: Similar to a CD-R drive, this type enables you to record music or data files both to CD-R and CD-RW disc media. *RW* stands for *rewriteable,* which means that you can write a CD-RW disc and then later wipe that disc and rewrite new material in its place.

central processing unit (CPU): The "brain" of a PC, which handles all the instructions and commands sent to it by the PC. The CPU is also called the *processor.* CPU types include the Intel Pentium 4 and Celeron and the AMD Opteron, Duron, Sempron, and Athlon.

COM port: A communications port typically available at the rear of a PC for connecting serial devices such as a modem and older-style computer mice and digital cameras.

combo drive: A drive that combines two or more drive types together, such as universal serial bus (USB) and IEEE 1394 combo external drives and drives that combine CD and DVD capabilities together.

compact disc (CD) drive: See **CD drive.**

CPU fan: A special type of fan specifically designed to attach to the heatsink of the CPU to move hot air away from the processor to prevent heat-related damage and early CPU hardware failure.

device driver: A special piece of software designed to allow the operating system and PC communicate with a hardware device.

Device Manager: A feature in recent versions of Microsoft Windows that enables you to check connected hardware, look for hardware conflicts or problems, and update device drivers.

digital camera: A camera designed to connect directly to and work with a PC using storage media rather than film. This can be either a still camera or a video camera.

drive bay: The compartments inside a PC case where drives — such as the hard disk and CD or DVD drive — are mounted.

driver: See **device driver.**

DVD drive: Short for *digital video disc* or sometimes *digital versatile disc*, this is the generic name given to any drive that can play both CD and DVD discs. A DVD drive cannot record to DVD disc media.

DVD-R drive: A DVD player that also enables you to record data and music files to DVD-R recording disc media as well as plays most types of CDs.

DVD-RW drive: A DVD player/recorder that enables you to record and rewrite to DVD-RW disc media, letting you re-record over an existing DVD-RW disc.

EIDE: see **IDE.**

expansion slots: Slots available in a motherboard that enable you to add adapters to provide video, audio, network, telecommunications via modem, and other capabilities not already available as chips integrated into the motherboard.

external drive: A drive of any type that is designed to sit outside the PC case, typically connected by a USB or IEEE 1394 port to the motherboard.

faceplates: PC case coverings that can be removed to give you access to drive bays or the connector edge of add-on adapters such as a graphics or sound card.

graphics card: An add-on adapter installed to the PC motherboard's expansion slots (or sometimes, integrated directly into the motherboard) that handles all the video demands of the PC, with one or more special processors built-in. The graphics card provides connections to install the PC monitor and special devices such as a video camera.

hard disk: A drive where your primary files, applications, and operating system are installed and run. Although many people confuse the hard disk with memory, they are not the same thing; however, part of a hard disk may be used as a form of virtual memory to let you quickly access files on your desktop.

headphones: Just like stereo headphones, PC headphones usually connect to the sound card on a PC and enable you to listen to music or audio privately rather than directly through the speakers.

heatsink: A special piece of metal that is attached to the CPU with a special thermal compound. The job of a heatsink is to draw heat away from a CPU to prevent heat-related damage.

high-definition (HD) TV: A newer standard for TV broadcasts with much greater resolution and definition than standard TV. Windows Media Center is the first operating system to support HDTV playing through a PC.

high-speed Internet connection: Often referred to as *broadband service*, this refers to any Internet service that provides connection speeds well above the 56KB limitations of dial-up telephone service and includes cable, digital subscriber line (DSL), and satellite.

IDE: Integrated drive electronics, a drive standard used by the majority of consumer-level drives including hard disks, CDs, and DVDs; this is also referred to as *EIDE* and *ATA*.

IDE controllers: This refers to two or more sockets located on the motherboard that allow the connection of IDE drives via ribbon cable.

IDE drive: Any drive that conforms to the IDE drive standard, including hard disks, CD and DVD drives, and other removable media drives.

IEEE 1394: Either of two versions of a high-speed external device type including drives and digital video cameras, sometimes referred to as *FireWire*, although *FireWire* is exclusively an Apple term. IEEE 1394 devices connect through an IEEE 1394 port found on many but not all motherboards. Sony calls IEEE 1394 *i.Link*.

IEEE 1394 port: The connection point for IEEE 1394 devices.

internal drive: Any drive that is installed inside the PC case.

keyboard: The primary input device for a computer, connected through either a PS/2 port on the back of a PC or through a USB port in the case of a USB keyboard. USB keyboards sometimes offer extra USB ports to plug in other devices.

memory: Special chips that handle the burden of your PC needs for desktop applications and programs that may run in the background for faster retrieval as basic and essential operating systems are performed. The contents of information stored in memory, also called *RAM,* are erased each time the PC is rebooted or powered down. Memory is different from a hard drive because a hard drive provides permanent storage capabilities whereas memory is usually just short term and used for applications running on the desktop.

microphone: A recording device usually connected through a jack on the sound card connector at the back of the PC that enables you to create your own audio files. Sometimes, a microphone is integrated into the motherboard itself.

modem: Short for *modulator-demodulator,* a modem acts as a translator between the binary format used by a PC and the communications medium such as a phone line, cable, or satellite connection. Modems can be either external or internal and are specific to the type of connection you are using, such as cable or DSL.

monitor: The TV-like device that displays your desktop. The graphics card does all the work related to drawing a visual representation of your programs and games, but the monitor serves as the display for what the graphics card produces and connects to one of the video ports located on the graphics card.

motherboard: Also called the *system board* or the *mainboard,* this is the primary printed circuit board inside your PC case to which almost everything else is directly or indirectly connected, including your drives, your CPU, memory, and add-on adapters. A motherboard can be upgraded by special software referred to as "flashing the BIOS."

mouse: A pointing device that enables you to point at and click on options on the screen. A mouse connects either through a PS/2 port at the back of the PC or through a USB port.

network interface card (NIC): An add-on adapter that provides the connection and support to run a network in your home or office. Sometimes the network capabilities are supplied not by an add-on adapter but are integrated directly into the motherboard or are available as an external device that connects through a USB port.

operating system: A special program that acts as a central manager for the rest of the computer. The operating system enables you to run applications; keeps track of hardware; coordinates services such as printing, telecommunications, and file management; and automatically loads as the PC boots up, which sets the stage for you to use the PC. Microsoft Windows XP Media Center Edition is an example of an operating system.

power supply: An essential PC component that draws in power from an outlet, converts it into a form your PC hardware can use, and then supplies that power through connectors out to other hardware including the motherboard, drives, the power button, and fans.

printer: An external device that enables you to print hard copies of your files and communications. Printers connect either through a printer port — sometimes referred to as an *LPT port* or *parallel port* — at the back of the PC or through a USB port.

printer port: The standard connection for installed printers; although some other devices, including older style drives and scanners, may connect through the printer port as well.

processor: See **central processing unit (CPU)**; today's PCs may actually include multiple processors, including one found on the graphics card and the sound card to handle video and audio demands so that the main CPU is not overburdened or slowed down.

random access memory (RAM): See **memory.**

ribbon cable: A thin flat cable composed of many parallel wires that are used to connect devices such as disk drives to the motherboard on a PC. One edge of a ribbon cable is usually color coded to help you install it properly.

Sempron CPU: An AMD-manufactured 32-bit Pentium-compatible central processing unit that offers good performance at a lower price and competes directly with the Intel Celeron CPU.

serial ATA (SATA): A higher-speed internal drive platform that connects through either a SATA connector on the motherboard or to a special adapter installed to the motherboard that enables you to connect SATA drives.

sound card: A multipurpose adapter that handles all sounds generated by the PC or its files, including the capability to record, play back, and manipulate sound. A sound card has several jacks or connections that enable you to connect headphones, speakers, and a microphone as well as some game devices and may be integrated directly into the motherboard rather than available as a separate installed adapter.

speakers: Much like your stereo speakers, PC speakers provide playback and volume/quality control for sounds played on the system.

surge protector/suppressor: A piece of hardware that acts to protect the PC or other electronics equipment from power surges and so-called *dirty power*. A surge protector is usually built into uninterruptible power supplies and into many of the power strips used to connect PC components such as the main system and the monitor to power.

system memory: See **memory.**

TV tuner card: An add-on adapter that enables you to connect TV input from something like a cable or satellite TV receiver directly to the PC. Using this adapter, you can watch your favorite programs right from your desktop.

uninterruptible power supply (UPS): An external power supply used in addition to a standard PC power supply to provide uninterrupted battery-powered support and protection for your PC when normal power is interrupted, such as during a blackout or brownout. This device blocks power surges from reaching the PC and gives you time to properly shut down the system.

universal serial bus (USB): One of two versions of external device types including a slower-speed version (1.1) that handles keyboards, mice, digital still cameras and Webcams, and more and a version 2.0 that is much higher in transfer speed for external drives, digital video cameras, and other devices. Desktop PCs usually offer at least two USB ports, and mobile devices such as a laptop have one USB port, but separately available USB hubs enable you to connect up to 127 USB devices simultaneously.

USB hub: A USB hub enables you to connect multiple USB devices — usually in increments of four — to a single USB port on your PC.

USB port: A connector for USB devices typically found either at the rear and/or front of the PC.

vent: One or more openings in a PC case, usually protected by a grill or filter, that allows the exchange of cooler air from the room and the hotter air that needs to exit the PC.

video adapter: See **graphics card.**

video cable: A heavy-duty cable that connects the monitor with the graphics card or integrated video chipset found inside the PC.

video capture card: A special type of graphics card that enables you to capture still images or snippets of video from a movie or TV broadcast, which can then be edited and changed through special software.

Windows Media Center: A special version of Windows XP designed specifically for multimedia playback and recording, including the ability to download and watch movies, play music, create movies and sound files, and incorporate your PC into your home or small-office entertainment equipment.

Index

A

adapters. *See* graphics cards; NICs; PCI adapters; sound cards
Add New Hardware Wizard, 286–287
AGP (accelerated graphics port), 19, 174, 308
AGP cards. *See* graphics cards
antistatic wrist straps, 50, 69
audio adapters. *See* sound cards
audio devices *See also* CD/DVD drives; speakers
    connecting, 226–227
    electric instruments, 183
    headphones, 25, 309
    microphones
        defined, 310
        overview, 25
        sound cards and, 183
        speech recognition and, 237
    music-play testing, 272
    personal media players, 27
    playback settings, 293
    sound mixing boards, 28, 227
    volume controls, 293

B

backup storage *See also* hard drives
    CD/DVD drives, 154, 303
    external hard drives, 136, 137, 165
    overview, 21
backups, 302–305
bootup problems, 253–257, 259
bootups, defined, 308
broadband/high-speed Internet access, 189, 190, 191, 309
building Media Center PCs *See also* shopping for parts; Windows Media Center PCs
    assessing needs, 7
    avoiding problems, 59
    checking hardware compatibility, 11
    connecting devices *See also* each device
        audio devices, 226–227
        digital cameras, 27
        IEEE 1394 devices, 243–245
        keyboard, 232–233
        microphones, 226–227
        monitors, 224
        mouse, 234–235
        other input devices, 236–237
        printers, 241
        speakers, 225
        USB devices, 243–245
    considering cost, 9
    using damaged parts, 57
    documenting the process, 51
    getting online help, 13
    getting tools together, 45, 48–51
    installing components *See also* drives; *each component*; hard drives
        CD/DVD drives, 156–161
        CPU, fan, heatsink, 92–97
        floppy drives, 166–169
        graphics cards, 176–177, 210–211
        memory, 102–103, 105
        modems, 190, 192–193
        motherboard, 114–117
        network cards, 196, 202
        power supply, 82
        sound cards, 184–187
    installing Media Center software
        and activating, 266–267
        changing boot sequence, 260–261
        changing CMOS Setup, 261
        checking system readiness, 258–259
        hardware setup, 265
        Internet connections, 266–267
        operating system setup, 260–265
        troubleshooting startup, 260–261
    learning from working PCs, 68–71
    planning carefully, 10
    preparing to boot
        checking your work, 250–251
        installing power cord/starting PC, 252
        moving PC out of workspace, 251
        troubleshooting bootup, 253–257, 259
    preparing yourself, 51
    receiving parts orders
        checking for damage, 53, 54–55
        inspecting, 52, 54
        replacing damaged parts, 56–57, 59
        storing until you build, 58
        taking inventory, 53–54
        unpacking, 53
    safety concerns, 45, 47
    setting up workspace, 44–47
    sticking to budgets, 11
    testing results, 268–269, 272
    versus buying, 8, 12

C

cables *See also* power cords
    CD/DVD-to-sound card cable, 25
    network cable, 198, 200–201, 203
    printer cable, 240
    ribbon cables
        affixing to floppy drives, 168
        attaching to CD/DVD drives, 158–159
        attaching to hard drives, 150–151
        checking, 142
        defined, 24, 311
        dual-drive cables, 129, 131, 151
    video cable, 25, 311
cases
    alternative back panels, 117
    alternative choices, 63
    author choice, 62
    case fans, 308
    defined, 16, 308
    hard drive setup, 127–129
    looking inside, 66–67
    opening up, 64–65
    piano cases, 62, 127–129
    removing faceplates, 72–73
    tower cases, 63, 127
    vents, 311
    visualizing assembly, 74–75
    warning, 69

312

CD/DVD drives **See also** audio devices; drives
    alternative choices, 155
    attaching ribbon cables, 158–159
    author choice, 154
    as backup storage, 154, 303
    CD drives, defined, 308
    connecting to power supply, 160
    connecting to sound cards, 186
    deciding where to mount, 131
    DVD drives, defined, 309
    enabling recording, 279
    installing, 157
    music/movie/game testing, 272
    preparing to install, 156
    setting jumpers, 156
    troubleshooting, 279
    verifying installation, 161
CD/DVD-to-sound card cable, 25, 159
color settings, 291
COM port, 71, 308
compatibility checking, 11, 75, 208
Control Panel
    Add Hardware, 286–287
    Display, 290–292
    Power Options, 295
    Printers and Faxes, 295
    Sounds and Audio Devices, 293–294
    System, 107, 306–307
cost considerations, 9
CPU (central processing unit)
    alternative choices, 90
    author choice, 90
    checking insertions, 96–97
    connecting fan/heatsink to, 94
    connecting fan to motherboard, 95
    CPU fan, defined, 18, 308
    defined, 18, 308
    heatsink, defined, 18, 309
    keeping CPU booklets, 97
    matching to motherboard, 17, 90
    memory and, 90, 99
    mounting into motherboard, 92–93
CPU Solutions. **See** shopping for parts

D

DDR SDRAM memory, 98–99
Design Studio online help, 13
device drivers
    defined, 308
    rolling back to previous, 285
    updating, 282–284
Device Manager. **See** Windows Media Center PCs
digital cameras, 27, 308
dirty power. **See** power fluctuations
Display Properties dialog box, 290–292
displays. **See** monitors
documenting build process, 51
documenting problems, 296
drive bays, 70, 309
Drive Image program, 302
drivers. **See** device drivers

drives **See also** CD/DVD drives; hard drives
    changing, 135
    checking cables, 142
    combo drives, 308
    connecting two to own IDE controllers, 133, 135
    connecting two to same IDE controller, 129, 131, 133–134, 151
    deciding where to mount, 130–131
    defined, 21
    external drives
        author choices, 163
        defined, 136
        installing, 165
        reasons to add, 137, 141
        versus internal drives, 124, 136
        ways to use, 137
    floppy drives
        affixing ribbon cable, 168
        connecting to power supply, 169
        defined, 162
        installing, 166–167
        overview, 21
    master/slave drives, 127, 131, 133–134
    online help
        drive software, 141
        installation instructions, 140
        jumper details, 141
        from manufacturers, 138–139
    overview, 124
    piano case issues, 127–129
    removing screws/retainers, 142
    tower case issues, 127
DVD drives. **See** CD/DVD drives
DVI connectors, 23, 218

E

expansion slots. **See** AGP; PCI expansion slots
external drives. **See** drives

F

faceplates, 72–73, 309
fans
    case fans, 308
    CPU fans, 95, 308
    and heatsinks, 18, 94
    specialty fans, 25, 206
Firewire. **See** IEEE 1394 devices
first aid kits, 45
floppy drives **See also** drives
    affixing ribbon cable, 168
    connecting to power supply, 169
    defined, 162
    installing, 149, 166–167
form factor, 63, 75

G

game devices, 26
game-play testing, 272
graphics cards **See also** PCI adapters
    adjusting video setup, 291
    AGP versus PCI cards, 174–175
    alternative choices, 173

Index

author choice, 172
checking seating of, 178
connecting monitors to, 224
defined, 19, 309
extra cables, 179
features, 175
installing AGP cards, 176–177
installing PCI cards, 177, 210–211
monitor ports, 23
monitors and, 218–219
TV tuner/video capture cards, 204, 207
video processing units, 19
graphics tablets, 27

H

hard drives *See also* drives
    adding more, 163–164
    alternative choices, 145
    author choice, 144
    checking available space, 303
    defined, 309
    IDE drives
        adding more, 164
        controllers, 124, 309
        defined, 124–126, 309
        reading label on, 132
        versus SCSI drives, 124–126
    installing IDE drives
        attaching ribbon cables, 150–151
        checking installation, 153
        connecting power supply, 152
        deciding where to mount, 131
        independent drives, 135
        master/slave drives, 133–134
        setting jumpers, 129, 132–134, 146–147
        steps in, 148–149
    SATA drives
        adapters, 126, 206, 207
        defined, 126, 311
        installing, 126, 164
        motherboard ports, 145
        SATA II drives, 127
        versus IDE drives, 126–127
    SCSI drives, 124–126, 206
    versus memory, 309, 310
HD (high-definition) TV support, 309
headphones, 25, 226–227, 309
heatsinks, 18, 94, 309
help online *See also* Web sites
    building Media Center PCs, 13
    with drives
        drive software, 141
        installation instructions, 140
        jumper details, 141
        from manufacturers, 138–139
    manufacturers, 298
    Microsoft sites, 299–301
    power supply specs, 81
high-speed/broadband Internet access, 189, 190, 191, 309

I

IDE drives. *See* drives; hard drives
IEEE 1394 devices
    adding ports for, 205–206, 207, 246
    connecting, 243–245
    defined, 242–243, 309
    disconnecting, 243
    I/O card adapters, 205–206, 207
    sharing with Macintoshes, 245
    versions of, 247
integrated components. *See* motherboard
Internet connections *See also* modems
    dial-up, 189
    free services, 29
    high-speed/broadband, 189, 190, 191, 309
    setting up in Media Center, 266–267
    sharing on networks, 188, 194–195
I/O card adapters, 205–206, 207

J

jumper settings
    for CD/DVD drives, 156
    for IDE drives, 129, 132–134, 146–147
    if changing drives, 135
    master/slave settings, 131, 133–134
    for motherboard, 113
    online help with, 141

K

keyboard and mouse
    alternative choices, 229
    author choice, 228
    connection types, 230, 235
    defined, 23, 310
    installing keyboard, 232–233
    installing other input devices, 236–237
    mouse pads, 235
    optical mouse, 231, 235
    setting up mouse, 234–235
    USB adapter for, 231
    USB keyboard, 231, 247

L

LCD monitors, 23, 215, 219
line conditioners, 87

M

Macintosh computers, 245
mainboard. *See* motherboard
master/slave drives, 127, 131, 133–134
Media Center PCs. *See* building Media Center PCs; Windows Media Center PCs
Media Center software. *See* Windows Media Center Edition
memory
    adding more later, 105
    alternative choices, 99
    author choice, 98
    avoiding damaging, 103

checking
    amount installed, 107
    memory sockets, 101
    seating, 104, 106
    when receiving order, 100
DDR SDRAM memory, 98–99
defined, 18, 310
installing, 102–103
motherboard/CPU and, 90, 99
problems with, 106
replacing, 105
versus hard drives, 309, 310
memory banks, 103
microphones *See also* audio devices
    connecting, 226–227
    defined, 310
    overview, 25
    sound cards and, 183
    speech recognition and, 237
Microsoft Knowledge Base, 299, 301
mixing boards, sound, 28, 227
modems *See also* Internet connections
    alternative choices, 189
    author choice, 23, 29, 188
    connectors, 191
    defined, 310
    dial-up modems, 189, 193
    external modems, 29, 189, 190, 192
    high-speed modems, 189, 190, 191
    installing, 192–193
    internal modems, 20, 190, 192
    network setup, 188, 194–195
monitor display settings
    color, 291
    refresh rate, 292
    screen resolution, 291
    screen savers, 290
monitors
    alternative choices, 215
    author choice, 214
    checking cables/cords, 220, 221
    connecting audio devices, 226–227
    connecting to graphics cards, 224
    controls, 223
    cost, 9
    defined, 22, 310
    documentation, 219, 220
    graphics cards and, 218–219
    items included with, 220–221
    LCD monitors, 23, 215, 219
    placement requirements, 222
    power cords, 24, 224
    troubleshooting, 293
    unpacking/cleaning/inspecting, 223
    VGA or DVI connectors, 23, 218
    video adapters and, 23
    video cable, 220, 221, 311
motherboard
    alternative choices, 109
    author choice, 108
    checking connections, 120, 121

checking installation, 120–121
connecting power supply, 118–120
defined, 17, 310
documentation, 110–111
features, 108
integrated components
    defined, 17, 108
    disabling, 279
    versus PCI adapters, 17, 19
matching to CPU, 17, 90
memory and, 90, 99
mounting
    being careful, 114
    CPU into, 92–93
    inserting motherboard, 116–117
    installing screws, 117
    installing standoffs, 115
    preparing for, 114
preparing for the case, 112
setting jumpers, 113
upgrading, 310
mouse. *See* keyboard and mouse
movie-play testing, 272
music-making devices. *See* audio devices; CD/DVD drives

N-O

network adapters. *See* NICs
network setup, 188, 194–195
NICs (network interface cards) *See also* PCI adapters
    alternative choices, 197
    author choice, 196
    cable/connectors, 200–201
    defined, 20, 310
    disabling onboard, 279
    inserting cable, 203
    installing, 196, 202
    RJ–45 jack, 200
    wireless networks, 198–199
Norton Ghost program, 302

operating systems, 310 *See also* Windows Media Center Edition

P-Q

parts. *See* building Media Center PCs; shopping for parts
PCI adapters *See also* graphics cards; NICs; sound cards
    checking system compatibility, 208
    cooling devices, 206
    defined, 308
    IEEE 1394 adapters, 205–206, 207, 245, 246
    I/O cards, 205–206, 207
    overview, 205
    rearranging, 209
    SATA adapter, 126, 206, 207
    SCSI host adapter, 206
    TV tuner/video capture card, 204, 207, 210–211
    versus AGP adapters, 174
    versus integrated components, 17, 19
    where they mount, 19
    wireless network adapters, 199, 206

315

Index

PCI expansion slots
    availability of, 21, 204, 209
    defined, 309
    installing in
        graphics cards, 177, 210–211
        internal modems, 190, 192
        network cards, 202
        sound cards, 184–185
    rearranging installed adapters, 209
power cords *See also* cables
    main power cords
        checking, 83
        connecting, 252
        defined, 24
        when to plug in, 67
    monitor power cords
        checking, 220, 221
        connecting, 224
        defined, 24
power fluctuations, 84–87
Power Options in Control Panel, 295
power-protection devices, 28–29, 87, 311
power supply
    alternative choices, 77
    author choice, 76
    connecting
        floppy drives, 169
        hard drives, 152
        motherboard, 118–120
    damaged connectors, 119
    defined, 16, 310
    finding specs online, 81
    how it works, 81
    importance of, 78, 81
    installing, 82
    label attached to, 80
    system need and, 80
    uninterruptible power supply, 28, 87, 295, 311
    what good ones do, 78
    what to look for, 78–80
printers
    alternative choices, 239
    author choice, 238
    cables, 240
    defined, 310
    installing, 241
    multiple printers, 240
    printing photos, 240
    troubleshooting, 251
    USB or LPT ports, 71, 240, 241, 310
    verifying setup, 295
processors, 310 *See also* CPU
PS/2 ports/connectors, 230, 235

R

RAM. *See* memory
refresh rate settings, 292
resolution settings, 291
Restore tool, System, 306–307
restoring from backups, 305

ribbon cables. *See* cables
RJ–45 jack, 200
RMA (return merchandise authorization), 56

S

SATA drives *See also* hard drives
    adapters, 126, 206, 207
    defined, 126, 311
    installing, 126, 164
    motherboard ports, 145
screen resolution settings, 291
screen saver settings, 290
SCSI hard drives, 124–126, 206
serial ATA. *See* SATA drives
shopping for parts *See also* building Media Center PCs
    alternative choices, 38
    author choices, 35
    avoiding missing parts, 11, 14
    avoiding sales hype, 12
    basic parts *See also* each part
        case, 16
        CD/DVD-to-sound card cable, 25
        CPU/fan/heatsink, 18
        drives, 21
        graphics card, 19, 23
        keyboard/mouse, 23
        memory, 18
        modem, 20, 23, 29
        monitor, 22
        motherboard, 17
        network adapter, 20
        overview, 15, 22
        power cords, 24
        power supply, 16
        ribbon cables, 24
        sound card, 19
        speakers, 23
        video cable, 25
    CPU Solutions online
        accessing, 32
        asking questions, 38, 39
        author-recommended parts, 34–35, 38
        Build It Yourself Visually link, 34–35
        by categories, 36
        checking your list, 11, 41
        comparing features/prices, 36–37
        contacting customer service, 32
        using coupons, 31
        customizing order, 34, 35, 36–38
        defined, 30
        by manufacturers, 36
        New Products link, 33
        placing your order, 42–43
        reading product details, 39, 208
        saving time, 34
        Specials links, 33
        troubleshooting help, 298
    extras *See also* audio devices; PCI adapters
        digital cameras, 27
        external hard drives, 163, 165

external modems, 29
headphones, 25
microphones, 25
overview, 26–27
power-protection devices, 28–29, 87
printers, 238–241
sound mixing boards, 28
specialty fans, 25, 206
uninterruptible power supplies, 28
USB hubs, 205, 246
USB/IEEE 1394 devices, 242–247
Media Center software, 40
preparing to shop, 30–31
sticking to budgets, 11
shunts, 113
sound cards *See also* PCI adapters
alternative choices, 181
author choice, 180
CD/DVD-to-sound card cable, 25
checking installation, 187
connecting CD/DVD drive, 186
connectors/plugs/jacks, 182
defined, 19, 311
installing, 184–185
microphones and, 183
speakers and, 183
sound devices. *See* audio devices; CD/DVD drives
Sound Recorder, 269
Sounds and Audio Devices dialog box, 293–294
speakers *See also* audio devices
alternative choices, 217
author choice, 216
defined, 23, 311
installing, 225
settings, 294
sound cards and, 183
standoffs, 66, 115
surge protectors/suppressors, 29, 87, 311
system board. *See* motherboard
System Properties dialog box, 107, 306
System Tools, 302–307

T
tools for building, 45, 48–51
troubleshooting. *See* Windows Media Center PCs
TV, high-definition (HD), 309
TV tuner card, 26, 204, 207, 210–211, 311

U
UPS (uninterruptible power supply), 28, 87, 295, 311
USB adapter for keyboards/mice, 231
USB devices *See also* audio devices
connecting, 243–245
defined, 242–243, 311
disconnecting, 243
sharing with Macintoshes, 245
versions of, 247
USB hubs, 190, 205, 246, 311
USB keyboards, 231, 247

USB ports
adding, 205–206, 246, 247
defined, 71, 311
keyboards/mice and, 230, 235

V
vents in case, 311
VGA connectors, 218
VGA ports, 23
video adapters. *See* graphics cards
video capture card, 26, 204, 207, 210–211, 311
video game/movie testing, 272
video (monitor) cable, 25, 220, 221, 311
volume controls, 293
VPU (video processing unit), 19

W-Z
Web sites *See also* help online
Biostar, 110–111
CPU Solutions, 30
drive manufacturers, 139
free Internet services, 29
Windows Media Center, 5, 13, 299–301
Windows Catalog, 208
Windows Media Center Edition
defined, 311
Design Studio online, 13
enhancements/features, 6
HDTV support, 309
how to get, 5, 40
installing
and activating, 266–267
checking system readiness, 258–259
hardware setup, 265
Internet connections, 266–267
operating system setup, 260–265
troubleshooting startup, 260–261
System Tools, 302–307
Windows Media Center PCs *See also* building Media Center PCs
backing up, 302–305
connecting to networks, 194–195
defined, 6
using Device Manager
changing settings, 275
defined, 273
disabling devices, 278, 279
enabling devices, 278, 279
opening, 273–274
removing device entries, 280, 281
rolling back to previous drivers, 285
scanning for hardware changes, 281
troubleshooting devices, 276–277, 280, 287
updating drivers, 282–284
viewing device properties, 275
fine-tuning
audio hardware, 294
audio playback, 293
cautions, 289
color settings, 291

Index

display properties, 290–292
using manufacturer sites, 289
monitor refresh rate, 292
overview, 288
power options, 295
printer setup, 295
screen resolution, 291
screen savers, 290
speakers, 294
forcing new hardware checks, 286–287
hardware needs, 4
Internet connections, 188, 195
problem causes
    changing CMOS Setup, 261
    changing Device Manager settings, 275
    using damaged parts, 57
    driver updates, 284
    hardware incompatibility, 11, 75, 208
    moving printers, 251
    not grounding yourself, 69
    using System Restore, 307
running Windows Update, 270–271
secure locations, 65
using System Restore, 306–307
troubleshooting
    approaches to, 296
    backing up before, 302–307
    boot issues, 253–257, 259
    devices, 276–277, 280, 287
    documenting problems, 296
    DVD drives, 279
    getting help with, 298–301
    memory, 106
    monitors, 293
    not finding new hardware, 287
    not recognizing installed devices, 287
    problems caused by driver updates, 284, 285
    tips for, 297
    Windows startup, 260–261
versus standard PCs, 4
Windows Update, 270–271
wireless networks, 198–199, 206

Everything you need
to build the perfect media PC!

Use this code when ordering and receive FREE SHIPPING: BIYMPC

CPU Solutions can take you from this...

...to this!

The AMD Athlon™ 64 processor offers exceptional performance, enhanced security*, a rich digital experience, and investment protection.

BIOSTAR

The Affordable Multi Media Solution!
ATi Radeon Xpress 200
Radeon® Xpress 200 + Theater 550 Pro = MCE Ready System

Quiet Computing™
Overture II
Minuet II
Stylish, whisper-quiet media center cases from **Antec**.

cpusolutions.com

Office Hours
Monday to Friday
9AM to 5PM
TEL 800-474-4278
Fax 608-824-9616

Tech Support Hours
9AM to 4PM   **608-831-3259**

Office & Mailing address:
CPU Solutions Inc.
8604 Fairway Place
Middleton, Wisconsin 53562

*Enhanced Virus Protection (EVP) is only enabled by certain operating systems, including the current versions of Microsoft® Windows®, Linux, Solaris, and BSD Unix. After properly installing the appropriate operating system release, users must enable the protection of their applications and associated files from buffer overrun attacks. Consult your OS documentation for information on enabling EVP. Contact your application software vendor for information regarding use of the application in conjunction with EVP. AMD and its partners strongly recommend that users continue to include third-party antivirus software as part of their security strategy.

Visit us online at cpusolutions.com